Flashes of Merriment

University of Oklahoma Press : Norman

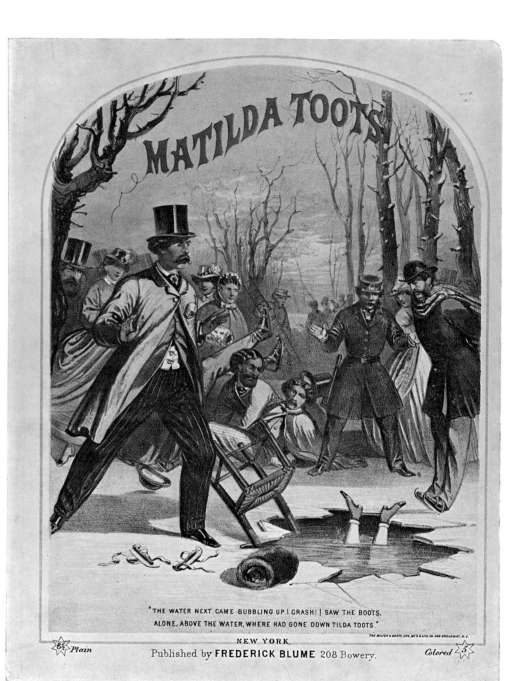

MATILDA TOOTS.

"THE WATER NEXT CAME BUBBLING UP ! CRASH ! | SAW THE BOOTS,
ALONE, ABOVE THE WATER, WHERE HAD GONE DOWN TILDA TOOTS."

NEW YORK,
Published by **FREDERICK BLUME** 208 Bowery.

FLASHES OF MERRIMENT

MERRIMENT

A Century of Humorous Songs in America
1805-1905

AS WRITTEN BY

LESTER S. LEVY

CALLIGRAPHY BY HENRY W. HOFFMAN

By Lester S. Levy

Grace Notes in American History: Popular Sheet Music from 1820 to 1900
(Norman, 1967)
Flashes of Merriment: A Century of Humorous Songs in America, 1805–1905
(Norman, 1971)

International Standard Book Number: 0–8061–0914–9

Library of Congress Catalog Card Number: 74–108805

To my grandchildren

Preface

THE PURPOSE of this volume is to examine the kind of musical humor that our progenitors found entertaining. Much of it is amusing even today if we are willing to put away for a moment our mid-twentieth-century sophistication and revert to the simpler days of the century that is gone.

This is not to say that anyone hearing the old songs now for the first time will double up with laughter. Amusement values change with generations. A teenager of the later 1960's and early 1970's squeals with delight when a long-haired Britisher yells unintelligible words into a microphone and beats on a guitar at the same time. In the late 1940's her mother had only to hear Frank Sinatra croon on a downtown stage to develop similar manic symptoms. In the 1920's her grandmother very likely felt a heartthrob when a handsome young singer like Dennis King flashed his eyes as he strutted across the boards in *The Vagabond King*.

But the audiences at Tony Pastor's in the 1880's and 1890's, who packed themselves in to hear the songs of Maggie Cline or May Irwin, came not to squeal or to sigh, but to smile and then to guffaw—and, as they left the theater, to buy the songs and take them home for further performances *en famille*.

In those days, when professional entertainment was not available to everyone and people had to "make for themselves a theater," singing was a popular pastime and sheet music was in great demand. Hundreds of thousands of Americans in homes all over the country sat down at the piano to hammer out the popular songs propped up over the keyboard, while millions more gathered around for loud and lusty vocal accompaniments.

For a comic song, a simple melody would suffice if the tune was gay and the good humor of the verses infectious. Thus the songs in this book are easy to sing and easy to remember. Nearly all of them are written in a major key—mostly in B-flat, C, D, F, or G—and can be played by a second- or third-year music student.

The arrangers, however, seem to have given more thought to the ability of the pianist than to the range of the amateur vocalist. Occasionally, the key in which a song is written makes a singer reach for the moon when the melody soars up to high F or even a high G, as in the national anthem at "the rockets' red glare" (a G in the original version).

But, in the main, nothing interfered with the easy flow of words (frequently misspelled) and music. Most of these songs were written in 4/4 or 6/8 time, the latter in a rollicking ibbity-zibbity rhythm which could excite a listener even before he heard the lyrics.

Although entertaining, the music of American comic song writers before 1875 was notably unoriginal, as were the earliest of the British humorous songs which found their way to this country. The work of Stephen Foster is, of course, an exception to this generalization, but rarely did any other composer stand out from the crowd.

There is a conspicuous absence of accidentals, save in the arrangements of a few of the more talented composers, such as Will S. Hays, who in the 1870's anticipated some of the diversions that would be employed by popular composers twenty to thirty years later (see his "Gay Young Clerk in the Dry Goods Store").

Now and then a composer deviated from the humdrum, as in the "Tee-To-Tal Society"—which is written, surprisingly, in 9/8 time—or in "Over There" and "Drill Ye Tarriers," both of which are delightfully developed in a minor key, yet are completely whistleable.

The later English comic songs were more sophisticated than the earlier ones, and they intrigued American listeners. "Johnny Sands," written in the 1840's, had a swing which Americans couldn't resist, as did "The Flying Trapeze," which has lasted for a century, and "Jenny Jones," whose melody —twenty years after it was composed—was appropriated by an American versifier for "The Charming Young Widow I Met in the Train." Not that the English were always so inventive. The writer of the verses for "All the World Is Scheming" set his words to the tune of "Here We Go Round the Mulberry Bush," a fortunate choice.

A song became a hit 75 to 125 years ago in much the same way it does today—because a popular performer "plugged" it. Just as Irving Berlin achieved his greatest successes with the help of the artists who introduced them—Emma Carus, singing "Alexander's Ragtime Band"; Fred Astaire, presenting "Top Hat, White Tie, and Tails"; Kate Smith, belting out "God Bless America"; Bing Crosby, crooning "White Christmas"—past generations of music men persuaded the ingratiating Billy Emerson, the buxom May Irwin, and the stentorious Maggie Cline to try to win an audience to their new numbers. Even the songs of Stephen Foster were first presented to the public by performers in minstrel troupes. (The black-face minstrel show, although it is the most important source of American musical humor, will not be discussed at length in this book. My earlier book *Grace Notes in American History* [Norman, 1967] devoted a chapter to the subject.)

The songs that appealed to nineteenth-century America had a simple humor which would not on first hearing snare many of today's sophisticates, but 100 years ago a song that started, "Oh where, and oh where, is my little wee dog," sung by a phony German with a phony German accent, would send an audience into gales of laughter. And 125 years ago, the story of a rich man with a cork leg which did not function properly was enough to convulse a crowd of listeners.

The songs discussed in this book are arranged in categories. First there is the humorous tale set to music; next, the comic situation of an awkward "boy and girl" relationship; then the funny accents of unassimilated foreigners (the Germans and the Italians); then the nonsense song with the silly, unintelligible punch line (the forerunner of "The Hut Sut Song," "Flat Foot Floogie with the Floy, Floy," and "Chim Chim Cheree"). Some of these songs have an animal as the hero or the villain, as the case may be. Some rare humorous pieces are embellished with title pages by Currier. Others spoof an incident in the administration of a President or poke fun at an enemy or parody a political involvement. Still others concern drinking and drunkards, subjects that were always good for laughs when acted out by veteran vaudeville performers. To conclude the volume, there are some well-remembered songs of our childhood that were crooned to us fondly by a devoted Grandma. We will be describing some of these in detail and will try to tickle, at one point or another, any funny-bones that may be exposed.

From time to time in the course of the text, when successful singers and song writers emerge, brief sketches tell something about them and what endeared them to their followers.

LESTER S. LEVY

Pikesville, Maryland
January 4, 1971

Contents

Illustrations

Flashes of Merriment

Where be your gibes now?
your gambols? your songs?
your flashes of merriment,
that were wont to set the
table on a roar?

—Hamlet
  Act V, Scene 1

The Comic Tale

1

SHEET-MUSIC PUBLISHING in the United States sprang up in the last decade of the eighteenth century. For a quarter of a century publishers were obliged to use songs and instrumental pieces popular in England; and with occasional exceptions the music first published in Boston, New York, Philadelphia, and Baltimore consisted of material imported from abroad, including not only English songs, but works of the great masters—such as Mozart, Haydn, and Handel—scored for piano solo. A number of American music publishers were from England, where their firms had originated. It was natural, therefore, for them to bring their tastes with them and to assume, rightly, that the people of the United States would accept the music that appealed to Londoners.

At the same time the American publishers were aware that along with the sentimental and occasionally patriotic pieces which were in brisk demand, the humorous song was beginning to establish its place in the hearts of their public.

The early eighteenth-century Englishman had sung many amusing ditties, frequently on the coarse side, set to sprightly tunes; and several hundred of these were assembled in half a dozen volumes—now collectors' items—called "Pills to Purge Melancholy."

From here it was but a short step to the comic tale, set to verse and scored for the piano early in the 1800's. Professional performers sang these songs on the English stage, and they were promptly transported across the Atlantic in sheet-music form to be reprinted and redistributed to the American public. Any trivial situation might serve for a plot, if it were deftly developed and then fully exposed—whether crudely, cruelly, or shamelessly—to tickle the ribs of an audience. True, the poetry could not be compared to that of John Keats, and the music was many notches below the work of George Frederick Handel. But still, the verses were entertaining and the music lively.

The first songs published in America were the work of anonymous English composers. Except for classical instrumental pieces, it was uncommon to see a composer's name on a song sheet. If a name *were* mentioned, it was usually that of the singer rather than the song writer, as in this excerpt from a cover sheet:

Oh! Cruel
A Comic Song,
as sung by Mr. Jefferson
in the character of a
Female Ballad Singer

And this:

Thimble's Wife
Sung by Mr. Blissett
in
Killing No Murder

Just *who* wrote *Killing No Murder* the public may never have known.

In 1824 a New York publisher (late of London) named Edward Riley placed on sale a song about a boat trip, with the title:

Oh, What a Row! or The Adventures of a Steam Packet
A New Comic Song
As sung by Mr. Barnes

The gentleman telling the story (see page 13) relates how he was coaxed into a sea excursion by his wife and daughter, and how the one-day voyage was fraught with unfortunate experiences.

The song is English in origin, but no matter; the gentleman's misadventures have a universal flavor. Unfortunately the name of the author remains shrouded in mystery. It is a shame not to know who thought up the delightful lines given to the man who falls over the side:

Dripping wet, and in a fret, with many more
distressables
A fellow took the long boat-hook, and caught
my inexpressibles.

Or, when the meal is served:

4

"I cannot eat, I loath my meat, I feel my
        stomach failing me,
Steward hasten, bring a bason, what the
        Deuce is ailing me?
If it is handy, get some brandy."—the malady
        to quench unable,
Down I lay, for a half-day—in pickle quite
        unmentionable.

(The misspelled words are the author's, or his printer's.)

Throughout the following two decades, musical stories of embarrassing or unfortunate episodes which originated in England were quickly adopted by performers in this country. Many of the title pages were illustrated with amusing sketches by American artists. True, some of them resembled rather closely the illustrations which appeared on the covers of the original sheets published in London, but it was more expedient to engage an American artist than to bring across the ocean the stones from which the lithographed title pages were run off.

One favorite English song which was written about 1840 and became popular here was "Tea in the Arbour." (See page 16.) It was composed by J. Beuler, and sung "with great applause" by Wm. Latham.

A gentleman who has been invited to tea in the arbor by a Miss Barber is subjected to all sorts of minor irritations, which mount to a crescendo in verse five:

In the fields at our back, boys were shooting at crows,
And a shot coming through, I was wounded,
To expostulate with them of course I arose,
And I climbed up the palings that bounded:
When, behold! my nankeens were bedaub'd and cross barr'd
"Oh I ought to be flogged!" said Old Barber,
"I neglected to tell you the palings were tarr'd
When I asked you to Tea in the Arbour."

"The Cork Leg" (see page 19) has an illustration on the title page with this description underneath it:

A Celebrated Comic Song
Sung with great Applause
by Mr. Burton
at the Philadelphia Theatres.

No author is mentioned.

The poor gentleman of the story, after requiring a leg amputation, gets a new artificial limb made of cork. There is only one difficulty; the leg never stops walking:

> Horror and fright were in his face,
> The neighbours thought he was running a race,
> He clung to a lamp post to stay his pace,
> But the Leg wouldn't stay, but kept on the chase.

A tale of a different kind was told by an English lyricist named Allridge, with music composed by a gentleman who called himself (pseudonymically?) M. T. A'Beckett. The title is "He Was Such a Nice Young Man." (See page 22.)

Upon development, it becomes clear that it isn't the daughter of the homeowners who has attracted the young man; he has other designs, for:

> From House He scarce was out of sight
> Whence from the lower rooms,
> A Servant Maid, came in a fright
> And cried He's stole the Spoons.

Incidentally, this song is 6/8 time.

What were the American comic song writers doing all this time? They were writing, of course, but much of their material was performed by the predecessors of our American minstrel troupes. Micah Hawkins, one of the best of our early song writers, had his songs popularized by a prominent comedian, James Roberts, who performed in blackface. "Jim Crow" was introduced in 1828—again in blackface—by Thomas "Daddy" Rice, its composer. Two other early minstrels each claimed authorship of "Zip Coon," written in 1834 and still featured at every American square dance under its better-known title "Turkey in the Straw."

There were a few writers who dared compete against the English without the assistance of a blackface comedian. Around 1836 one J. C. White teamed up with an associate (who is listed on the title page as T. Ball, but on an inside sheet as Tom Moody) to write "When We Were Out a Fishing!" (see page 25) described on the cover as:

> A Comic Song,
> As Sung with rapturous applause
> Mr. W. F. Johnson,
> at the National Theatre

The lyrics describe the fishing expedition of three somewhat incompetent anglers, who catch few fish but experience a number of catastrophes. One of the trio, Snooks, falls into the stream and has to be rescued, as follows:

> You've heard about too many Cooks,
> And as we strived to land old Snooks,
> We stuck him full of little hooks,
> With which we had been Fishing.

It was not unusual for comic songs to be interspersed with spoken monologues. A performer and song writer of 1841, a Mr. Winchell, used this procedure in his "Niagara Falls" (see page 28), which was, reports the title page:

> sung by him with tremendous applause at
> Harrington's New Museum,
> and at the
> Principal Western Theatres.

It starts routinely enough:

> From Buffalo my labour done,
> For curiosity and fun,
> I took the cars the morning run;
> To go to Niagara falls sirs.

He describes the passengers. Among them:

> A charming Lady of fifty-one,
> Whose volubility of tongue
> Reminded me of a chinese gong.

Then he breaks into his monologue, which develops into a conversation between the passengers, starting with an "Old Gent":

(*Spoken*) "My dear I told you not to bring that child along this frosty morning, you might just as well left it tew hum with the sarvent gall as not."

And so on, for four verses, with interpolations.

An English comic ballad, immensely popular in this country in the 1840's, was "Johnny Sands" (see page 32), which relates the amusing story of a husband and wife whose marriage has gone on the rocks, and who have chosen a most unusual method to dissolve it. The husband agrees to let his wife lead him to the bottom of a hill, tie his hands behind his back, and push him into the water, where he will, of course, drown. But the story does not end quite that way:

7

All down the hill his loving bride
Now ran with all her force
To push him in—he stepped aside,
And she fell in of course.
Now splashing, dashing, like a fish,
"Oh save me Johnny Sands."
"I can't my dear tho' much I wish,
For you have tied my hands."

In the 1850's the "pathetic ballad" (according to the title page) of "Reuben and Phoebe" (see page 34), composed by one D. B. Tenney, was introduced to the American public by W. F. Durant, a concert artist with a traveling group called "Whitehouse's New England Bards." The origin of this entertaining story, which like "Niagara Falls" has much spoken material between the verses, is something of a mystery, for at approximately the same time Durant was performing before American audiences, another singer was presenting the same song on the English stage with a slightly different title: "Reuben Wright & Phoebe Brown, A Tale of a Dismal Swamp." The Englishman was Sam Cowell; and not only was he the singer, but he claimed to be the composer as well. This could well be, because the melodies of the American and English versions differ, though the words are the same for the most part. The English version adds four years to Phoebe's age—twenty-one against seventeen for the American girl—and brings in a bit of British tootling between the verses. For example, to quote from Cowell's song:

In Manchester a maiden dwelt,
Her name was Phoebe Brown;
Her cheeks were red, her hair was black,
(*Spoken*) And she was considered by good judges to be
by all odds the
(*Sung*) best-looking girl in town.
Ri chooral, li chooral, ri chum chooral lay [repeated].

Now even in the nonsense songs which appealed to us in later years, it would seem pretty difficult for Americans to shout "ri chum chooral lay." At any rate, destiny pursues its relentless course, and Reuben, Phoebe, and Brown Senior are all slated to become its victims—in the American version, that is. Here is their terrible fate:

Old Brown then took a deadly aim
Towards young Reuben's head;
But, oh! it was a burning shame, He

(*Spoken*) made a mistake and shot his only daughter,
    and had the unspeakable anguish of seeing her
 (*Sung*) Drop right down stone dead.

    Then anguish fill'd young Reuben's heart,
    And vengeance craz'd his brain;
    He drew an awful jack knife out, and
(*Spoken*) plunged it into old Brown about fifty
    or sixty times, so that it is very doubtful
    about his ever
 (*Sung*) Coming to life again.

Cowell, on the other hand, treats us to a surprise ending, possibly as a predecessor to the English movies which allow Alec Guiness to wind up a performance with a totally unexpected denouement, witness herewith:

    Then Reuben Wright in frenzy tore
    The hair from off his head,
    And, when half scalp'd, the pain was such
 (*Spoken*) That he awoke, and discovered himself lying flat
    on his back, with his bootjack on his chest, and
    his nightcap brimful of the briny torrents,—
    having been out to a tea party, and so regaled
    himself on muffins and crumpets hot, that the
    nightmare he had got on
 (*Sung*) Getting into bed.

Cowell claimed other compositions of considerable importance on the British music-hall scene, one being the successful "Ratcatcher's Daughter," which proved so entertaining that it was published and republished in the United States, once with a title page by Winslow Homer. The authorship of "Vilikins and His Dinah," another number of enormous popularity, was attributed by some to Cowell but by others to John Parry, whose name appears on the copy which is reproduced in a later chapter of this book.

Cowell and his wife toured the United States in 1860 and 1861. Mrs. Cowell kept a copious diary of the trip in which she reported many odd occurrences. For example, when Cowell was insulted by a colonel in Alabama and wanted to retaliate, he was warned to be "well prepared." "What do you mean 'prepared' "? inquired Sam. "Why," cautioned his adviser, "that black cane he carries is both a sword and an air gun; he also carries two revolvers and a bowie knife; and he has a big mastiff, that will seize the throat of anyone who is against his master." Cowell did not pursue the quarrel further.

9

In an Arkansas backwoods settlement the Cowells discovered, on a Sunday morning, that a series of arguments had resulted in the death of three men and the wounding of two others. "Don't you arrest anybody here?" they inquired incredulously. "Oh, no," they were told, "we ain't incorporated yet."

One American ballad with a tune unmistakably from across the ocean is "The Charming Young Widow I Met in the Train." (See page 37.) The rollicking melody was written in the 1840's by John Parry for a Welsh ballad called "Jenny Jones," whose opening words are:

> My name's Edward Morgan, I live at Llangollen
> The vale of St. Tafyd, the flow'r of North Wales.

Edward roves the sea, but eventually returns to his love, Jenny Jones.

Like other good English tunes "Jenny Jones" came to America, was circulated by an American music publisher, and enjoyed mild popularity. Twenty-five years later, a song writer named W. H. Cove put a new set of verses to the old melody to create one of the most entertaining little musical stories of the period, "The Charming Young Widow I Met in the Train." which commences:

> I live in Vermont And one morning last summer,
> A letter inform'd me my uncle was dead,
> And also requested I'd come down to Boston
> As he'd left me a large sum of money it said.

Hardly has the hero entered his railway carriage

> Before a fresh passenger enter'd the door,
> 'Twas a female—a young one—and dress'd
> in deep mourning
> An infant in long clothes she gracefully bore.

Of course the narrator falls madly in love, and as the dialog between the two progresses, the lady becomes emotional and bursts into tears.

> She choking with sobs laid her head on my
> waistcoat—
> Did the Charming Young Widow I met in the Train.

The lady finds an excuse to leave the compartment, entrusting the child to the gentleman. When she fails to reappear, he discovers the loss of his watch and his purse, and learns at the same time that the "child" is a dummy.

Moralizing comes a bit too late:

> And I now wish to counsel young men from the country
> Lest they should get served in a similar way.
> Beware of Young Widows you meet on the Railway
> Who lean on your shoulder, [etc.].

Another great English tale we have not been allowed to forget is one popularly known in recent years as "The Daring Young Man on the Flying Trapeze." (See page 40.) With music arranged by Alfred Lee and lyrics by George Leybourne, it was published as "The Flying Trapeze" in 1868. Its popularity spread to this country almost immediately, and it was distributed by several music publishers simultaneously.

Johnny Allen, a favorite comedian who had been on the minstrel circuit for a number of years, put "Trapeze" into his repertoire and helped the song achieve nationwide recognition.

When Walter O'Keefe, a star of the Rudy Vallee 1939 radio program, re-introduced it on the show, the public reception was so favorable that once again, seventy years after it was written, it skyrocketed past every other song then being promoted. Of all the songs mentioned here, none will be more familiar to the modern reader than:

> Oh he flew through the air with the greatest of ease
> This daring young man on the flying trapeze.

"Matilda Toots" (see page 43), whose author is unknown, relates the breathless adventure of a young couple on an ice-covered park lake. It is a pity that the lyricist of this engaging tale did not reveal his name, for the story is a nice period piece of a hundred years ago. It relates the meeting of the song writer and his girl on the ice, and the near tragedy that ensues. A peculiar taste has our hero: apparently he is not attracted by the lady's face and figure, but rather by her shoes. Had there been a pre-Freudian psychoanalyst present to observe this unorthodox attachment, he would certainly have drawn some strange conclusions. Our young gentleman's fancy runs along these lines:

> Oh! Matilda Toots
> You should have seen her boots,
> Upon the ice they look'd so nice,
> Did the boots of 'Tilda Toots.

And near the end, when cute Miss Toots is headed for a watery grave, she is rescued. How? By the boots, of course!

Many of the nineteenth-century comedians wrote their own material.

One well-known and versatile performer of the 1870's was Charles A. Reade. He was described on the title pages of his songs as "The Great German Star and Ethiopian Comedian" (quite a combination!), and many of his songs are in German dialect. "I Lose Me Mine Vife" (see page 46) tells the sad story of a saloonkeeper's broken marriage, which has monologs between the verses, such as:

> (*Spoken*) a couple days after I opened I don't hardly got enny more customers except tree: me und mine vife vos der best customers und anoder feller we use to bring his dinner mit him und steal all mine sausages, bumpernickels, soup spoons und kiss mine frou by der door. . . .

> (*Sung*) But I'm sorry to say mine vife's gone avay
> Und left me forlorn in dis vide vorld to mourn,
> But how can I tell she's gone with some swell
> Or I may hear before long dot she's married
> Brigham Young.

Sometimes a song writer would be impelled to write about important events reported in the newspapers. Usually such songs dealt with serious subjects such as a war or a president or the death of a prominent individual. But occasionally an event warranted a light-hearted composition, and one of these was an around-the-world trip, some ninety years ago, by a newspaperwoman named Nelly Bly. The song, written by Joe Hart, an erstwhile blackface minstrel and member of the vaudeville team of Hallen and Hart, was dedicated to the young lady's employer, the *New York World*, and was called "Globe Trotting Nelly Bly." (See page 49.) After explaining that she is attempting to circle the world in a record-breaking seventy-five days, the song tells of her experiences:

> When she landed in Cork, to Killarney took a walk,
> And kissed the blarney stone with her sweet lips;
> She told funny tales to the Prince of Wales,
> And left him laughing almost in a fit.
> She did the Gaiety dance and set Paris in a trance,
> Sang "Little Annie Rooney" to Jules Verne.

And so on, introducing the topical personalities and subjects of the period.

To some present-day readers these songs may be as far-out as Never-Never Land. But our fun-loving great-grandfathers relished them, and so may we if we will play the melodies, sing the verses, and smile, smile, smile.

OH, WHAT A ROW!

or the

ADVENTURES OF A STEAM PACKET

A NEW

Comic Song

As Sung by Mr. Barnes.

New-York: Engraved, Printed, & Sold by E. RILEY, No. 29 Chatham Street.

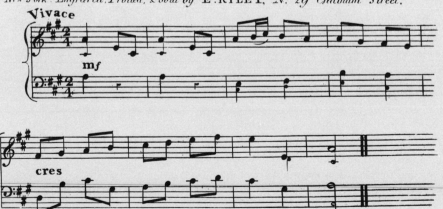

Oh, What A Row!

Oh! what a row! what a rum-pus and a riot-ing, All those en-dure, you may be sure, that go to sea. A ship is a thing that you nev-er can be qui-et in, by wind or steam, it's all the same, 'twas so with me. Wife and daugh-ter on the wa-ter, said they'd like to sail a bit. I con-sent-ed, soon re-pent-ed, soon be-gan to rail a bit; Pa, now pray! go to-day, the wea-ther's so in-vit-ing, lauk I'm sure t'will do such good to you, they feed you like a fight-ing cock. Oh what a row what a rum-pus and a ri-ot-ing, all those en-dure, you may be sure that go to sea.

2. In a boat, I got afloat, as clumsy as an Elephant,
   So spruce and gay, to spend the day, and make a splash,
   Gad! it's true, I did it too, for stepping in, I fell off on't
   And overboard, upon my word, I went, slap dash,
   Wife squalling, Daughter bawling, every thing provoking me,
   Called "a Hog, a Poodle dog," all the sailors joking me.
   Dripping wet, and in a fret, with many more distressables
   A fellow took, the long boat-hook, and caught my inexpressibles.
                        Oh! what a Row! &c.

14

3. Such a gig, without a wig, on deck I was exhibited,
   Laughed at by the Passengers, and quizzed by the crew;
   Raved and swore, that on the shore, I rather had been gibbetted,—
   Than thus, half drown'd, by all around, be roasted too;
   Danger past, and dry at last, indulging curiosity,
   I stared to see, the Vessel flee, with such a strange velocity;
   "Pray" said I, to one just by, "What power can impel us so,"
   "The smokey Devil goes by steam, at least the Lubbers tell us so."
                                        Oh! what a Row! &c.

4. Not a sail, to catch a gale, yet magically on I went,
   'Gainst wind and tide, and all beside, in wonder quite;
   Cast my eye, up to the sky, and tall as Trinty's Monument,
   I saw the Kitchen Chimney smoke, as black as night.
   People toiling, roasting, boiling, bless us! such a rookery,
   They'd soup and fish, and fowl and flesh, and Niblo's Tavern cookery;
   Then the noise, of Men and Boys! a din to rival Hell's Hubbub,
   I thought the crew, were Devils all, the master Captn. Belzebub.
                                        Oh! what a Row! &c.

5. Wife to me, says—says she "Now's your time to pick a bit,
   "The dinner's serving up below—and we must fly."
   Says I, "My dear I'm very queer, I'm going to be sick a bit,
   I'm seized with an *alloverness,* I faint! I die!
   I cannot eat, I loath my meat, I feel my stomach failing me.
   Steward hasten, bring a bason, what the Deuce is ailing me?
   If it is handy, get some brandy"—the malady to quench unable,
   Down I lay, for a half-day—in pickle quite unmentionable.
                                        Oh! what a Row! &c.

6. As to dinner, I'm a sinner, if I touched a bit of it,
   But anchor cast, and home at last, I'm safe once more;
   In the packet, such a racket! crowding to get quit of it,
   Like cattle from a coaster, we were hauled on shore.
   With "how d'ye do," and "how are you, I see your better *physically,"*
   "Zounds *be still,* I'm very ill, you're always talking quizzically,
   Some with glee, may go to sea, but I shall not be willing, Sir,
   For *such a day,* again to pay, just Two pounds fifteen shillings, Sir."
                                        Oh! what a Row! &c.

TEA IN THE ARBOUR,

A Comic Song,

Written by

J. BEULER,

and Sung with great applause!

by

M.r W.m LATHAM.

PHILADELPHIA,

G. W. Hewitt & Co. 70 South Third Street.

Come And Take Tea In The Arbour

What plea-sure folks feel, when they live out of town, in the cul-ture of tur-nips and

flow — ers   And get-ting a friend, now and then to come down to look at their walks and their

bow-ers, And such is the taste of some dear friends of mine, Mister, Mis-tress, and Miss Ma-ry

Bar - ber, who will oft have me come to their vil-la to dine, and then to take tea in the ar-bour;

Where there are sweet Bil-lies and Daf-fy down dil-lies Per-fumes like the shop of a bar-ber; And

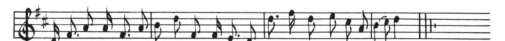

ro-ses and po-sies to scent up your no-ses Then come and take tea in the ar-bour.

2. As oft as I can I decline their invite,
For of rural delights I'm no lover;
Of insects and reptiles I can't bear the sight,
Oh, they e'er make me shudder all over.
However last Monday I went there to dine;
"I am glad you are come," said Miss Barber,
"I know you will like it, the weather's so fine,
And we will all take Tea in the Arbour."
Sweet Billies and Lillies and Daffydowndillies, etc.

3. I had on thin shoes and the gravel was damp,
   The thought of it made me quite nervous,
   From a cold, or a fit of the gout, or the cramp,
   I said to myself "Lud preserve us!"
   And when we went there a great frog made me jump
   Which was excellent fun to Miss Barber;
   Then there was a long caterpillar fell plump
   In my first cup of tea in the Arbour.
   Sweet Billies and Lillies and Daffydowndillies, etc.

4. Of little green flies on my dress came a host,
   And a bee put me all in a flutter;
   A great daddy long legs stuck fast on my toast,
   And left one of his limbs in the butter.
   On the sugar six blue bottles sat hob a nob,
   And while I discours'd with Old Barber,
   From above a black spider swung hibbity bob
   In my chops as I sat in the Arbour.
   Sweet Billies and Lillies and Daffydowndillies, etc.

5. In the fields at our back, boys were shooting at crows,
   And a shot coming through, I was wounded,
   To expostulate with them of course I arose,
   And I climb'd up the palings that bounded:
   When, behold! my nankeens were bedaub'd and cross barr'd
   "Oh I ought to be flogg'd!" said Old Barber,
   "I neglected to tell you the palings were tarr'd
   When I ask'd you to Tea in the Arbour."
   Sweet Billies and Lillies and Daffydowndillies, etc.

6. Then I happened to tread where a man trap was set,
   Which snapping, my leg held fast in, Sirs,
   And ere I got out, it came on heavy wet,
   And soon I was soaked to the skin, Sirs.
   In rather bad temper I homewards did jog,
   And next morning I wrote to Miss Barber,
   That squash'd in my pocket, I found the great frog,
   Which had frighten'd me first in the Arbour.
   And though there be lillies and daffydowndillies,
   Said I, in my note to Miss Barber,
   And roses perfuming, excuse me from coming
   Again to take Tea in the Arbour.

J. H. Buffard, del. & lith.

"He clung to a Lamp Post
To stay his Pace"

THE CORK LEG,

A CELEBRATED COMIC SONG

Sung with great Applause,

BY

Mr BURTON

at the Philadelphia Theatres.

NEW YORK.

Munson Bancroft. 395. Broadway.

I'll tell you a tale now with-out an-y flam, In Hol-land there dwelt Myn-heer Von Clam, Who

ev'ry morn-ing said, I am the rich-est mer-chant in Rot-ter-dam, Ri tu, di nu, di nu, di nu,

Ri tu, di ni, nu, ri tu, di nu, ri na.

2. One day, when he had stuff'd him as full as an egg,
   A poor relation came to beg,
   But he kick'd him out without broaching a keg,
   And in kicking him out he broke his leg,
     Ri tu, di nu, &c.

3. A surgeon, the first in his vocation,
   Came and made a long oration,
   He wanted a limb for anatomization,
   So he finish'd his jaw by amputation,
     Ri tu, di nu, &c.

4. "Mr. Doctor" says he, when he'd done his work,
   "By your sharp knife I lose one fork,
   "But on two crutches I never will stalk,
   "For I'll have a beautiful leg of Cork,"
     Ri tu, di nu, &c.

5. An Artist in Rotterdam, t'would seem,
   Had made Cork Legs his study and theme,
   Each joint was as strong as an iron beam,
   And the springs were a compound of clockwork & steam,
     Ri tu, di nu, &c.

6. The Leg was made, and fitted right,
   Inspection the Artist, did invite,

Its fine shape gave Mynheer delight,
As he fix'd it on and screw'd it tight,
     Ri tu, di nu, &c.

7. He walked through squares and pass'd each shop,
Of speed he went to the utmost top,
Each step he took with a bound and a hop,
And he found his leg he could not stop!
     Ri tu, di nu, &c.

8. Horror and fright were in his face,
The neighbours thought he was running a race,
He clung to a lamp post to stay his pace,
But the Leg wouldn't stay, but kept on the chase,
     Ri tu, di nu, &c.

9. Then he called to some men with all his might,
"Oh! stop this Leg or I'm murder'd quite!"
But though they heard him aid invite,
In less than a minute he was out of sight,
     Ri tu, di nu, &c.

10. He ran o'er hill and dale and plain,
To ease his weary bones he'd fain,
Did throw himself down—but all in vain,
The Leg got up and was off again!
     Ri tu, di nu, &c.

11. He walk'd of days and nights a score,
Of Europe he had made the tour,
He died—but though he was no more,
The Leg walk'd on the same as before!
     Ri tu, di nu, &c.

12. In Holland sometimes it comes in sight,
A skeleton on a Cork Leg tight,
No cash did the Artist's skill requite,
He never was paid—and it sarv'd him right,
     Ri tu, di nu, &c.

13. My tale I've told both plain and free,
Of the rummest merchant that could be,
Who never was buried—though dead we see,
And I've been singing his L. E. G. (elegy.)
     Ri tu, di nu, &c.

'HE WAS SUCH A NICE YOUNG MAN'

From the House he was scarce out of sight,
When from the lower room
A servant maid came in a fright,
And cried he stole the spoons.

A Celebrated Comic Song.

WRITTEN BY

R. W. ALLDRIDGE,

The Music Composed & Arranged

BY

M. T. A'BECKETT.

Pr. 50 cts.

NEW YORK,

Published at ATWILL'S MUSIC SALOON, 201, Broadway.

Lith.d of Endicott N.Y.

He Was Such A Nice Young Man

If pi-ty dwell with-in your breast, some sym-pa-thy pray spare, Of love that breaks

young ladies' rest, in-deed I've had my share, His form is e-ver in my sight, For-get I

nev-er can; I'm haunt-ed by him day and night, He was such a nice young man.

2. 'Twas at a Ball held in the West,
   On me He first did glance,
   So gently He my fingers prest
   And ask'd me out to dance.
   I blush'd and whisper'd no, no, no.
   Then smiling drop'd my fan,
   For how cou'd I refuse to dance,
   He was such a nice young Man.

3. When growing late, about to leave
   It rain'd in torrents fast,
   Said He, dear Miss I really grieve
   I fear that it will last,
   Then quick he hurri'd from the room
   And for a Coach he ran,
   His kindness quite o'erpower'd me
   He was such a nice young Man.

4. As through the Hall we went along
   He beg'd for my address
   I gave him it, not thinking wrong
   He was in such distress
   His card emboss'd he handed me

   With Captain Miss I am
   My stars! thought I oh here's a chance
   He was such a nice young Man.

5. Next morning dress'd and breakfast
      done
   Heart beating with desire,
   The Hall door Bell was loudly rung
   Enough to break the wire,
   I thought I should have died with
         fright
   Up come our Servant Ann,
   A Gentleman Miss waits below
   He is! such a nice young Man.

6. Almost had sunk 'twixt hope and fear
   I wish'd I was afar,
   Guess my surprise Him now to hear
   Conversing with Mamma,
   Such language elegant he used
   Her Heart He did trepan,
   She said She no objection had
   He was such a nice young Man.

23

7. Now stop to dine with us you must
   I will not take denial
   Excuse me Mam this visit first
   Is far too great a trial,
   Well call again whene'er you please
   For visit here you can,
   I'll call again tomorrow Mam
   Said my very nice young Man.

8. From House He scarce was out of sight
   Whence from the lower rooms,
   A Servant Maid, came in a fright
   And cried He's stole the Spoons.
   Ah! fetch him back Mamma she cried

Off went our footman Dan
Who brought him back—we found the
   Spoons
Yes, upon the nice young Man.

9. A caution Ladies give I must
   The Moral I well know
   'Tis never the appearance trust
   Of any dashing Beau,
   For this is what I should have done
   When to notice He began
   But who'd have thought he was a
      thief,
   He was such a nice young Man.

"WHEN WE WERE OUT A FISHING!"

A COMIC SONG,

As Sung with rapturous applause,

MR. W. F. JOHNSON,

at the

NATIONAL THEATRE

Music by J. C. WHITE, *Words by* T. BALL.

NEW YORK

Published by ENDICOTT, 359 *Broadway.*

When We Went Out A Fishing

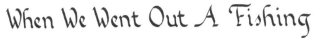

Last night Tom Snooks says he to me, If you've a mind some fun to see, I'll take you out with

two or three, who mean to go a fish-ing. So get a rod, a can, and bait— We start from town pre-

cise at 8, Then mind Friend Muggs you aren't too late, to go with us a fish-ing; Says I, I will so

up I goes, to Mr.— Spout with my best cloathes, and bor-rowed what you may sup-pose, to

rig me out for fish-ing; With rods and lines and bait a store— E-nough for half a doz-en more, I

nev-er shall for-get the bore, of go-ing out a fish-ing

2. Then off we trudged thro' dust and sun,
The perspiration off me run,
Thinks I, I hope this ar'nt the fun
Of going out a Fishing,
At length we reached the River side,
And soon upon the glittering tide,
Our Floats like little boats did ride,
As Floats do when you're Fishing.
I felt a Tug—I tugged again,
And pulled away with might and main,
When up I bring's a Dog and Chain,
When we were out a Fishing.
With Rods and Lines, &c.

26

3. Lord how they laughed to see the prize,
   When, Snooks (you know he's such a size)
   Soused in the stream to our surprize,
   As tho to spoil our Fishing.
   You've heard about too many Cooks,
   And as we strived to land old Snooks,
   We stuck him full of little hooks,
   With which we had been Fishing.
   At length our Friend on shore we brought,
   He puffed and blowed, you would have thought,
   A full grown Porpoise we had caught
   When we were out a Fishing.
   With Rods and Lines, &c.

4. We brandy'd Snooks he soon was well,
   We plied away and must I tell,—
   What next to Jemmy Higgs befell,
   When we were out a Fishing.
   The sun was hot, the grass was green,
   He set him where the cows had been,
   And such a sight was his nankeen,
   When we were out Fishing.
   I warning took and on a rail,
   I like the bird in Nursery Tale,
   What wagged about his little tail,
   Perched me up for Fishing.
   With Rods and Lines, &c.

5. But sad mischance the rail was old,
   It broke and down the bank I rolled,
   Look here! I'm sure I shall catch cold,
   From going out a Fishing.
   The mud was soft, my legs are thin,
   And farther I kept sinking in,
   Until I thought t'would reach my chin,
   When we were out a Fishing.
   At last, says I this will not suit,
   So out I bawls, when Higgs the brute,
   He lugged me out but left my boot,
   Where I had been a Fishing.
   With Rods and Lines, &c.

27

Niagara Falls

From Buf-fa-lo my la-bour done. For cur-i-os-i-ty and fun, I took the cars the
morn-ing run; to go to Ni-ag-a-ra Falls, sirs, The morn was cold the snow fell fast,
Old Bor-eas blew a piping blast, with two horse powr sat off at last. We'd pas-sen-gers of
ev-ry cast; There was M-r and M-rs Frost and son. A charm-ing La-dy of fif-ty
one, whose vol-u-bil-i-ty of tounge re-mind-ed me of a Chi-nese gong.

The following conversation took place in the Cars, between an old Lady and Gentleman.

(*Spoken*) OLD GENT: "My dear I told you not to bring that Child along this frosty morning, you might just as well left it tew hum with the sarvent gall as not, and it would have been well taken care of; let me hold it that's a dear."

OLD LADY: "No Mr. Frost I'll carry it myself so I will, the ony dony lettle huny-buny, I did not want to set off for the falls so early in the spring, but you are an untimely frost Mr. Frost as your conduct sufficiently evinces; last fall you were for going to the springs and this spring you are for going to the falls, last winter you went to Sum-

NIAGARA FALLS,

Written by

MR WINCHELL,

And sung by him with tremendous applause at

HARRINGTON'S NEW MUSEUM,

and at the

PRINCIPAL WESTERN THEATRES.

BOSTON.

Published by **HENRY PRENTISS**, 33 Court St.

Entered according to Act of Congress in the year 1841 by Henry Prentiss in the Clerks office of the District Court of Massachusetts.

B.W. Thayer's Lithog.^y Boston.

mertown we put up at Mr. Snows Hotel where we had all like to have frozen to death." (*Child cries.*) "There there yes Mamas dear pet shall go and see the"

> Rumbling tumbling tearing away,
> Wallowing bellowing wet with spray
> Like aunt Deborahs washing day;
> This trip to Niagara falls.

2. The driver did his horses crack,
   But the snow kept drifting o'er the track,
   Which made our travelling rather slack,
   Going to Niagara falls sirs.
   At length we arrived in time to dine.
   The Cateract hotel is fine;
   We'd flesh and fish of ev'ry kind,
   And negro waiters to stand behind
   The Landlord he procured a guide,
   Who took us down to the water side
   Where we rock'd and pitch'd in the foaming tide,
   As through the surge our boat did glide.

OLD LADY: "Dont sit over there sir, if you do we shall overset." OLD GENT: "Billy my boy set up out of the bottom of the boat." BOY: "Oh no Pa I'm afraid I shall upset oh! mama! see what a sight of ice there is all around the boat." "Sartain" (observed a Yankee). "This is an ice boat wherry." OLD GENT: "Dont be making fun its punishment enough crossing this pond tis pon my word Ah! theres the English 'hallo' I wonder whats the reason they are not as high as the American falls." YANKEE: "Well as nigh as I can callate 'tis because they haint got so far to fall." OLD LADY: "How is it possible you can jest in the midst of this

> Rumbling tumbling, &c.

3. Midst foaming billows at length we land,
   On cakes of rocky ice and sand,
   We all got safe upon the strand,
   Going to Niagara falls sirs.
   We gazed upon the English falls,
   Tumbling over natures walls;
   The noise of which your heart appalls,
   Just like the thousand thunder squalls,
   A red coat sentry bid us stand,
   A froth of a boy from Paddys land;
   With bayonet fix'd and pen in hand,
   To sign our names did us command.

Sentry: "Ladies and Gentleman won and all ye's cant pass here any way ye's can fix it 'till ye's all put down your names, 'tis for that reason I'm placed here on guard by her Majestys government and am bound to enforce the commands of my superior officer, ye's have all written down but divil the word can I wread but I spose its all right or ye's wouldnt write it. A little silver in my hand by way of keeping the divil out of my stomach, I know the Yankees would rather it were lead than silver, but long life to ye's if ye's die tomorrow you can all walk up and see the"

Rumbling tumbling, &c.

4. Stuck fast in mud with sad turmoil,
Some lost a shoe, amidst the toil,
At length we reach'd the topmast soil,
That leads to Niagara falls sirs.
The rival cateracts in view,
Roaring and rushing ever knew;
Goat Island stands betwixt the two;
The English falls they call horse shoe,
Near Table Rock we all descend,
Down winding steps that never end,
The Ladies our aid we had to lend;
Each begging the other her pace to mend.

Old Lady: "Oh! dear I cant go under there, wont that rock fall on us? does nobody never get kill'd under here nor nothing?" Yankee: "Nobody I guess that ever liv'd to tell on it." Guide: "Don't be frightn'd Ladies you are now in sight of the sublimest of spectacles." Old Gent: "I left my spectacles to hum." Frenchman: "Heres von grand plaze pour de contemplation." Yankee: "Grand for washing sheep." Dutch-man: "Dish falls is pig." Dandy: "Oh! de'ah I am really distracted with this"

Rumbling tumbling, &c.

Johnny Sands

COMIC BALLAD

Composed by

JOHN SINCLAIR.

25 net

PIANO.   GUITAR.

BOSTON. *Published by* OLIVER DITSON *115 Washington St.*

J. E. GOULD.
Philadelphia. T. T. BARKER. *Boston.* D. A. TRUAX. *Cincinnati.* C. C. CLAPP & Co. *Boston.* T. S. BERRY. *N.York.*

Entered according to act of Congress AD 1842 by O. Ditson in the Clerks Office of the Dist. Court of Mass.
B F Greene. Eng.

Johnny Sands

A man whose name was John-ny Sands, had mar-ried Bet - ty Hague And though she brought him gold and lands, she prov'd a ter-ri-ble plague, For Oh! she was a scold-ing wife, full of ca-price and whim. He said that he was tired of life, and she was tired of him, and she was tired of him, and she was tired of him. Says he "then I will drown my-self - The ri-ver runs be-low," Says she, "pray do you sil-ly elf I wished it long a-go," Says he, "Up-on the brink I'll stand, do you run down the hill, and push me in with all your might," Says she, "My love I will," Says she, "My love I will," Says she, "My love I will."

"For fear that I should courage lack
And try to save my life,
Pray tie my hands behind my back."
"I will," replied his wife.
She tied them fast as you may think,
And when securely done,
"Now stand," she says, "Upon the brink
And I'll prepare to run,
And I'll prepare to run,
And I'll prepare to run."

All down the hill his loving bride
Now ran with all her force
To push him in—he stepped aside,
And she fell in of course.
Now splashing, dashing, like a fish,
"Oh save me Johnny Sands."
"I can't my dear tho' much I wish
For you have tied my hands,
For you have tied my hands,
For you have tied my hands."

Reuben and Phoebe

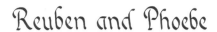

In Man-ches-ter a mai-den dwelt whose name was Phoe-be Brown. Her cheeks were

red, her eyes were black, and she was acknowledged by good judges to be by all odds the best

look-ing girl in town. Her age was on-ly se-ven-teen, her eyes were spark-ling bright. A

very lovely girl she was, and for about a year and a half there had been a young fellow paying

attention to her, by the name of Reuben Wright.

2. Now Reuben was a nice young man,
   As any in the town;
   And Phoebe loved him very dear, But
(*Spoken*) on account of his being obliged to work for a living, he never could make himself agreeable to
   (*Sung*) old Mr. and Mrs. Brown.
   Her cruel parents were resolved
   Another she should wed,
   A rich old miser in the place, And
(*Spoken*) old Brown has frequently been heard to declare that rather than have his daughter marry Reuben Wright he'd sooner . . . .
   (*Sung*) Knock her in the head.

34

REUBEN WRIGHT & PHŒBE BROWN,
A Tale of a Dismal Swamp.

S. ROSENTHAL LITHO.   Sam Cowell — From a Photograph by La Roche.   2 RED LION SQUARE, HOLBORN.

Composed and Sung by
SAM COWELL.

ENT. STA. HALL.   PRICE. SIXPENCE.

3. But Phoebe's heart was bold and strong,
   She feared not parents frowns;
   And as for Reuben Wright so brave, I've

(Spoken) heard him say more than fifty times that with the exception of Phoebe, he didn't care a snap for

(Sung) All the race of Browns.
   So Phoebe Brown and Reuben Wright
   Determined they would marry;
   Three weeks ago last Tuesday night They

(Spoken) started for old Parson Wheeler's determined to be united in the holy bonds of matrimony although it was tremendous dark and rained

(Sung) like the old Harry.

4. But Captain Brown was wide awake,
   He loaded up his gun,
   And then persued the loving pair, He

(Spoken) overtook 'em when they'd got about half way there, and then Phoebe and Reuben started

(Sung) Off upon a run.
   Old Brown then took a deadly aim
   Towards young Reuben's head;
   But oh! it was a bleeding shame, He

(Spoken) made a mistake and shot his only daughter, and had the unspeakable anguish of seeing her

(Sung) drop right down stone dead.

5. Then anguish filled young Reuben's heart,
   And vengeance crazed his brain,
   He drew an awful jacknife out, And

(Spoken) plunged it into Old Brown about fifty or sixty times, so that it was very doubtful about his ever

(Sung) coming to life again.
   The briny drops from Reuben's eyes
   In torrents poured down,
   He yielded up the ghost and died, And

(Spoken) in this melancholy and heart rending manner terminates the eventful history of Reuben and Phoebe, and like

(Sung) Wise Old Captain Brown.

THE CHARMING YOUNG WIDOW I MET IN THE TRAIN

BOSTON & NEW YO

HE'S MY LATE HUSBANDS BROTHER DEAR WOULD YOU KINDLY
MY BEST BELOVED CHILD FOR A MOMENT SUSTAIN,

OF COURSE I COMPLIED, THEN OFF ON THE PLATFORM
TRIPPED THE CHARMING YOUNG WIDOW I MET IN THE TRAIN.

BY

W. H. GOVE

J.H. BUFFORD'S LITH.

BOSTON:
Published by OLIVER DITSON & CO. 277 Washington St.

W. A POND & CO.
N. YORK.

J. C. HAYNES & CO.
BOSTON.

JOHN CHURCH JR.
Cinn.

G. W. A. TRUMPLER.
Phila.

LYON & HEALY.
Chicago.

The Charming Young Widow I Met In The Train

I live in Ver-mont, and one morn-ing last sum-mer, a let-ter in-form'd me my Un-cle was dead,

and al-so re-quest-ed I'd come down to Bos-ton as he'd left me a large sum of mon-ey   it

said. Of course I de-ter-min'd on mak-ing the jour-ney and to book my-self by the "first

class" I was fain   Tho' had I gone "se-cond" I had nev-er en-coun-ter'd The Charm-ing Young

Wi-dow I met in the Train.

2. Yet scarce was I seated within the compartment,
   Before a fresh passenger enter'd the door,
   'Twas a female—a young one—and dress'd in deep mourning
   An infant in long clothes she gracefully bore,
   A white cap surrounded a face oh so lovely!
   I never shall look on one like it again
   I fell deep in love over head in a moment,
   With the Charming Young Widow I met in the Train.

3. The Widow and I side by side sat together
   The carriage containing ourselves and no more,
   When silence was broken by my fair companion
   Who enquired the time by the watch that I wore.
   I of course satisfied her, and then conversation
   Was freely indulged in by both, 'till my brain
   Fairly reeled with excitement, I grew so enchanted
   With the Charming Young Widow I met in the Train.

4. We became so familiar I ventured to ask her
   How old was the child that she held at her breast.
   "Ah Sir!" she responded, and into tears bursting
   Her infant still closer convulsively pressed.
   "When I think of my child I am well nigh distracted
   Its Father—my Husband—oh my heart breaks with pain."
   She choking with sobs leaned her head on my waistcoat—
   Did the Charming Young Widow I met in the Train.

5. By this time the Train had arrived at a Station
   Within a few miles of the great one in town
   When my charmer exclaimed, as she looked through the window
   "Good gracious alive! why there goes Mr. Brown.
   He's my late Husband's Brother—dear Sir would you kindly
   My best beloved child for a moment sustain?"
   Of course I complied—then off on the platform
   Tripped the Charming Young Widow I met in the Train.

6. Three minutes elapsed when the whistle it sounded
   The Train began moving—no Widow appeared.
   I bawled out "stop! stop," but they paid no attention
   With a snort, and a jerk, starting off as I feared.
   In this horrid dilemma I sought for the hour—
   But my watch! ha! where was it? where where was my chain!
   My purse too, my ticket, gold pencil-case—all gone!
   Oh that Artful Young Widow I met in the Train.

7. While I was my loss thus so deeply bewailing
   The Train again stopped and I "tickets please" heard.
   So I told the Conducter while dandling the infant
   The loss I'd sustained—but he doubted my word.
   He called more officials—a lot gathered round me—
   Uncovered the child—oh how shall I explain!
   For behold 'twas no baby—'twas only a dummy!
   Oh that Crafty Young Widow I met in the Train.

8. Satisfied I'd been robbed they allowed my departure
   Though, of course I'd to settle my fare the next day.
   And I now wish to counsel young men from the country
   Lest they should get served in a similar way.
   Beware of Young Widows you meet on the Railway
   Who lean on your shoulder—whose tears fall like rain.
   Look out for your pockets in case they resemble
   The Charming Young Widow I met on the Train.

To the HANLON BROS.

THE FLYING TRAPEZE

Comic Song & Chorus

AS SUNG WITH IMMENSE APPLAUSE

BY JOHNNY ALLEN.

ARRANGED BY R. FRANK CARDELLA

Mallory

ST. LOUIS
Published by COMPTON & DOAN, 205 N. Fourth St.

ENT'D ACCORDING TO ACT OF CONGRESS IN THE YEAR 1868 BY COMPTON & DOAN, IN THE CLERK'S OFFICE OF THE U.S. DIST. COURT FOR THE EAST. DIST. OF MO.
STUDLEY & CO., LITH.

Flying Trapeze

Oh once I was hap-py but now I'm for-lorn Like an old coat that is tat-ter'd and torn

Left in this wide world to fret and to mourn Be-tray'd by a girl in her teens — The girl that I

love she is hand-some I tried all I could her to please But I could not court her so

well As that man on the fly-ing trap-eze Oh he flew through the air with the great-est

of ease This charm-ing young man on the fly-ing trap-eze His name was Au-gus-tus the

girls he could please And my love he stole a-way. —

2. This man by name was Segnor Von Slum,
   Tall, big and handsome as well made as Chum,
   Whene'er he appeared, the halls loudly rang
   With cheers from the people there.

   He looked from the bar on the people below
   And then he looked at my love,
   She smiled back at him and shouted bravo
   As he hung by his ear from above.

   CHORUS

3. I once went to see if my love was at home
   I found there her father and her mother alone,
   When I asked for my duck they soon made it known
   That she had bolted away;
   She packed up her box and eloped that night
   With him with the greatest of ease,
   He lowered her down from a two pair back
   To the ground with his flying trapeze.

   CHORUS

4. One night I went out to a popular hall
   Was greatly surprised to see on the wall
   A bill in large letters which did my heart pall
   To see that she was playing with him.
   He taught her gymnastics and dressed her in tights
   To swing with the greatest of ease,
   He made her assume a masculine name
   And now she floats on the trapeze.

   CHORUS

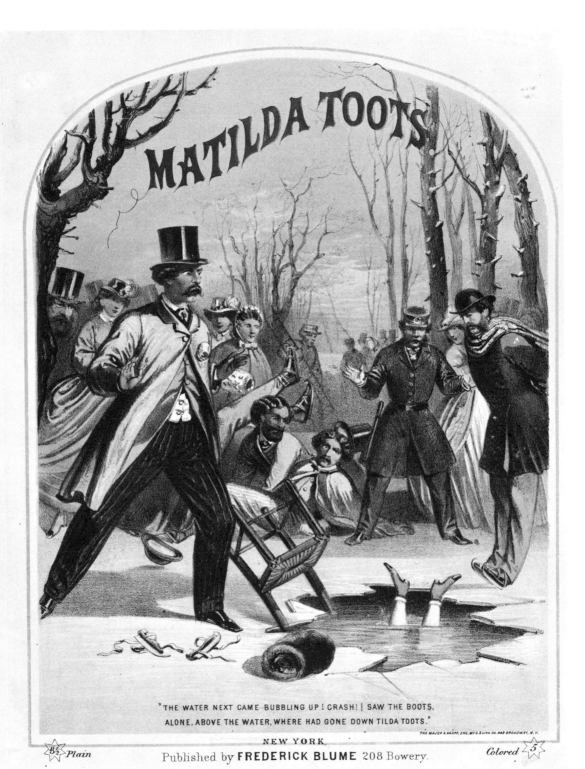

MATILDA TOOTS

"THE WATER NEXT CAME BUBBLING UP! CRASH! | SAW THE BOOTS,
ALONE, ABOVE THE WATER, WHERE HAD GONE DOWN TILDA TOOTS."

NEW YORK,
Published by **FREDERICK BLUME** 208 Bowery.

Plain

Colored

Tilda Toots

One fros-ty day on plea-sure bent I stroll'd in to the park   with skates in hand up-on the ice

to have a skat-ing lark   Some were whirl-ing round like tops, some dart-ing like a flash   Oth-ers

cut their names out, too, and oth-ers cut a dash   But not a-lone was I that day, for there in fur-topp'd

boots   and four rows of pearl but-tons was my own Ma-til-da Toots. Oh! my own Ma-til-da

Toots,   you should have seen her boots! Up-on the ice they look'd so nice, did the boots of

Chorus

Til-da Toots   Oh! Ma-til-da Toots,   you should have seen her boots,   Up-on the ice they look'd

so nice, did the boots of Til-da Toots.

44

2. She had the prettiest pair of skates of highly polish'd steel,
   And gracefully in chair she sat while I prepar'd to kneel
   Down at her feet to put them on, by boring in the soles
   Of those fur-topp'd pearl button'd boots the smallest gimlet holes;
   But just as I upon my knee had got one of her boots,
   A skater from behind upset *me*, *chair*, and 'Tilda Toots.

CHORUS

3. As I, the chair, and 'Tilda Toots, were struggling in a heap,
   A dozen skaters, more or less, came o'er us with a sweep.
   Some went tumbling head o'er heels, others on the back,
   When suddenly where 'Tilda lay the ice began to crack!
   The water next came bubbling up! *crash!* I saw the boots,
   Alone *above* the waters where had *gone down* 'Tilda Toots.

CHORUS

4. " 'Scape ladders, grappling hooks, help! help!" I roar'd with all my might.
   A squad of gallant "Park Guides" then quickly hove in sight!
   They ran a ladder cross the hole, the men aside I cast,
   I scarcely think I touch'd a rail, I rush'd along so fast;
   But I was there in time to save the soul of my pursuits,
   For by those boots, those fur-topp'd boots, I dragg'd out 'Tilda Toots.

CHORUS

5. With 'Tilda in my arms to the Refreshment House I flew—
   They us'd the proper remedies, and quickly brought her to.
   I call'd a cab and saw her home—and saving thus her life,
   Matilda Toots agreed next day to be my darling wife;
   And as the water did not spoil those fur-topp'd button'd boots,
   Why in those boots—identical boots—I married Matilda Toots.

CHORUS

I Lose Me Mine Vife

I dink me vone day dot dere bis-ness would pay to keep a sa-loon in der town—— So I went right a-way der wer-ry next day to rent a base-ment what's close by der ground When I rent me dot blace then I bot Swi-zer-kase, Lag-er beer und plak pud-dings ten pound—— Und I open'd right a-vay der wer-ry next day und asked der poys all to come down.

Chorus

But I'm sor-ry to say mine wife's gone a-vay und left me for-lorn in dis vide vorld to mourn, But how can I tell she's gone with some swell or I may hear before long dot she's mar-ried Brigham Young.

(*Spoken*) Yes! und der night I opened dot saloon you ought have seen der croud vot come down dere, I dought dot I vould be a rich man soon if I would sell so much beer efery day. For I vos going to take all der money vot I could make and buy stock in Chinese laundries but a couple days after I opened I don't hardly got enny more customers except tree; me and mine vife vos der best customers und anoder feller we use to bring his dinner mit him und steal all mine sausages, bumper-nickels, soup spoons und kiss mine frou by der door when I vos going und becase I scold me mine frou about dot she got mad und now

2. Von afternoon about five I said to my vife,
   I must valk me avhile by der street;
   Und ven I cum out I meet mister Stout;
   Who said Yacop jost go down und see Pete.

Vhile in Peters we sat dot come in my head,
Dot my frou Katharine vos alone;
Vhen I dink me dot I hurried right back;
But I found my frou she vos gone.

(*Spoken*) Yes! Vhen I come down to Peters mit mister Stout he vanted me to play cards mit dem for one hundred dollars a site. But I say, gentlemen, I dont got me some money; but mister Stout he say Yakob dots all right I'll put up a hundred dollars against your vife. I say dots all right then so ve commenced to play. I vos 2 points ahead of him der first ding, and thought sure I vos going to win der 100 dollars, but all by sudden he beat me und the first ding vot I know he had won my vife. So he vent mit me down by the saloon to get her but vhen ve come down there vot you dink: mine frou vos gone. She rode me a note and left it on der counter for me. She rode in der note: Yakob, I heard vot you've been doing so I thought I vould go before you come after me, I'm going up to Oshkosh to marry a feller vot keeps a cheese factory. I hope you'll be a good man und dont commit sunnysid und this will give you opportunity.

CHORUS: To be sorry to say dot your wife's gone away,
        Und left you alone in dis wide world to mourn;
        But how can you tell, I'm gone mit some swell;
        Or you may hear before long dot I married Brigham Young.

3. Then I hear me of dot I feel me so bad,
   But I dont could drop me a dear;
   But I got drunk like a loone the same afternoon;
   For you bet I dhrank plenty of Soda and Beer.
   I write me a letter for I dink'd 'tvos bedder,
   To let her know dot I dont care;
   For sly like a mouse I married miss Krouse:
   Und mit her I keep der saloon.

(*Spoken*) Now! I've married Miss Krouse und I vont play cards again mit mister Stout, for her you bet. But I often tell him why Jack the chief of the Modoe Inshuns represented 4 points in a game of cards vhen he vos hung. It goes dis way. Vhen he vos hung, he was *high*; when he vos cut down, he vos *low*, und his name vos *Jack*, und he died *game*. Dot's: high, low, *Jack* und der game. Und I told mister Stout if he ever ax me to play cards mit him again for mine frou I make him play the same game as Inshun Jack. Und I tell Miss Krouse efery day dot

CHORUS: I'm habby to say dot mine wife's gone avay,
        Und left me der hous so I could marry Miss Krouse;
        Und I hope she's vell if she's gone mit some swell;
        Or dot she may live long if she's married Brigham Young.

48

DEDICATED TO
The New York World.

GLOBE TROTTING

Nellie Bly.

AS SUNG BY

HALLEN & HART,

WORDS & MUSIC
BY
JOE HART.

④

NEW YORK,
WILLIS WOODWARD & CO.
842 & 844 BROADWAY.

Globe Trotting Nellie Bly

I hold here in my hand a lengthy ca-ble-gram, That came from far a-cross the sea— It's from Miss Nellie Bly, and its contents I will try to tell if you will listen unto me— She's trying very hard to beat the world's re-cord to round the world in sev-en-ty five days— Of the many funny sights in her ca-ble-gram she writes, of the people and their very curious ways— With an um-brel-la and a grip, she gave her friends the slip, far a-cross the deep blue sea;— It was a pleasant trip for her grip was not "La Grippe," con-se-quent-ly she was happy as could be——

Chorus

2. When she landed in Cork, to Killarney took a walk,
   And kissed the blarney stone with her sweet lips;
   She told funny tales to the Prince of Wales,
   And left him laughing almost in a fit.
   She did the Gaiety dance and set Paris in a trance,
   Sang "Little Annie Rooney" to Jules Verne;
   She would have spoken French and Greek, if she could have stayed a week.
   But she knew fond hearts for her at home did yearn.

CHORUS: She cheered up all the crew
        With a little song or two,
        At sea she ate three times a day,
        From the bottom of the sea,
        Up came McGinty,
        To wish her luck upon her way.

3. When she landed in Hong Kong, she rang the dinner gong,
   And they thought her quite a curiosity.
   To see our Nelly hustle, and she did not wear a bustle,
   A sight which even here we rarely see.
   When she reached Yokohama she met a Jersey farmer,
   And together they sipped too-long boo-long tea;
   She was courted by a Jap—sat in the old King's lap,
   And he wanted her to marry him, you see.

CHORUS: But when the Oceanic sailed,
        How that poor fellow wailed,
        Now she's on the ocean blue,
        She's a box of chewing tu-lu
        For each one in Honolu;
        I wish she'd bring some back to me and you.

Men and Women

2

IN THE REALM of comic songs, two subjects have always held sway over all others— men and women. The song writer with a sense of humor could always develop a situation out of the ludicrous predicaments in which unfortunate members of the human race found themselves, and as a rule, it was two for the show.

If an embarrassing incident befell a man, it was likely due to his entanglement, in or outside marriage, with a lady. "The Colonel from Constantinople," sung by the famous Mrs. Florence, and "Fifty Cents," sung by Dan Lewis, described such entanglements. An unfulfilled desire almost always had to do with a person of the opposite sex. A girl in 1810 lamented "Nobody Coming to Marry Me," and a gentleman in the 1870's declaimed, wistfully, "I Wish I Were Single Again."

In "Of Thee I Sing," the Pulitzer Prize winning musical of 1932, George and Ira Gershwin introduced a great song called "Love Is Sweeping the Country." Although the song was new then, the theme was as old as time. Love and popular music had always gone steady. The earliest sheet music distributed in this country in the last decade of the eighteenth century, except for a smattering of patriotic songs, had a decidedly sentimental flavor, and during that time it would have been almost sacrilegious to poke fun at lovers. But the young people of the young United States were too high-spirited to confine their musical taste to sentimental songs for long. Their sense of humor had to find means of expression, and soon after the 1800's were on their way, songs satirizing the man-woman relationship began to be performed on the concert stage and to be available in sheet music.

"Nobody Coming to Marry Me" (see page 68), one of the very earliest of these songs, was sung by a Mrs. Clark in New York and elsewhere, "with unbounded applause at the Public Concerts," according to the description on the sheet music.

> The dogs began to bark;
> And I peep'd out to see
> A handsome young man a hunting
> But he was not hunting for me.
> And it's oh! what will become of me?
> Oh! what shall I do?
> Nobody coming to Marry me,
> Nobody coming to woo.
>
> The first time I went to my prayers
> I pray'd for half a year,
> I pray'd for a handsome young man
> With a meikel deal of gear.
>
> The last time I went to my prayers
> I pray'd both night and day
> Come blind come lame come cripple,
> Come some one, and take me away!

Other songs, developed along a similar line, appeared in the 1820's and 1830's. Two of the most popular were "The Old Maid" and "The Old Bachelor," companion songs by two different composers.

"The Old Maid" (see page 69), related by a spinster of fifty-three who in her youth was altogether too particular, starts:

> When I was a Girl of Eighteen years old,
> I was scornful as scornful could be,
> I was taught to expect wit, wisdom and gold,
> And nothing less would do for me.

After eight verses of proposals and rejections, the lady resigns herself to her unwedded fate.

As for "The Old Bachelor" (see page 72), he keeps reiterating throughout his young manhood, "There'll be time enough for that," until time is about to run out on him. His recollections, like the old maid's, run on for eight verses, and conclude sadly:

54

I am sixty today not a very young man,
And a bachelor doom'd to die;
So youths be advised and marry while you can,
There's no time to be lost say I.

A hundred years and more later, these same themes have been developed by some of our most celebrated musical comedy composers. In 1950, in "Out of This World," Cole Porter wrote his entertaining number, "Nobody's Chasing Me." And in 1939, Maxwell Anderson wrote the touching words of "The September Song" to one of Kurt Weill's most memorable melodies. These are modern-day counterparts of the songs just outlined.

In the 1820's, too, an unknown writer, probably a Baltimorean, wrote about another lady who wouldn't marry because she didn't like her gentleman friend's name. The song was "Mrs. Poe" (see page 76), and it commenced:

Mister Poe was a man of great credit and fame,
And I lov'd him I own, but I lov'd not his name;
When he ask'd me to wed, in a pet I said, no,
I'll never marry you and be call'd Mistress Poe.
(*Spoken*) How ridiculous it would sound in the village to hear the
children say one to another as we pass—
(*Sung*) That's Mistress Poe, Goody Poe, Cousin Poe, Gaffer Poe!
No, I never will be married and be call'd Mistress Poe.

A lady with a different outlook on life was Miss Wrinkle (see page 77), the subject of an 1808 song in the farce of "Arbitration, or Free and Easy."

In a village there liv'd an old maid
Who was ne'er known for trifles to fret,
But yet she was sadly afraid
That a husband she never should get.

Yet Miss Wrinkle, who wasn't a bit finicky, in the end gets a man.

But there have been songs about some men who take no personal interest in women. One such character is Paul Pry (see page 78), whose adventures are written up by "Peter Pigwiggin the Younger," though the appellation sounds like a pseudonym. Mr. Pry is inquisitive about everybody else's doings, as may be deduced at once by the song's opening lines:

I've just dropped in to make a Call, I hope
I don't intrude now,
'Tis but Paul Pry, how are you all, Pray
do not think me rude now.

Paul admits that his curiosity gets him into difficulties:

> Because I take an interest in other People's
>   business,
> I'm bump'd and thump'd and snubb'd and drubb'd
>   until I feel a dizziness.

Nevertheless he winds up:

> I'll still continue—Prying.

Some years after the composition about Paul, another anonymous writer, who did not even resort to a pen name, brought out a very popular song entitled "The Washing Day" (see page 80), which he called "A Ballad for Wet Weather." Each edition of "The Washing Day" was illustrated by a clever artist; the one reproduced in this book is the most elaborate. A devoted husband, who tells the story, relates how his "bonny Kate" is a veritable Jekyll and Hyde, a "good creature" except when the washing day dawns:

> And then she is the devil!
> The very kittens on the [h]earth
> They dare not even play,
> Away they jump with many a bump
> Upon the Washing day.

The pianist's instructions for playing the verses are "Misericordia Allegro." The chorus goes:

> For 'tis thump, thump, scrub, scrub, scold, scold away
> [instructions for the piano read "con thumpo et scoldrino."]
> The de'il a bit of comfort's here, upon a Washing day!
> [*Piano*—"con Furio."]

But sometimes it is the man's turn to get out of sorts, as is evidenced by "The Dissatisfied Man," or "Anything to Make a Change" (see page 82), which appeared late in the 1830's, a few years after "The Washing Day." J. Bruton wrote the words to this one; J. Monro arranged the music; W. Burton was the artist who popularized it. The song concerns the feelings of an excessively grouchy young man, who finds fault with all aspects of normal living:

> The joys of having constant health,
> I've heard the ailing often praise:
> I'm thirty turn'd, yet ne'er have had
> A whole hour's illness all my days!

56

All suffer something but poor I,
Which is most vexing, sad and strange:
I can't e'en get a broken leg—
Or anything to make a change!

In the preface to this book it was noted that only rarely were the earliest humorous songs composed in a minor key. One such rarity emerged in 1859, performed by a comedian named E. F. Dixey. Dixey had been a member of minstrel troupes, a "bones" performer of outstanding ability, and a great delineator of "wench" types for half a dozen years before presenting to his audiences "The Boy with the Auburn Hair" (see page 84). He was a gentleman of intellect and culture, which could hardly have been surmised from the many mispronounced words in the body of the song. Neither the author nor the composer is known, but the latter has developed a merry tune in D minor to complement the engaging lament of a "damsuiel," apparently a Philadelphian, searching for the boyfriend who has deserted her. The short chorus has the distinction of consisting of five bars, an almost unheard of characteristic then, and one seldom seen even today.

It is difficult to learn which young man—the song mentions three—is the girl's favorite, but if we stick with the one in the chorus:

Oh, he was her darling boy,
He was the boy with the auburn hair, his name
was Mcavoy

One of the most popular couples on the American stage in the mid-nineteenth century were the W. J. Florences. W. J. Florence was born Bernard Conlin in 1831 in Albany, New York. He grew up on the East Side of New York City, the oldest of eight children. At fifteen he went to work as a cub reporter to help support his widowed mother and the family. At nights he rehearsed to prepare himself for the stage, and when he was eighteen, he made his first theatrical appearance—in Richmond, Virginia. Four years later he married a popular dancer named Malvina Pray, and soon they were starring in a play Florence wrote called *The Irish Boy and the Yankee Girl*. For almost ten years they confined themselves, in America and later in London, to Irish-American comedy, with a little melodrama on the side.

The *Dictionary of American Biography* calls "Billy" Florence one of the four leading comedians of the American stage. He was a great joker and at times enjoyed inscribing guest books with brief rhymes. For example, in a guest book of the famous nineteenth-century actor Lawrence Hutton he wrote:

When in after years you see
The page I mutilate for thee
Let cheery tears flow fast in torrents
At thoughts of
                    Yours forever
                    Florence (W. J.)

His last joke was prophetic. Stopping in New York on his way from Boston to Philadelphia, he checked in at the Fifth Avenue Hotel, where he was told that the barber who had shaved him for years had just passed away and was to be buried the following afternoon. Florence could not go to the funeral because of professional commitments, but he wanted to do something for the barber. When he learned that the boys in the barbershop had subscribed for a floral tribute and had raised twenty-three dollars, Florence told them grandly: "Here are $27, make it something handsome." Because he was the largest contributor, he was asked to suggest the motto to be fixed across the mass of flowers, something the barber himself would have liked. "Next!" Florence said, without hesitation. The suggestion was unanimously adopted. Unfortunately for Florence, he himself was the next to go, being taken ill the same week in Philadelphia, and dying within a few days' time.

The Florences had introduced in the early 1850's an entertaining comic song called "Bobbin' Around." "The Colonel from Constantinople" (see page 86), an even more popular number, came more than ten years later. Florence wrote the words, and his wife sang them:

I met the Colonel at a ball;
To him I was presented;
Upon his knees the youth did fall,
And lots of stuff invented;

              . . . . .
So I accepted the young Colonel who
From Constantinople came.

CHORUS: C, O, N, with a Con,
With S, T, A, N, with a stan,
With a Con-stan, T, I, ti, with a Con-stan-ti,
N, O, no, with a no,
With a Con-stan-ti-no, P, L, E, with a pull,
Con-stan-ti-no-ple.

One evening, while we sat at tea,
We'd a visit most informal;
The police came, and gracious me,

58

They took away the Colonel;
I soon found he a swindler was,

. . . . .

And so I lost my Colonel who
From Constantinople came.
(*Repeat chorus.*)

The Florences were at the top of the ladder in the 1860's, with songs like "Way Down in Maine" and "The Captain" published and republished, each title page bearing the facsimile inscription by Billy himself, "Authorized edition, W. J. Florence."

At the time of "The Colonel's" success, the country was trying to recuperate from the Civil War, and it was only natural that many light-hearted and jocular songs were being presented to, and appreciated by, a battle-weary public. One which was published in Philadelphia in 1868, "The Girl That Keeps the Peanut Stand" (see page 88), bore on its title page the names of the composer, "Blasee," and the author, "Albert Harry," both suspiciously pseudonymic.

Our hero met "the blooming lass that keeps the peanut stand," and he describes her appearance:

Her hair was frizzled o'er her brow,
Her eyes were slightly cross'd,
Her face was thickly freckled o'er
Like mildew mix'd with frost,
Her gown of richest calico
Hung low upon her neck,
And sundry graces round her shed,
With spots of grease bedeck'd.

CHORUS: Oh! She dress'd so neat, she look'd so sweet
I couldn't hardly stand,
My heart it palpitated so,
It shook the peanut stand.

But our boy had no chance:

I asked her if she'd like to have
A man of my estate,
She monched a handfull of peanuts,
And said, "You've come too late.
I am the organ grinders girl
And him I mean to wed."

59

One sees from the picture of the peanut-stand girl on the title page that the organ-grinder was not getting any Miss America.

From time to time, a favorite topic of public relations men has been the color of a woman's hair. The tint to restore faded locks tempts ladies of all ages. And apparently, the most enticing color, in hair as in jewelry, is gold. The slogan "Is it true that blondes have more fun?" has been a devilish come-on. But don't think for a moment that such sales promotions are new, for we can turn back a hundred years to find that the women of the 1870's had the same thoughts about making themselves more attractive.

In 1870, Bobby Newcomb, a popular comedian of the day, wrote a set of verses for "The Blonde That Never Dyes" (see page 90):

> As I strolled out the other day,
> In fashion's best arrayed,
> I passed and looked and list'd to gents,
> As compliments they paid.
> And one that pleased me most of all,
> Was spoken with such sighs;
> A nice young man says there she goes,
> The Blonde that never dyes.

This young lady was the exception; most women without the sought-after natural golden tresses had no compunction about using whatever means were necessary to achieve the desired result. For example, examine the words of a song written in 1872, "O Let Me Be a Blonde, Mother" (see page 93):

> I know I'm called a gay brunette,
> With jetty, curly hair;
> But, O, I'm weary of dark curls,
> And wish that they were fair;
> O I must be a blonde, Mother,
> O let me be a blonde!
>
> . . . . .
> Do Ma! Please Ma! Now Ma!
> Let me be a blonde!
>
> . . . . .
> And Frederic Jones who waits on me,
> You think of me he's fond;
> But oft I find him slighting me,
> And smiling on a blonde;
> You surely won't say no, Mother,
> But let me be a blonde!

Do Ma! Please Ma! Now Ma!
Let me be a blonde.

Fashion, too, became a major feminine subject, and the most elaborate costumes made their appearance. One of the most popular was the Dolly Varden ensemble. Since the song writers poked fun at the styles of the day, Dolly Varden came in for plenty of ribbing. A team composed of Frank W. Green and Alfred Lee scored a hit, about 1872, with their "Dolly Varden" number (see page 95). Their description of the well-dressed girl of the period is not flattering.

> She's got a monstrous flip-flop hat
> With cherry ribbons on it.
> She dresses in bed furniture
> Just like a flower garden,
> A blowin' and a growin' and
> They call it "Dolly Varden."

During this period there had to be songs about the young gentleman, too. One writer who usually had great popular appeal was Will S. Hays, whose output was prodigious. His themes ranged from banal sentimentality, as in "Nora O'Neal," his most successful song, to comedy for the minstrels of the day. Among the latter, one of the favorites was "The Gay Young Clerk in a Dry Goods Store" (see page 98), which Hays wrote in 1868. The lively young hero is described in these words:

> His eyes they are of a dark sky-blue,
> How are you ladies, Howdy;
> His hair light brown and his mustache too,
> Ah! ladies ha-ha!
> And he wears eye-glasses on his nose,
> And he never looks down at his toes,
> For fear he'll fall on a cellar door,
> This dashing clerk in a Dry-Goods Store.

> CHORUS: O! Augustus Dolphus is his name,
> From Skiddy-ma-dink they say he came,
> He's a handsome man and he's proud and poor,
> This gay young clerk in the Dry-Goods Store.

> He smiles at all the girls he meets,
> How are you ladies, Howdy;
> And you smile at him in the crowded streets,

> Ah! ladies ha-ha!
> Why don't you make him "come to taw,"
> I know he wants a mother-in-law,
> Do as your parents did before,
> You . . . and the clerk in the Dry-Goods Store.
> (*Repeat chorus.*)

On the other side of the coin, there is the gentleman who found a wife but lived to regret it. J. C. Beckel, a song writer of the seventies with a number of successes to his credit, produced in 1871 "I Wish I Were Single Again" (see page 101), a lively lament which goes:

> I wish I were single, oh then, oh then!
> I wish I were single, oh then!
> When I was single my pockets did jingle,
> And I wish I were single again.
>
> I married a wife, oh! then, oh then!
> I married a wife, oh! then!
> I married a wife, she's the plague of my life,
> And I wish I were single again.
>
> When my wife died, oh! then, oh! then!
> When my wife died, oh! then!
> When my wife died, I'll be hanged if I cried,
> So glad to be single again.

Unfortunately the poor fellow didn't know what was best for him, so he made the same mistake again, and as the song puts it:

> I married another, she's worse than the tother!

And the writer concludes:

> Be kind to your first, or the last will prove worse!

And again, these outpourings bring to mind songs written two or three generations later, such as George Gershwin's first published piece, entitled "When you Want 'Em You Can't Get 'Em, When You Get 'Em You Don't Want 'Em."

In the seventies, eighties, and nineties no comedian could consider himself an unqualified success unless he had played at Tony Pastor's. The name of Pastor was synonymous with "variety show." For Pastor, after a spectacular rise as a performer himself, became the operator of the most popular theater in New York, presenting humorous acts that drew the whole family to his box office. The entertainment world knew Pastor as the father of vaudeville, although Tony, until the last, called his house a "variety theater."

Pastor was the promoter of so many actors who became famous under his tutelage that we should know something about the great man's background. He was born in the 1830's and made his first public stage appearance at the age of six. His father, a violinist, opposed his son's predilection for the theater, but Tony had a strong will.

In his early teens he joined a minstrel troupe. Shortly, he deserted the minstrels for the circus, where he rode elephants and practiced tumbling. By the time he had reached sixteen, he was a ringmaster, but that was only another way station on his road to the top.

In 1861 he attended a Union rally at the Academy of Music on Broadway. Suddenly he grabbed a flag, leaped on the stage, and electrified the vast audience by singing "The Star-Spangled Banner." The crowd went wild, and Tony was famous.

He quit the circus to enter the variety field, where he sang topical songs and acted in humorous sketches. On stage he was an immaculate dresser. Out he would glide from the wings, in full evening dress, holding a collapsible silk hat over his not inconsiderable paunch. Bowing to the thunderous applause that customarily greeted him, he would snap open his hat, cock it over one eye, break into a brief dance routine, and start his songs. The audience loved him.

He opened his first theater in 1865, moving from one location to another as the city spread northward. His most famous "variety" theater was located on East Fourteenth Street. Opened in 1880, it developed into the great "family" theater of the era. Parents could take their children to any of Tony's shows without fear of embarrassment.

Pastor's personality was so engaging that his most ordinary activities attracted attention. Every day he made it his business to walk four miles. As he strolled, he would lift his hat constantly, for he was convinced that his hair would fall out unless it was exposed periodically to fresh air.

He enjoyed a game of pinochle more than almost anything else in the world. One of his regular pinochle gang, Lew Fields—who, with his partner, Joe Weber, performed at Pastor's—used to say that anyone who let Tony beat him at pinochle could have a lifetime engagement at his theater.

One of Pastor's most popular songs was "The Poor Girl Didn't Know" (see page 102), composed in the late seventies by John Cooke. Tony would amble out on the stage in formal attire and inform the audience of the misadventures of his sister, who was not exactly on the bright side. She has just come to New York and has been hired as servant in a private home. Her mistress, with the best of intentions, insists that, once a week, her servant girls go to church, where they can "put in a good hour's sleep." But when Tony's sister goes off and doesn't come back, he recounts:

> They search'd for her, such a hub-bub.
> When after two good solid hours on the scout,
> They found her inside of a "pub."
> CHORUS: But the poor gal didn't know, you know,
> She hadn't been in New York long.
> I'm always a-telling her she must wake up,
> And she ought to know right from wrong;
> For any gal would see by the sign outside,
> 'Twas a different kind of a show,
> Her eyes were red, and she did look tired,
> But the poor gal didn't know.

Another song which Pastor used in his acts apparently originated in England but was even more popular in America. This was, "Oh Fred, Tell Them to Stop!" (see page 105), by George Meen, written in the same period as "The Poor Girl Didn't Know." The narrator takes his girl to the Fair Grounds, and inspects the menagerie and other places of amusement. The girl wants, more than anything else, to have a ride in a swing, called at that time a "Roundabout." Once she is deposited in it, however, she changes her mind and cries out:

> "Oh! Fred, tell them to stop!"
> That was the cry of Maria,
> But the more she said "Wo!" they said, "Let it go!"
> And the swing went a little bit higher.

In 1878 there appeared a ditty which is recognized even today when the first eight notes are played. A hitherto unknown composer, William Gooch, was responsible for the tune, and another unknown, Harry Birch, wrote the verses of a song ostensibly about a Quaker couple, called "Reuben and Rachel" (see page 108), a piece known today as "Reuben, Reuben." Birch had Rachel start out:

> Reuben, I have long been thinking,
> What a good world this might be,

64

If the men were all transported
Far beyond the Northern Sea.

To which Reuben replies:

Rachel, I have long been thinking,
What a fine world this might be,
If we had some more young ladies
On this side the Northern Sea.

Finally Rachel comes to the point:

Reuben, what's the use of fooling,
Why not come up like a man?
If you'd like to have a "lover"
I'm for life your "Sally Ann."

Naturally, Reuben says yes:

We will live on "milk and honey,"
Better or worse, we're in for life.

Rachel was not as demanding as another girl whose appetite a versifier named Billy Mortimer (a devotee of phonetic spelling) described in detail. Dan Lewis, a well-known entertainer of the seventies and eighties, wrote the melody and presented the song "Fifty Cents" (see page 110) on the stage. Sang Lewis:

I took my girl to a fancy ball,
It was a social hop.
We staid until the folks went out
And the music it did stop.
Then to a restaurant we went
The best one on the street.
She said she was not hungry,
But this is what she eat.
A dozen raw, a plate of slaw,
A chicken and a roast.
Some sparrow grass with apple sass,
And soft shell crabbs on toast.
A big box stew with crackers, too;
Her hunger was immense.
When She called for pie, I thought I'd die,
For I had but fifty cents.

Being polite, our hero inquired if she would have something to drink, too:

65

I asked her what she'd have to drink,
She's got an awful tank.
She said she was not thirsty
But this is what she drank.
A glass of jin, a whiskey skin,
It made me shake with fear.
Some gingerpop, with rum on top,
A schooner, then, of beer.
A glass of ale, a gin cocktail,
She ought to have had more sense.
When she called for more, I droped on the floor
For I had but fifty cents.

The final verse describes, in detail, what happened when the bouncer took charge of our boy and literally swept up the floor with him before heaving him over the fence.

A collateral subject which proved entertaining was the mother-in-law. One lyricist of the seventies (see page 113) wrote:

My mother-in-law . . . in-law,
Oh, her icy face can never thaw,
She is the worst that I ever saw.

Another (see page 115) declared:

But I'll stand interference no longer;
To me she's a terrible bore;
So now, on my life, I'll boss my own wife,
And get rid of my mother-in-law.

In the 1890's the song writers gave a new twist to the husband and wife quarrel. They introduced Negro participants, and did not hesitate to use dialect which today would be regarded as racially offensive. Ned Wayburn, who later became a great showman of "girlie" shows and one of Florenz Ziegfeld's most successful rivals, was a little-known song writer when, in 1898, he produced a "coon" song entitled "He Ain't No Relation of Mine." (See page 116.) The words:

I beat mah wife an' I beat her good,
An' den in de police court I stood,
De Judge axed me what had I done,
"Nothin' at all jes' havin' some fun;"
He said dat he would set me free,
If mah wife could stand for me,

66

She said dat I to her was dead,
An' in dat court dese lines she read.

CHORUS: "He ain't no relation of mine,
He ain't no relation of mine,
From dis day forth I'm not his wife,
Mister Judge please send him up for life;
I can't stand his abuse,
If ever he gets loose,
I'll let him be—he's nothin' to me
He ain't no relation of mine."

During this same period, however, there were some couples who did not fight. Cupid was taken seriously, and the comic songs were toned down considerably when he was a participant. This was the decade of waltzes, and a song written in 3/4 time was off to a good start. When "The Band Played On" (see page 119) appeared in 1895, its composer, Charles B. Ward, struck a happy combination—a verse was developed in 2/4 time, then switched over to waltz time for the lively chorus. The lyrics described a social club formed by Matt Casey, and told how Casey's friends would dress up for the Saturday night parties, and how

When Casey led the first grand march
    they all would fall in line,
Behind the man who was their joy and pride, For

CHORUS: Casey would waltz with a strawberry blonde,
And the Band played on,
He'd glide cross the floor with the girl he ador'd,
And the Band played on.
But his brain was so loaded it nearly exploded,
The poor girl would shake with alarm.
He'd ne'er leave the girl with the strawberry curls
And the Band played on.

Eventually Casey won his inamorata, and:

The blonde he used to waltz and glide with on
    the ball-room floor,
Is happy missis Casey now for life.

This is perhaps the best way to end a comic ballad about two people. But then again, if all such songs ended happily, they would cease to be funny. So here's to old maids and mothers-in-law and cat-and-dog fights and blonde-jealous brunettes! In the world of music, they add up to a lot of fun.

Nobody Coming To Marry Me

The dogs be-gan to bark, and I peep'd out to see,—A hand-some young man a
hunt-ing But he was not hunt-ing for me—And its oh! what will be-come of me
Oh! what shall I do— No-bo-dy com-ing to mar-ry me No-bo-dy com-ing to woo——
———— No-bo-dy com-ing to woo—

2. The first time I went to my prayers
   I pray'd for half a year,
   I pray'd for a handsome young man
   With a meikel deal of gear.
   And its Oh, &c.

3. The last time I went to my prayers,
   I pray'd both night and day,
   Come blind come lame come cripple
   Come some one and take me away.
   And its Oh, &c.

4. And now I have sung you my song
   I hope it has pleas'd you so well
   That a husband for me you will find,
   Or soon you will hear of my knell.
   And its Oh, &c.

THE OLD MAID

When I was a Girl of eighteen years old.

Published by Geo. Willig Jr. Baltimore.

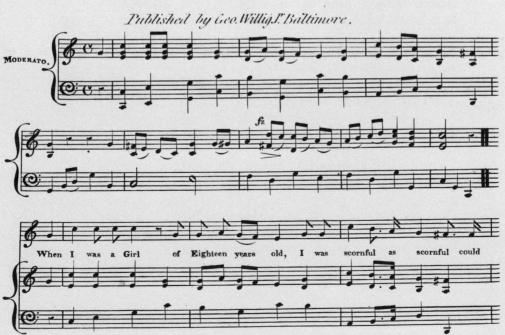

When I was a Girl of Eighteen years old, I was scornful as scornful could

The Old Maid

When I was a girl of eigh-teen years old, I was scorn-ful as scorn-ful could be

I was taught to ex-pect wit, wis-dom and gold, and no-thing less would do for me.

2. Ah! those were the days when my eyes beam'd bright,
   And my cheek was like the rose on the tree;
   And the ringlets they curl'd o'er my forehead so white,
   And lovers came courting to me.

3. The first was a youth any girl might adore,
   And as ardent as lover could be;
   But my mother having heard that the young man was poor,
   Why! he would not do for me.

4. And then hobbled in, my favour to beg,
   An officer in our navy;
   But tho' famous in arms, he wanted a leg,
   So he would not do for me.

5. And now came a lawyer, his claims to support,
   By precedents from Chancery;
   But I told him I was judge in my own little court,
   And he would not do for me.

6. The next was a dandy, who had driven four in hand,
   Reduced to a Gig—d'ye see;
   In getting o'er the ground, he had run thro' his land,
   So he would not do for me.

7. I'd a suitor from the South, and another from the West,
   I think, from the state of Tennesee;
   But one was rather old, the other badly drest,
   So neither of them suited me.

70

8. These were nearly the last—I was then forty-four,
   I am now only just fifty-three;
   But I really think that some, I rejected before,
   Would now do very well for me.

9. Then all ye young ladies, by me warning take,
   Who scornful, or cold chance to be;
   Lest ye from your fond silly dreams should awake,
   Old Maidens of Fifty-three.

THE OLD BACHELOR,

Written & Dedicated

TO THE

Author of the Old Maid

BY

T. H. BAYLY.

Baltimore, Published by Geo. Willig Jun.[r]

The Old Bachelor

When I was a school-boy a-ged ten, Oh! migh-ty lit-tle Greek I knew; With my short strip'd trow-sers and now and then, with stripes up-on my jack-et too! When I saw oth-er boys to the play-ground run, I threw my old gra-dus by, and I left the task I had scarce be-gun, "There'll be time e-nough for that" said I,— "There'll be time e-nough for that" said I.

2. When I was at college my pride was dress,
   And my groom and my bit of blood;
   But as for my study, I must confess
   That I was content with my stud;
   I was deep in my tradesmen's books, I'm afraid;
   Tho' not in my own, by the bye;
   And when rascally tailors came to be paid,
   "There'll be time enough for that," said I.
   "There'll be time enough for that," said I.

3. I was just nineteen when I first fell in love,
   And I scribbl'd a deal of rhyme,
   And I talk'd to myself in a shady grove,
   And I thought I was quite sublime:
   I was torn from my love! 'twas a dreadful blow,
   And the Lady she wiped her eye;
   But I didn't die of grief, Oh dear me no,
   "There'll be time enough for that," said I.
   "There'll be time enough for that," said I.

4. The next was a lady of rank, a Dame,
   With blood in her veins you see;
   With the leaves of the Peerage she fann'd the flame,
   That now was consuming me:
   But tho' of her great descent she spoke,
   I found she was still very high;
   And I thought looking up to a wife no joke,
   "There'll be time enough for that," said I.
   "There'll be time enough for that," said I.

5. My next penchant was for one whose face,
   Was her fortune, she was so fair!
   Oh! she spoke with an air of enchanting grace,
   But a man cannot live upon air:
   And when poverty enters the door, young love,
   Will out of the casement fly;
   The truth of the proverb I'd no wish to prove,
   "There'll be time enough for that," said I.
   "There'll be time enough for that," said I.

6. My next was a Lady who lov'd romance,
   And wrote very splendid things;
   And she said with a sneer when I ask'd her to dance,
   "Sir I ride upon a horse with wings."
   There was ink on her thumb when I kissed her hand,
   And she whisper'd, "If you should die,
   I will write you an epitaph gloomy and grand,"
   "There'll be time enough for that," said I.
   "There'll be time enough for that," said I.

7. I left her and sported my figure and face,
   At Opera party and ball;
   I met pretty girls at ev'ry place,
   But I found a defect in all!
   The first did not suit me I cannot tell how,
   The second I cannot say why;
   And the third, bless me I will not marry now,
   "There'll be time enough for that," said I.
   "There'll be time enough for that," said I.

8. I look'd in the glass, and I thought I could trace,
   A sort of a wrinkle or two;
   So I made up my mind that I'd make up my face,
   And come out as good as new.

74

To my hair I imparted a little more jet,
And I scarce could suppress a sigh,
But I cannot be quite an old Bachelor yet,
"No there's time enough for that," said I.
"No there's time enough for that," said I.

9. I was now fifty one, yet I still did adopt,
   All the airs of a juvenile beau,
   But somehow whenever a question I popp'd
   The girls with a laugh said "No."
   I am sixty today not a very young man,
   And a bachelor doom'd to die;
   So youths be advised and marry while you can,
   There's no time to be lost say I.
   There's no time to be lost say I.

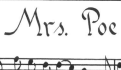

Mrs. Poe

Mr. Poe was a man of great cre-dit and of fame, and I lov'd him I own, but I lov'd not his name;

When he ask'd me to wed, in a pet I said, no, I'll nev-er mar-ry you and be call'd Mis-tress Poe.

Mis-tress Poe, Good-y Poe, Cous-in Poe, Gaf-fer Poe! No I nev-er will be mar-ried and be

call'd Mis-tress Poe.

2. In a passion he flew and he cruelly said,
   In my heart do I wish you may die an old maid;
   You may wish what you please, still my answer is no!
   For I'll never marry you and be call'd Mrs. Poe.
(Spoken) How ridiculous it would sound in a Ball-room, to hear the company
   whisper one to the other—that's
(Sung) Mistress Poe, Goody Poe, Cousin Poe, Gaffer Poe!
   No, I never will be married to be call'd Mrs. Poe.

3. So I said, and I thought, about twelve years ago,
   And refus'd the kind offers of sweet Mr. Poe;
   Now I think I was wrong and greatly to blame,
   To refuse a good man on account of his name.
(Spoken) Now I'd give the world to hear the people say as I pass them—that's
(Sung) Mistress Poe, Goody Poe, Cousin Poe, Gaffer Poe,
   Oh! I wish that I had married the gallant Mr. Poe.

Miss Wrinkle

In a vil-lage, there liv'd an old Maid who was ne'er known for tri-fles to fret, But yet she was sad-ly a-fraid that a hus-band she nev-er should get: Miss Wrin-kle was fif-ty, it can't be de-nied, Sing fal de ral lal de ral de, Yet still to be mar-ried she con-stant-ly sigh'd,—— Sing fal de ral lal de ral de.

2. She went in the Garret to pray,
   And hoping her pray'r may be granted,
   She never omitted a day,
   To name in her pray'rs what she wanted,
   For though she was fifty, it can't be denied,
   Sing fal de ral lal de ral de,
   That still to be married she constantly sigh'd
   Sing fal de ral lal de ral de.

3. A thatcher, one day thro' the roof,
   At her pray'rs did espy this old dove,
   Then popp'd in his head gave her proof
   Her devotions were heard from above.
   Will a Thatcher do for you? Miss Wrinkle quoth he,
   Sing fal de ral lal de ral de.
   "For better or worse, I'll consent," reply'd she,
   Sing fal de ral lal de ral de.

I just dropped in! Hope I don't intrude!

The

ADVENTURES OF PAUL PRY;

written expressly for

MR. LISTON,

BY

PETER PIGWIGGIN

the Younger.

BALTIMORE

Published and Sold by John Cole.

C. C. CHRISTMAN
404
PEARL
ST.
NEW YORK.

Paul Pry

I've just dropp'd in to make a call, I hope I don't in-trude now, 'Tis but Paul Pry how are you all, Pray do not think me rude now, They say that I've gone out of town, but that in-deed's a sto-ry, or how could I ap-pear to make my hand-some bow be-fore ye, Poor Paul Pry, Ev'-ry bo-dy laughs when they be-hold Paul Pry

2. Because I take an interest in other People's business,
   I'm bump'd and thump'd and snubb'd and drubb'd until I feel a dizziness,
   Which makes me vow I'll never do a kind and worthy action,
   For whatsoe'er I meddle in—I ne'er give satisfaction.
   Poor Paul Pry.
   Every body fleers and jeers at Poor Paul Pry.

3. One night as next the wall I walk'd—my way in caution groping,
   I spied a ladder next a window—placed there for eloping,
   I knew this was not Quite Correct so to the top did clamber,
   And as I just dropp'd in I saw a man hide in a chamber.
   Poor Paul Pry.
   What a situation 'twas for Poor Paul Pry.

4. Who should the Lady's father be but my friend Colonel Hardy,
   I pointed to his daughter's room and bid him not be tardy,
   He quickly kick'd me out of doors and call'd me lying fellow,
   But I came back—because I had forgot my umbrella.
   Poor Paul Pry.
   Every body's mischief falls on Poor Paul Pry.

5. This umbrella cost me one and ninepence in the city,
   To lose an article so useful would be shame and pity,
   I often too forget my gloves—affairs my mind distract so,
   While people can't forbear from laughing when they see me act so.
   Poor Paul Pry.
   Every body laughs when they behold Paul Pry.

6. One lucky act has crown'd my life—I sav'd a man from marrying,
   By fishing up some letters that down the stream were hurrying,
   A Housekeeper she tried to hook her gudgeon of a Master,
   But I saved the old Bachelor from such a sad disaster.
   Poor Paul Pry.
   Every body laughs when they behold Paul Pry.

7. They've got me in the Picture Shops—they have upon my honor,
   I'm next to Venus—which they say is quite a libel on her,
   No matter if my friends still smile—their plaudits ne'er denying,
   To yield them more amusement—why I'll still continue—Prying,
   Pry Pry Pry.
   Every body laughs when they behold Paul Pry.

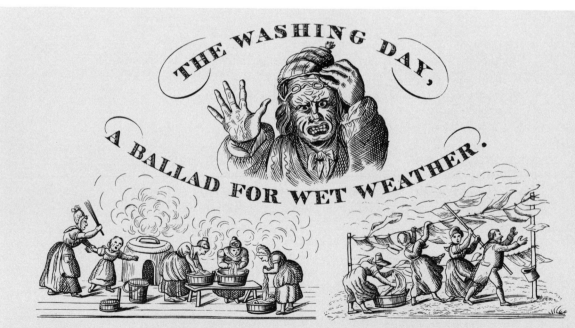

THE WASHING DAY, A BALLAD FOR WET WEATHER.

Philad.ª Published by G.E.Blake. 13 so: Fifth st.

The Washing Day

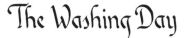

The sky with clouds was ov-er-cast, The rain be-gan to fall; My wife she whipp'd the child-ren, and

rais'd a pret-ty squall; She bade me with a frown-ing look, to get out of her way; Oh! the deuce a bit of com-

fort's here, up-on a wash-ing day! For 'tis thump, thump, scrub, scrub, scold, scold a-way, The de'il a bit of

com-fort's here, up-on a wash-ing day!

2. My Kate, she is a bonny wife,
   There's none so free from evil
   Unless upon a Washing day,
   And then she is the devil!
   The very kittens on the [h]earth
   They dare not even play,
   Away they jump with many a bump
   Upon the Washing day,
   For 'tis thump &c.

3. I met a friend who ask'd of me,
   "How long's poor Kate been dead?"
   Lamenting the good creature, gone
   And sorry I was wed
   To such a scolding vixen, while
   He had been far away!
   The truth it was, he chanced to come
   Upon a Washing day!
   When 'tis scrub, scrub &c.

4. I ask'd him then, to come and dine,
   "Come, come," quoth I, "Ods buds!
   I'll no denial take, you must;
   Tho' Kate be in the suds!"—
   But what we had to dine upon,
   In truth I cannot say,

But I think he'll never come again,
Upon a Washing day!
When 'tis scrub, scrub &c.

5. On that sad morning, when I rise,
   I put a fervent prayer,
   To all the Gods, that it may be
   Throughout the day quite fair!
   That not a Cap or Handkerchief
   May in the ditch be laid—
   For should it happen so egad,
   I get a broken head!
   For 'tis thump, thump &c.

6. Old Homer sang a royal wash,
   Down by a chrystal river;
   For dabbling in the palace halls
   The King permitted never—
   On high Olympus, Beauty's queen
   Such troubles well may scout,
   While Jove and Juno with their train
   Put all their washing out!
   Ah! happy gods, they fear no sound,
   Of thump and scold away;
   But smile to view the perils of
   A mortal Washing day!

THE DISSATISFIED MAN

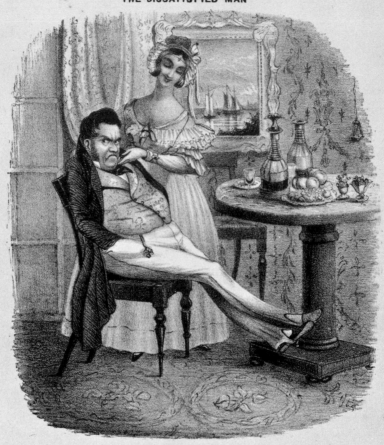

OR

"ANY THING TO MAKE A CHANGE"

Comic Song

WRITTEN BY J. BRUTON SUNG BY W. BURTON

Arranged by

J. MONRO.

PHILADELPIHA

Published by L. MEIGNEN & Cº Chesnut St.

Anything To Make A Change

Ex-ist-ence is mo-not-on-ous, to me at least, I must con-fess; To dress and sleep, to eat and

drink, to drink and eat, to sleep and dress. The same dull la-bor o'er a-gain, Day af-ter day,

the self same range; I'm real-ly tired, and fair-ly sigh for an-y thing to make a change.

2. I've got a wife who's amiable—
   Does ev'ry thing my mind to sooth;
   No earthly thing can ruffle her,
   Her temper is so very smooth!
   Now, other men can meet with scolds,
   Who'll fight, and drink, and from
         them range;
   I wish my wife would thrash me well—
   Oh! anything to make a change!

3. The joys of having constant health,
   I've heard the ailing often praise:
   I'm thirty turn'd, yet ne'er have had
   A whole hour's illness all my days!
   All suffer something but poor I,
   Which is most vexing, sad and strange:
   I can't e'en get a broken leg—
   Or any thing to make a change!

4. An accident by flood or fire,
   Every one but I can meet;
   Can fall into the river, or
   Can get burnt out, or some such treat!
   I leave a candle carelessly,
   At home when out at night I range;
   But I ne'er find my house burnt down—
   Or any thing to make a change!

5. For years have I belong'd to Clubs,
   And money paid, and pay it still;
   But ne'er have had a farthing out,
   For luck I ne'er had to be ill!
   'Tis not that I the money want—
   But I'd this sameness disarrange:
   Oh! for a little wholesome pain—
   Or, any thing to make a change!

6. Munching ravenously, I've seen,
   A bak'd potatoe some poor wight;
   And I have look'd with envy, at
   The ragged rascal's appetite!
   On luxuries I feast each day—
   Just like the dainty bee can range;
   But oh! for bread and water fare—
   Or any thing to make a change!

7. This tedium is intolerable
   I'll on some alteration hit;
   Like Megrim, I must kill myself,
   Just to enliven me a bit!
   But there's a sameness here, good folks,
   From which I hope I ne'er may range
   Your happy smiling faces round—
   I never can wish them to change!

Philadelphia.
Publish'd by WM. H. COULSTON, 147 N th 8 th St

25 Cts. Nett.

Entered according to act of Congress AD 1859, by W H Coulston in the Clerks Office of the District Court of the Eastern District of Pa

The Boy With The Auburn Hair.

It was on a sum-mer's morn-u-i-ing all in the month of May, and in those flow-ery gar-du-i-

ing where Bes-sie she did stay, I o-ver heard a dams-u-iel in sor-row to com-plain, All for the

sake of her lov- ier he ploughed the roar-ing main With his Oh, oh, oh oh oh oh oh, ho, he

was her dar-ling boy, He was the boy with the au-burn hair his name was Mea-voy.

2. I step't up to this damsuiel and did her much surprise,
   Because she did not know me I being in singular disguise.
   Says I my charming creature my gay young hearts delight,
   How far have you to travuiel this dark and stormy night.

CHORUS

3. The way kind sir to Manniyunk, If you will please to show,
   And pity a poor distracted maid for there I have to go.
   In search of the faithless heartless young man and Snicklefritz is his name
   All on the banks of the Schullikill I'm told he does remain.

CHORUS

4. If Johnny Kizer he was here he'd keep me from all harm,
   But he's on the field of battuiel with his gallant uniform,
   He's on the field of battuiel his foes he will destroy
   Like a roaring boy from Darbia he fought in Germantown.

CHORUS

SONGS OF

The Florences.

AS SUNG BY THEM IN THE PRINCIPAL THEATRES OF

EUROPE AND AMERICA.

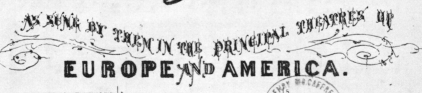

1. THE COLONEL FROM CONSTANTINOPLE   3.
2. HE VOWED HE NEVER WOULD LEAVE ME   4.

J H BUFFORD LITH BOSTON

BOSTON:
Published by OLIVER DITSON & CO. 277 Washington St.

N.YORK: CINN: PHILADA: BOSTON: CHICAGO.
W. A. POND.   JOHN CHURCH JR.   C.W. A. TRUMPLER.   J.C. HAYNES & CO.   LYON & HEALY.

Entered according to Act of Congress in the year 1867 by O. Ditson & Co. in the Clerks Office of the Dist. Court of the Dist. of Mass.

Constantinople

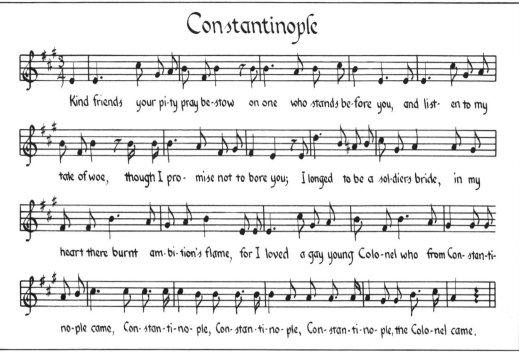

Kind friends your pi-ty pray be-stow on one who stands be-fore you, and list-en to my tale of woe, though I pro- mise not to bore you; I longed to be a sol-diers bride, in my heart there burnt am-bi-tion's flame, for I loved a gay young Colo-nel who from Con-stan-ti-no-ple came, Con-stan-ti-no-ple, Con-stan-ti-no-ple, Con-stan-ti-no-ple, the Colo-nel came.

CHORUS: C, O, N., with a Con, with S, T, A, N, with a stan,
With a Con-stan, T, I, ti with a Con-stan-ti,
N, O, no with a no,
With a Constantino,
P, L, E, with a pull,
Constantinople.

2. I met the Colonel at a ball;
To him I was presented;
Upon his knees the youth did fall,
And lots of stuff invented;
He said he was a Turkish prince,
And begg'd that I would bear his name,
So I accepted the young Colonel who
From Constantinople came,
Constantinople, Constantinople,
Constantinople, the Colonel came.

CHORUS

3. One evening while we sat at tea,
We'd a visit most informal;
The police came, and gracious me,
They took away the Colonel;
I soon found he a swindler was,
And long had carried on that game,
And so I lost my Colonel who
From Canstantinople came,
Constantinople, Canstantinople,
Constantinople, the Colonel came.

CHORUS

87

THE GIRL THAT KEEPS THE PEANUT STAND

SONG AND CHORUS

Words by BLASEE   Music by ALBERT HARRY

PHILADELPHIA.
Published by W. R. Smith No. 135 North 8th Street

NEW YORK   BOSTON   HARRISBURG   CLEVELAND
W. A. Pond & Co.   G. Ditson & Co.   H. C. Orth   S. Brainard & Sons

The Girl That Keeps The Peanut Stand

I wan-der'd down the oth-er day, a-long the ri-ver strand, And there I met the pret-ty maid that keeps the pea-nut stand. I o-gled her, she o-gled me, She looked so ve-ry grand. None can sur-pass the bloom-ing lass that keeps the pea-nut stand, Oh! She dress'd so neat, she look'd so sweet I could-n't hard-ly stand, My heart it pal-pi-ta-ted so, it shook the pea-nut stand.

2. Her hair was frizzled o'er her brow,
Her eyes were slightly cross'd,
Her face was thickly freckled o'er
Like mildew mix'd with frost,
Her gown of richest calico
Hung low upon her neck,
And sundry graces round her shed,
With spots of grease bedeck'd, Oh!
(*Spoken*) You just ought to have seen
her.
She dress'd so neat, &c.

3. I mosied up, "How do you do,
My pretty lass I pray."
"I'm hunkadora how are you,
Come buy some nuts today."
Said I, "I'll take a half a pint

If you will sell 'em low,
And throw me in a kiss to boot,"
Said she, "Go long old blow."
She dress'd so neat, &c.

4. I asked her if she'd like to have
A man of my estate,
She monched a handfull of peanuts,
And said, "You've come too late,
I am the organ grinders girl
And him I mean to wed,
Do you suppose I'd give him up
And marry you instead?"
She dress'd so neat, &c.

5. Oh! how I love that peanut girl
No one can ever know,

89

I wish that organ grinder man
Was grinding down below;
And now a broken hearted man,
I wander through the land,
My soul a busten for the gal
What keeps the peanut stand.
She dress'd so neat, &c.

Encore:

If I could play the organ well
I'd go to grinding too,
And I would cut as big a swell
As other grinders do,
But as I didn't go to war,
And lose a leg or hand,
I've lost for aye my pretty lass
That keeps the peanut stand.
She dress'd so neat, &c.

The Blonde That Never Dyes

As I strolled out the oth-er day, in fash-ion's best ar-rayed, I passed and looked and list'd to gents, as com-pli-ments they paid, And one that pleased me most of all, was spoken with such sighs; A nice young man says there she goes, The Blonde that nev-er dyes. The Blonde that nev-er dyes, the Blonde that nev-er dyes; Both far and near I'm sure to hear, The Blonde that nev-er dyes.

(*Spoken after 1st verse*) He was a real nice young fellow, and I felt quite taken with him, especially when he spoke the truth so charmingly in saying that I was—

(*Spoken in middle of 1st chorus*) And really it is quite charming to hear the dear fellows positively assert that I am the identical—

90

Songs & Ballads

As Sung by

Miss Eliza Weathersby.

Naughty Prince Pippin . . . 4   Coming from the Matinee. 4
The Blonde that never dyes. 4

NEW YORK,
Published by Wm. A. Pond & Co 547 Broadway.

BOSTON,   CINCINNATI,   SAN FRANCISCO,   NEW ORLEANS,   MILWAUKEE,
KOPPITZ, PRÜFER & Co   C. Y. FONDA.   M. GRAY.   L. GRUNEWALD.   H. N. HEMPSTED.

Entered according to Act of Congress AD 1877 by Wm A Pond & Co in the Clerks Office of the District Court for the Southern District of New York.

Robert Teller 107 Prince St. New York.

2. What's in a name Shakespeare said
   But with him I dont hold
   For some have styled my hair of late
   As quite a rise in gold.
   Yet I dont mind them not a bit
   But wonder at their eyes
   To think I die while yet I live
   The Blonde that never dyes.

(*Spoken*) And it is so funny to hear the different remarks that are passed as I go by, I heard a young fellow the other day lisp out to his companion, I thay "Charlie" ith that hair vermillion? No replied his friend, I think its wed, but at that moment a third party tapped him on the shoulder and said you are quite mistaken for that Lady is—

CHORUS: The Blonde that never dyes,
   The Blonde that never dyes;
   Both far and near that's what I hear,

(*Spoken*) And even the little boys in the street are equally as annoying for when ever they see me they cry out I say? Jimmy? do yer know who that is, why thats—

(*Sung*) The Blonde that never dyes,
   The Blonde that never dyes;
   Both far and near I'm sure to hear,
   The Blonde that never dyes.

3. To use a phrase I call my own
   And one of which I'm fond
   At once proclaims to all my friends
   I'll live and die a Blonde.
   Yet some will say that cannot be
   And add to my surprise
   That I must live the same as now
   A Blonde that never dyes.

(*Spoken*) So I suppose my friends you may congratulate me as I shall in all probability live forever—that is it must be so when I hear it daily announced that I am—

(*Sung*) The Blonde that never dyes,
   The Blonde that never dyes,
   Both far and near that's what I hear;

(*Spoken*) And if such a thing should be that I survive the fabled thousand years, why I trust all here likewise will be present, and still proclaim me—

(*Sung*) The Blonde that never dyes,
   The Blonde that never dyes;
   Both far and near I'm sure to hear,
   The Blonde that never dyes.

O let me be a blonde, O THER!

A Modern Ballad

A la Valse

Words by
GRACE H. HORR.

Music by
F. W. ROOT.

③

Published by S. BRAINARD'S SONS. _ Cleveland.

Chicago.   Austin, Texas.   Milwaukee.   San Francisco.
Geo. F. Root & Sons. C. T. Sisson.   H. N. Hempsted. A. L. Bancroft & Co.

Entered according to act of Congress A.D. 1872, by S. Brainard's Sons, in the office of the Librarian of Congress at Washington.

O Let Me Be A Blonde, Mother

I know I'm called a gay bru-nette, with jet-ty, curl-y hair;   But O, I'm wea-ry

of dark curls, and wish that they were fair;   O I must be a blonde, Mo-ther, O

let me be a blonde!   O I must be a blonde, Mo-ther, O let me be a blonde!

ad lib.

Do Ma! Please Ma! Now Ma!   Let me be a blonde!

2. There's little swarthy Katie Jones
O no one calls her fair;
Was bleached and blanched for just
three days,
And now has yellow hair;
Just think of Katie Jones, Mother,
And let me be a blonde!
Just think of Katie Jones, Mother,
And let me be a blonde!
Do Ma! &c.

3. And Frederic Jones who waits on me,
You think of me he's fond;
But oft I find him slighting me,
And smiling on a blonde;

You surely wont say no, Mother,
But let me be a blonde!
You surely wont say no, Mother,
But let me be a blonde!
Do Ma! &c.

4. You know that when to Lucy Brown
A new hat was denied,
She threw herself in Dreamer's Lake,
And sank beneath the tide!
Remember Dreamer's Lake, Mother,
And let me be a blonde!
Remember Dreamer's Lake, Mother,
And let me be a blonde!
Do Ma! &c.

DOLLY VARDEN

WRITTEN AND COMPOSED

by

Dressed in a Dolly Varden

G. W. MOORE.

G. W. HUNT.

Dolly Varden

ALFRED LEE.

PHILADELPHIA. LEE & WALKER 922 CHESTNUT ST.

Wm H. BONER & Co 1102 CHESTNUT St

BOSTON. O. DITSON & CO.

T. SINCLAIR & SON PHIL

Dolly Varden

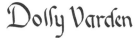

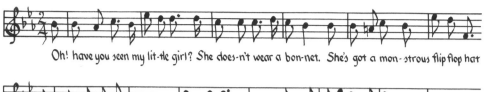

Oh! have you seen my lit-tle girl? She does-n't wear a bon-net. She's got a mon-strous flip flop hat

with cher-ry rib-bons on it, She dress-es in bed fur-ni-ture just like a flow-er gar-den, a blow-in' and

Chorus

a grow-in' and they call it "Dol-ly Var-den." Dol-ly, Dol-ly, Dol-ly, Dol-ly Var-den Dress-es like a

lit-tle flow-er gar-den, When she goes a-bout, all the peo-ple shout Dol-ly, Dol-ly, Dol-ly, Dol-ly,

Var-den

2. She started it one fatal day
Immediately her mother
Whose weight is over sixteen stun
Rush'd out and bought another,
The cook of course must have one next
As bold as a brass farden,
And now I'm bless'd if grandmother's
Not got a "Dolly Varden."

CHORUS

3. To walk with them about the streets
Is anything but jolly,

When crowds of dirty little boys
Will follow, shouting "Dolly!"
I dare not pass a rag-shop now
My fate's indeed a hard un,
The black dolls hanging up all seem
To shout, "How's Dolly Varden."

CHORUS

4. O'er come by Dolly Varden here
I rush'd away a Kiten,
The frightful dresses swam'd about

My shatter'd nerves to frighten.
At Saratoga and Cape May,
And even Castle Garden,
I was a wretched victim to
That awful Dolly Varden.

CHORUS

5. I see it in my dreams at night
No rest I ever find sirs,
I've Dolly Varden on the brain,
And chintz upon the mind sirs,
This fearful fashion haunts me now,
I really beg your pardon,
But is there anybody here
Who wears a "Dolly Varden?"

CHORUS

(*Spoken*) If so put it away, hide it before
the next fashion comes out or
you'll hear, "Miss, what have you
done with your"
(*Sung*) Dolly, Dolly, Dolly, Dolly
Varden
Dresses like a little flower
garden,
All the boys will cry,
How is that for high,
Dolly, Dolly, Dolly, Dolly
Varden.

TO ALL GAY YOUNG CLERKS.

The Gay Young Clerk in the Dry Goods Store

As sung by Emerson, Allen AND Manning's Minstrels

Written and Composed BY Will. S. Hays.

Author of: "Driven from Home", "Mrs Jinks of Madison Square", "Jessie Dean", "Kitty Ray", "Nora O'Neal", "My Father's growing old", "When I went home with Belle", "A Heart that beats only for thee", &c. &c.

SWACOTT, FORBRIGER & CO. LITH. CINCINNATI.

Piano.
Guitar.

NEW YORK,
Published by J.L. PETERS, 198 Broadway.

| CHICAGO. | CINCINNATI & ST LOUIS. | GALVESTON. | BOSTON. |
| De Motte Bros, | J.J.Dobmeyer&Co. | T. Goggan. | White, Smith & Perry. |

Entered according to Act of Congress in the year 1868 by J.L. Peters in the Clerks Office of the U.S. Dist. Court for the District of N. Jersey.

Gay Young Clerk In A Dry Goods Store

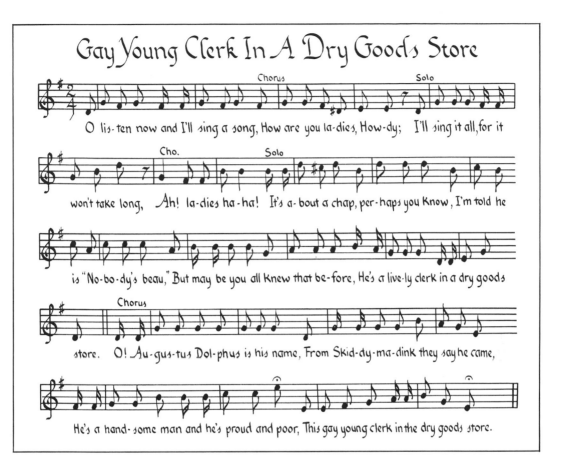

O lis-ten now and I'll sing a song, How are you la-dies, How-dy; I'll sing it all, for it
won't take long, Ah! la-dies ha-ha! It's a-bout a chap, per-haps you know, I'm told he
is "No-bo-dy's beau," But may be you all knew that be-fore, He's a live-ly clerk in a dry goods
store. O! Au-gus-tus Dol-phus is his name, From Skid-dy-ma-dink they say he came,
He's a hand-some man and he's proud and poor, This gay young clerk in the dry goods store.

2. His eyes they are of a dark sky-blue,
   How are you ladies, Howdy;
   His hair light brown and his mustache too,
   Ah! ladies ha-ha!
   And he wears eye glasses on his nose,
   And he never looks down at his toes,
   For fear he'll fall on a cellar door,
   This dashing clerk in a Dry-Goods Store.

   Chorus

3. He wears side whiskers on his jaws,
   How are you ladies, Howdy;
   Wont none of you hear him for his cause,
   Ah! ladies ha-ha!

99

Why almost ev'ry lady knows
He's a nice young man, for he wears good clothes,
He's a handsome chap as I said before,
He's a gay young clerk in a Dry-Goods Store.

Chorus

4. He smiles at all the girls he meets,
   How are you ladies, Howdy;
   And you smile at him on the crowded streets,
   Ah! ladies ha-ha!
   Why don't you make him "come to taw,"
   I know he wants a mother-in-law,
   Do as your parents did before,
   You and the clerk in the Dry-Goods Store.

Chorus

I Wish I Were Single Again

I wish I were sin-gle, O then, O then! I wish I were sin-gle O then! When I was

sin-gle my poc-kets did jin-gle, and I wish I were sin-gle a-gain.

2. When I was single, oh then, oh then!
   When I was single, oh then!
   I liv'd at my ease and I went where I pleas'd
   And I wish I were single again.

3. I married a wife, oh! then, oh then!
   I married a wife, oh! then!
   I married a wife, she's the plague of my life,
   And I wish I were single again.

4. And now I am married, oh! then, oh! then!
   And now I am married, oh! then!
   If I go any where, my wife's sure to be there,
   And I wish I were single again.

5. When my wife died, oh! then, oh! then!
   When my wife died, oh! then!
   When my wife died, I'll be hanged if I cried,
   So glad to be single again.

6. I went to the funeral, oh! then, oh! then!
   I went to the funeral, oh! then!
   The music did play, and I danced all the way,
   So glad to be single again.

7. I married another, oh! then, oh! then!
   I married another, oh! then!
   I married another, she's worse than the tother!
   And I wish I were single again.

8. Now all ye young men, oh! then, oh! then!
   Now all ye young men, oh! then!
   Be kind to your first, or the last will prove worse!
   And you'll wish for the old one again.

Poor Gal Didn't Know

My sis-ter's a-bout the most sim-ple of girls that ev-er a per-son could get,— She's not ver-y old, so

there's time to im-prove, She is-n't quite twen-ty-one yet;— She had a new sweet-heart, she'd known but

two days, and he asked her "what mon-ey she'd got?" She says "look for your-self" and she gave him her

Chorus

purse, and the fel-low walk'd off with the lot — But the poor gal did-n't know, you know, She

had-n't been in New York long,— I'm al-ways a-tel-ling her she must wake up, and she ought to know right

from wrong; For an-y gal would know what the fel-low was at, but she stood there and watch'd him go,

and stared like this, with her fin-ger in her mouth, but the poor gal did-n't know.

2. Her "Missis" is careful with fresh servant girls
   Once a week she insists that they go
   To Church, where they put in a good hour's sleep,
   And back by nine-twenty or so;
   Poor girl she went off, as she didn't come back.
   They search'd for her, such a hub-bub.
   When after two good solid hours on the scout,
   They found her inside of a "pub."

Compliments of JERSEY CITY BAZAAR.

POOR GIRL ✳ ✳

DIDN'T KNOW

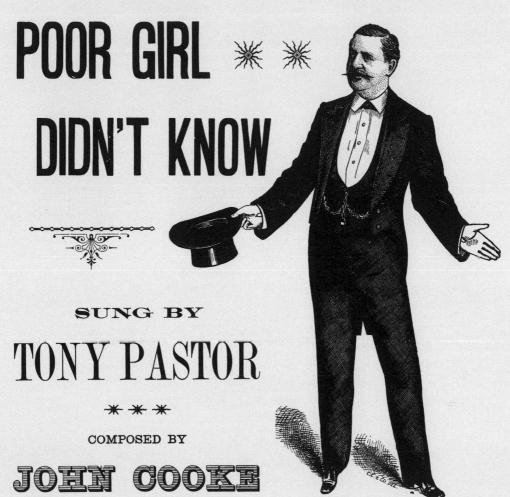

SUNG BY

TONY PASTOR

✳ ✳ ✳

COMPOSED BY

JOHN COOKE

—Song, - 40.   Schottische Caprice, - 40.

NEW YORK:

HITCHCOCK'S MUSIC STORES,

385 SIXTH AVENUE,

11 PARK ROW,   283 SIXTH AVENUE,

294 GRAND STREET.

Chicago, Ill.: NATIONAL MUSIC CO., 215 Wabash Avenue.

CHORUS: But the poor gal didn't know, you know,
    She hadn't been in New York long,
    I'm always a-telling her she must wake up,
    And she ought to know right from wrong;
    For any gal would see by the sign outside,
    'Twas a different kind of a show,
    Her eyes were red, and she did look tired,
    But the poor gal didn't know.

3. Her fortune she had it told on the quiet,
 By a woman who came to the gate;
 She told her she'd marry a fellow in blue,
 A P'liceman she tho't was her fate;
 She swore she would find out which fellow it was,
 So she started on Division A,
 Her rule is to walk out with two every week,
 And next week she'll be right up to J.

CHORUS: But the poor gal doesn't know, you know,
    She hasn't been in New York long,
    I'm always a-telling her she must wake up,
    And she ought to know right from wrong;
    She says, "They're the nicest men in the world,"
    And she'll follow where'er they go,
    They never tell lies and never go wrong,
    But the poor gal didn't know.

4. I think it must be that her memo'ry's bad,
 For one night we went out for a walk,
 When all of a sudden a man gave a shout,
 And soon put an end to our talk;
 He said "Ha! I've found you at last, have I dear?
 I've led such a miserable life,
 O come home at once." I said, "What do you mean?"
 He said, "That young person's my wife!"

CHORUS: But the poor gal didn't know, you know,
    She hasn't been in New York long,
    I'm always a-telling her she must wake up,
    And she ought to know right from wrong;
    She must know, he said, if we've met before,
    The marriage lines will show,
    So I said, "You let my sister alone,"
    For the poor gal doesn't know.

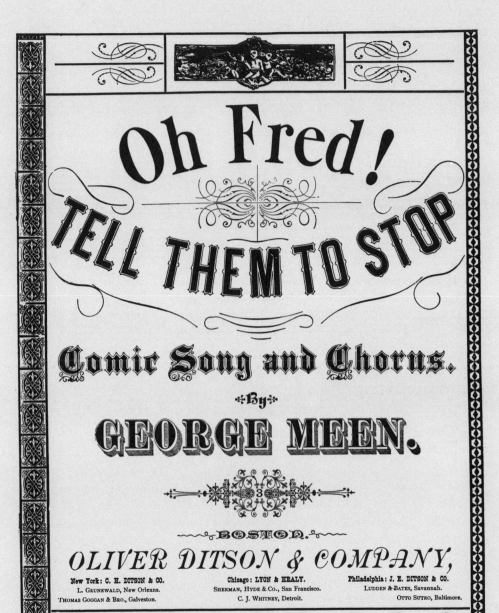

Oh Fred!
TELL THEM TO STOP

Comic Song and Chorus.

By

GEORGE MEEN.

BOSTON.

OLIVER DITSON & COMPANY,

New York: C. H. DITSON & CO. Chicago: LYON & HEALY. Philadelphia: J. E. DITSON & CO.
L. GRUNEWALD, New Orleans. SHERMAN, HYDE & CO., San Francisco. LUDDEN & BATES, Savannah.
THOMAS GOGGAN & BRO., Galveston. C. J. WHITNEY, Detroit. OTTO SUTRO, Baltimore.

O, Fred, Tell Them To Stop!

No doubt you have heard of the Great Fan-cy Fair, that used to take place ev'ry day,— Well I thought

for a-muse-ment I'd take my girl there, to pass a dull hour a-way;— We went in you must know,

and saw Rich-ard-son's show, and Fore-paugh's Me-nage-rie as well—— There were round-a-bouts,

swings, and all kinds of things; For-get the day I nev-er shall——

Chorus

"Oh! Fred, tell them to stop!" That was the cry of Ma-ri-a, But the more she said "Wo!" they

said, "let it go!" and the swing went a lit-tle bit high-er.

(*Spoken after 1st verse*) Yes, when we got in the Fair, my girl wanted to have a ride on one of the Roundabouts; I said, "All right, my darling," and we had a swing, but directly the swing went to and fro, she lustily called out—

Chorus

2. The people that stood round of course they all laughed,
But I only said, "Stop the swing";
There were four or five others in the *boats* beside us,
Saying, "Master, don't do such a thing."
Then four or five roughs caught hold of the ropes,

106

Maria fell down on her knee,
And one of them said, the young man's turning red,
But isn't he having a spree?

Chorus

3. They soon stopp'd the swing and Maria got out,
And quickly fell down on the floor,
They brought her some water, which soon brought her to,
This girl whom I now do adore.
Should you ever go there, to the great Fancy Fair,
Friends, take advice, whilst I sing
Of the great Roundabout, it's the best fun that's out,
And finish the day with a swing.

(*Spoken*): Mark now before you get into the *swing boat,* make a bargain with
your young lady not to call out—

Chorus

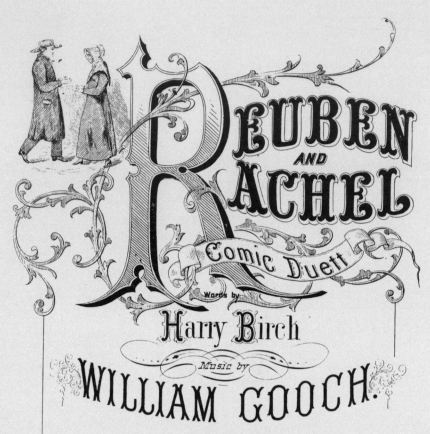

REUBEN AND RACHEL

AND

Comic Duett

Words by

Harry Birch

Music by

WILLIAM GOOCH.

Send for the Companion Duett

※ 34 ※

WHO'S TO BLAME.

BOSTON

WHITE, SMITH & CO.

298, 300 Washington St

Wm. A. Pond & Co. N. York

Send for the Companion Duett Who's to Blame.

Price 35¢

Reuben And Rachel

Reu-ben, I have long been think-ing, what a good world this might be, if the men were all trans-port-ed far be-yond the North-ern Sea. Rach-el I have long been think-ing, what a fine world this might be, if we had some more young la-dies on this side the North-ern Sea.

Rachel   Too ral loo ral,   Too ral lee, If the men were all trans-
Reuben   Too ral loo ral loo,   Too ral loo ral loo,   If we had some more young

port-ed far be-yond the North-ern Sea.
la-dies on this side the North-ern Sea.

RACHEL

2. Reuben, I'm a poor lone woman,
   No one seems to care for me,
   I wish the men were all transported
   Far beyond the Northern Sea.

3. Reuben, what's the use of fooling,
   Why not come up like a man?
   If you'd like to have a "lover"
   I'm for life your "Sally Ann."

4. Reuben, now do stop your teazing,
   If you've any love for me;
   I was only just a fooling,
   As I thought of course you'd see.

REUBEN

2. I'm a man without a victim,
   Soon I think there's one will be,
   If the men are not transported
   Far beyond the Northern Sea.

3. Oh my goodness! oh my gracious!
   What a queer world this would be
   If the men were all transported
   Far beyond the Northern Sea!

4. Rachel, I will not transport you,
   But will take you for a wife,
   We will live on "milk and honey,"
   Better or worse, we're in for life.

Fifty Cents

I took my girl to a fan-cy ball, It was a so-cial hop. We staid un-til the folks went out and the mu-sic it did stop. Then to a res-tau-rant we went, the best one on the street. She said she was not hun-gry, but this is what she eat. A doz-en raw, a plate of slaw, a chick-en and a roast, some spa-row grass with ap-ple sass, and soft shell crabs on toast. A big box stew with crack-ers, too; Her hun-ger was im-mense. When she called for pie, I thought I'd die, for I had but fif-ty cents

2. She said so sweet that she was not well,
And did not care to eat
Now I have money in my clothes
That says she can't be beat.
I asked her what she'd have to drink,
She's got an awful tank.
She said she was not thirsty
But this is what she drank.
A glass of jin, a whiskey skin,
It made me shake with fear.

Some ginger pop, with rum on top,
A schooner, then, of beer.
A glass of ale, a gin cocktail,
She ought to have had more sense.
When she called for more
I droped on the floor
For I had but fifty cents.

3. I told her that my head did ache,
And I did not care to eat

DAN LEWIS',

Popular Songs of the Day

1. ARE YOU GOING TO THE MAT THIS AFT.   35
2. OH SHE IS.   - - - - -   35
3. MOSES CART DEM MELONS DOWN.   -   35
4. IT DON'T BELONG TO ME.   - -   35
5. MOTHER'S REQUEST.   - - -   35
6. THE WHALE GOT JONAH DOWN.   -   35
7. OUT IN THE CHILLY NIGHT.   - -   35

8. KEEP YOUR TEMPER, JOHNNY.   - -   35
9. WHEN YOU HEAR THE LITTLE BIRDS
     SING. (Song and Dance.)   - -   35
10. WAY OVER YONDER. (Song and Chorus.)   35
11. FIFTY CENTS.   - - - - -   35
12. OH ! LOUISA.   - - - - -   35
13.

WHITE, SMITH & COMPANY.

BOSTON: CHICAGO: .
516 WASHINGTON STREET.   188 & 190 STATE STREET.

Expecting every moment to get kicked
        into the street.
She said she'd bring her fam'ly round,
Some day and have some fun.
I gave the clerk the fifty cents
And this is what he done.
He smashed my nose and tore my clothes
And hit me in the jaw.
He put my eyes in mourning deep
And with me swept the floor;
He grabbed me where my pants were
        loose
And kicked me o'er the fence.
Take my advice don't try it twice
When you have but fifty cents.

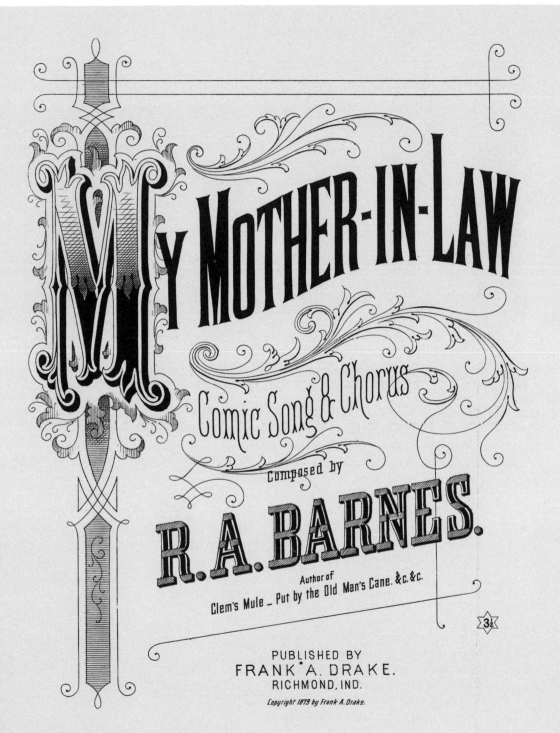

My Mother-in-Law

Comic Song & Chorus

Composed by

R. A. BARNES.

Author of
Clem's Mule – Put by the Old Man's Cane. &c. &c.

3½

PUBLISHED BY
FRANK A. DRAKE.
RICHMOND, IND.

My Mother-In-Law

My mo-ther-in-law, with the chat-ter-ing jaw, has ears that are made for to hear;——

She u-ses her tongue, like a dou-ble barr'ld gun, and speaks to all that are near;—— She's

brave to a fault, and nev-er will halt, to lis-ten to what you would say,—— What her eyes can not

see, is a won-der to me, for I've known her a ma-ny long day —— My mo-ther-in-law, in law — My

mo-ther-in-law, in law— Oh, her i-cy face can nev-er thaw, She is the worst that I ev-er saw.

2. My mother-in-law, with the double gear'd jaw,
   Takes pleasure in making me mad,
   And just for my good, let it be understood,
   I ought to be more like my dad,
   She says I'm red-hair'd, and ought to be scar'd,
   To think of my sins so complete,
   That I'm lazy and strong, and I'm not worth a song,
   And too shiftless to stand on my feet.

   CHORUS

3. My mother-in-law, with the light'ning clad jaw,
   And owl-screeching voice 'tis so shrill;
   Her queenly career, is to me very dear,
   Her reign has quite made me ill,
   I hope she will roam, to some other home,
   That is she'll drop off with out pain,
   I'll remember the boss, and consider the loss,
   For to be just some other one's gain.

   CHORUS

I'll Get Rid Of My Mother-In-Law

If you please, some time since I was mar-ried   to a young and most beau-ti-ful girl;   But now I do wish I had tar-ried, for my brain's in a ter-ri-ble whirl.   Her mo-ther, a-las! is a tor-ment She wor-ries me out of my life;   My feel-ings are all in a fer-ment, from the trou-ble I have with my wife.   But I'll stand in-ter-fer-ence no lon-ger: To me she's a ter-ri-ble bore;   So now, on my life, I'll boss my own wife, and get rid of my Mo-ther-in-law.

(*Spoken after 1st verse*) Yes! I have had more trouble with that wife of mine than one mortal can stand. Every time I wish any thing done to suit me, her old woman always sticks in her gab.

2. I ne'er shall forget our first baby,
   A bouncing, blue-eyed little boy:
   The actions then of the old lady
   Brought me torment instead of great joy.
   The neighbors all said, "He's a darling,
   "The image of his pap-pap-pa";
   The old woman she argued contrary,
   And said he looked like his mamma.

(*Spoken*) Yes! She swore he looked like his mamma; and I'll be———, Well, he didn't look like his mamma, nor any of her family; but he was the perfect image of his papa.

CHORUS

Belle Davis's Big Success in "Brown's in Town.

He Aint No Relation O' Mine.

Coon Song & Chorus

By **Ned Wayburn**
Composer of "Syncopated Sandy." Etc.

BELLE DAVIS
The Premiere
Coon-Song Cantatrice.

1260-1266 Broadway
New York.
Masonic Temple, Chicago.   Chas. Sheard & Co., London.

5

He Ain't No Relation Of Mine

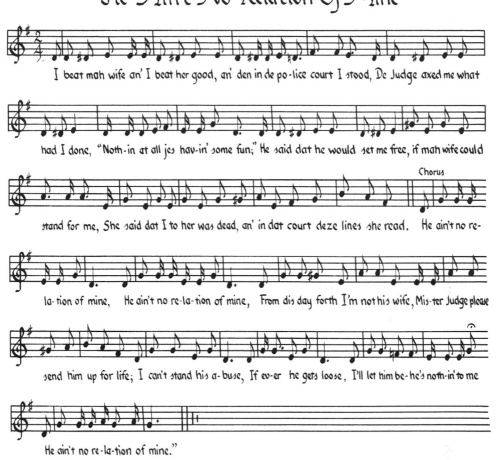

I beat mah wife an' I beat her good, an' den in de po-lice court I stood, De Judge axed me what had I done, "Noth-in at all jes hav-in' some fun;" He said dat he would set me free, if mah wife could stand for me, She said dat I to her was dead, an' in dat court deze lines she read. He ain't no re-la-tion of mine, He ain't no re-la-tion of mine, From dis day forth I'm not his wife, Mis-ter Judge please send him up for life; I can't stand his a-buse, If ev-er he gets loose, I'll let him be-he's noth-in' to me He ain't no re-la-tion of mine."

2. I left dat jail an' I fell in love,
An' soon was wed to a turtle dove,
My first wife thought she had me "cinched"
So for bigamy she had me "pinched."
De same ole Judge when he saw my face,
Said, "Madam, I dismiss dis case
Dis gemman I declare is free
Kase once dese words you said to me."

CHORUS

117

3. I dreamt dat I to Heav'n had been,
   Dat old St. Peter wouldn't let me in,
   When I axed him to decide my fate,
   He brought mah new wife to de gate,
   Said he to her, "It rests wid you,
   Ef you say yes I'll let him through."
   He axed her dere, was she mah wife,
   An' she said, "No not on your life."

   CHORUS: "He ain't no relation of mine,
           He ain't no relation of mine,
           He's just as warm as he can be,
           In de summer time he's too warm for me,
           I can't stand his abuse,
           If ever he gets loose,
           I'll let him be—he's nothin' to me
           He ain't no relation of mine."

The BAND

PLAYED ON

WORDS BY

JOHN F. PALMER.

MUSIC BY

Chas.B.Ward.

5

Published by

THE NEW-YORK MUSIC CO.,
57 WEST 28TH ST. NEW-YORK.
CHAS. SHEARD & CO. LONDON, ENGL.

The Band Played On

Matt Ca-sey formed a so-cial club that beat the town for style,— and hi-red for a meet-ing place a

hall —— When pay day came a-round each week they greased the floor with wax, and danced with noise

and vig-or at the ball—— Each Sat-ur-day you'd see them dressed up in Sun-day clothes,—— Each

lad would have his sweet-heart by his side—— When Ca-sey led the first grand march, they all would fall in

Chorus

line, be-hind the man who was their joy and pride;—— For —— Ca-sey would waltz with a

straw-ber-ry blonde, and the band played on—— He'd glide cross the floor with the girl he a-dored,

and the band played on—— But his brain was so load-ed it near-ly ex-plod —ed, The poor girl would

shake with a-larm— He'd ne'er leave the girl with the straw-ber-ry curls, And the band played on.——

2. Such kissing in the corner and such whisp'ring in the hall,
   And telling tales of love behind the stairs.
   As Casey was the favorite and he that ran the ball,
   Of kissing and lovemaking did his share.
   At twelve o'clock exactly they all would fall in line,
   Then march down to the dining hall and eat.
   But Casey would not join them although ev'ry thing was fine,
   But he stayed upstairs and exercise his feet, For

   CHORUS

3. Now when the dance was over and the band played home sweet home,
   They played a tune at Casey's own request.
   He thank'd them very kindly for the favors they had shown,
   Then he'd waltz once with the girl that he loved best.
   Most all the friends are married that Casey used to know,
   And Casey too has taken him a wife.
   The blond he used to waltz and glide with on the ball room floor,
   Is happy missis Casey now for life, For

   CHORUS

Dialect

3

Time was when no burlesque show was complete without its quota of comedians with foreign accents. The slapstick Dutchman and Jew were much more entertaining to a large part of the audience at Minsky's than were the girls. Vaudeville, too, banked on them for comic relief, and welcomed as well the purveyors of Irish, Italian, Chinese, Greek, and Negro humor.

Today the earthy humor generated by these ghosts of the stage's past glories is absent. The various nationalist protective societies and antidefamation groups will not permit performers to poke fun at anyone with a funny accent, except for the French, who are proud of their unique pronunciation of our language.

Our present-day concept of bad taste would have amazed the song writer of the nineteenth century. He could mock or make fun as he chose, without the slightest regard for the individual or the nationality derided. In fact, the more awkward the writer made the situation, the bigger chance there was that the song would appeal to those millions of red-blooded, second- or third-generation Americans who liked "gutsy" entertainment.

It was reasonable to expect that the most popular of these songs were in exaggerated Negro dialect, which had attracted audiences since early in the nineteenth century and had pre-dated the formation of the blackface minstrel troupes in the 1840's. The blackface comedians had a sizable repertoire, and from the 1820's on, for more than a century, they were welcome entertainment.

One of their songs that went over very big in the 1850's was written by Dan Emmett, a member of one of the first minstrel troupes, who was destined to achieve musical immortality with "Dixie." As a pioneer of minstrelsy in America, Emmett had early in his career composed a happy song entitled "Old Dan Tucker," which so caught the public fancy that the melody was used, with new, appropriate words, in presidential campaign songs of the period. In 1853, Emmett scored another success with "Jordan Is a Hard Road to Travel." (See page 130.) The tune was uninspiring but the swing was catchy, and the words for several of the verses were timely. For example:

> If I was de legislator ob dese United States
> I'd settle de fish question accordin.
> I'd give de British all de bones and de Yankees
>   all de meat
> And stretch de boundary line to de oder side
>   ob Jordan.

CHORUS: So take off your coat boys,
> And roll up your sleeves
> For Jordan is a hard road to travel.

> Louis Napoleon after all is emperor of France
> And all Europe begins to tremble accordin.
> But the Yankees dont care for if with us he
>   wants to fight
> He'll wish he'd staid on de oder side ob Jordan.

In the 1860's one of the stage's popular comedians was Dave Reed. He had started as a minstrel in the 1840's, and in the middle fifties had organized his own minstrel company which performed on a Mississippi steamboat, the *James Raymond*. In 1863 he joined the famous troupe run by Dan Bryant, where as a bones player he had no peer. Later he, his wife, and his four clever children appeared as the "Reed Birds."

His greatest success was with Negro dialect songs, simple in construction and in words and melodies. This was the period of the Civil War, when people craved light-hearted entertainment to counteract the anguish and the bitterness of the awful conflict. Probably the two best-received songs of Reed's were "Nancy Fat" (see page 132) and "My Polly Ann." Reed would deliver these numbers dressed in a short dark coat, light striped pants, and a cap that was a travesty of that worn by the Union soldier. He wrote the words himself; the music was by T. McNally. "Nancy Fat" went:

She says this darkey am so sweet
She loves me like molasses,
Dat small machine she calls her heart,
Goes pit pat as it passes.

. . . . .

And as we march unto de church,
And hear de bells a ringin,
De joy will break dis Niggar's heart,
To hear de darkies singin.

In 1896, Barney Fagan, one of the outstanding acrobatic dancers of his day as well as a top theatrical producer, showed his versatility by writing the song hit of the year.

Fagan had joined a blackface minstrel troupe at the age of fifteen and worked his way up through the ranks. His greatest achievement was the organization, in 1887, of the largest minstrel company that had ever traveled; their first parade in Albany, New York, included 105 people. The title of his very popular composition was "My Gal Is a High Born Lady" (see page 134), a dialect song of subtle humor, with a catchy tune that was shortly to be whistled and sung across the land. It starts:

Thar' is gwine to be a festival this evenin'
And a gatherin' of color mighty rare,
Thar'll be noted individuals of prominent
     distinctiveness,
To permeate the colored atmosphere.

The festival mentioned is a society wedding attended by "Africa's Four Hundred," and the bridegroom exults:

My gal is a high born lady,
She's black, but not too shady,
Feathered like a peacock, just as gay,
She is not colored, she was born that way.
I'm proud of my black Venus,
No coon can come between us,
'Long the line they can't out shine,
This high born gal of mine!

For the next few years other songs featuring Negro characters were in the spotlight. One of the most amusing was written by two veterans, Harry B. Smith and John Stromberg. Neither of these men had a minstrel background, but they had the "feel" for a "coon" song, and they built up a nice touch of comic drama in one entitled "What! Marry Dat Gal?" (See page 136.)

It seems that the singer, after being mistreated by a certain young lady, received a communication from her asking him to marry her. The chorus describes his reaction to her proposal:

> What! marry dat gal? wal I guess no,
> Not if she grubbled on her knees to ax me.
> What! me tie up to a bleach blon' coon
> What works me to de limit an' sacks me.
> I may not be so particklar wahm
> But I guess I know 'nuff to keep out of de stohm
> What! marry dat gal when she used me so?
> I'm some kinds o' fool but dat kind? No!

Comic songs about the Irish-American started to appear in the 1840's. One of the first was a parody on a popular piece of the period, "The Fine Old English Gentleman." John Brougham, a well-known song writer of the times, wrote it, and called it "The Fine Ould Irish Gintleman." (See page 139.) The old gentleman was "one of the rale ould stock" who "stood with a glass of fine ould Irish whiskey in his fist." Eventually he overdid it, and on a spree "he got about as dhrunk as he could be. His senses were complately mulvathered and the consequence was that he could neither hear nor see." He was laid out for dead with candles at his heels and head. "But, when the whiskey bottle was uncorked he couldn't stand it any longer so he riz right up in bed, and when sich mighty fine stuff as that is goin' about says he you don't think I'd be such a soft headed fool as to be dead!"

In 1888 a non-Irishman named Leopold Jordan brought out "Finnegan's Musketeers," possibly in an attempt to recapture some of the enthusiasm that had attended the presentation of Harrigan and Hart's great "Mulligan Guards." It did not approach in popularity this earlier favorite, but the tune, which at times ran perilously close to "The Wearing of the Green," had a nice swing, and the story was typically Irish. The musketeers, after their corps had grown to great strength, started fighting among themselves, until "the looks of it you ne'er saw! the dying and the dead!" And, sings the soloist, "So me friends if you will read in history it appears / That I'm the sole survivor of Finnigan's Musketeers." (See page 142.)

One of the great names in show business was Pat Rooney. In fact, there were two great Pat Rooneys, for Pat I had a son equally gifted. The soft patter and twinkling toes of father and son danced through half a century of stage appearances. Both men completely captivated their audiences and left only pleasant memories behind them.

Pat Sr.'s most popular portrayal was of a gentleman named Reilly; and whenever he sang—and danced—"Is that Mr. Reilly?" (see page 145), his audience was in for a rare treat. Pat sang:

> I'm Terence O'Reilly, I'm a man of renown,
> I'm a thoroughbred to the backbone.
> I'm related to O'Connor, my mother was queen
> Of China, ten miles from Athlone.
> But if they'd let me be I'd have Ireland free,
> On the railroads you would pay no fare
> I'd have the United States under my thumb
> And I'd sleep in the President's chair.

Soon he would break into a delicate soft-shoe dance that would have the audience applauding and squealing with delight.

Felix McGlennon, a song writer whose compositions were presented by some of the "big name" performers of his time, was impressed and amused by the introduction of the eight-hour workday in American industry around 1890.

His opinions were aired and illustrated in specific examples, as in a song entitled "I've Worked Eight Hours This Day" (see page 146), performed by the vaudeville team of Collins and Welch, in stage-Irish dialect:

> Have ye heard the rule, me boys, . . . ?
> Ye mustn't work more than eight hours any day or
>   else you're fined;
> Eight hours work a day, then eight hours to
>   play,
> Ye must work no more d'ye mind.

Another popular performer was Thomas O. Seabrooke, who took advantage of the poor Irishman to exploit his own talents. One song which appealed to his audiences was "Swim Out O'Grady" (see page 149), written in 1894 by two hitherto unknowns named Smith and Tracy. Poor O'Grady was a sailor who tumbled into the sea and who had the misfortune to see his ship continue on its way without him. As he was floundering, a little fairy whispered in his ear:

> Swim out O'Grady, you have no time to spare.
> You're stranded on the billow, twenty miles from anywhere.

> If you don't mind your business there will be one vacant chair,
> So swim out O'Grady swim out.

Poor O'Grady has one rendezvous after another, with mermaids, a codfish, a whale, a seal, and other individuals. We finally leave him still being admonished to swim out!

With somewhat less frequency, performers attempted to deride the English; but apparently American audiences were less receptive when their English cousins were ribbed than when fun was poked at other nationalities. Occasionally they enjoyed a bit of spoofing at the Englishman's expense, as in "Cawn't Do It Ye Know" (see page 152), a rollicking little number introduced in 1886 by R. E. Graham, in a successful comic opera, *The Little Tycoon*. In this ditty the Englishman admits that his compatriots are no match for the Americans when, for instance, he alludes to a recent yacht race between American and English boats:

> They say that John Bull can outsail
>   Uncle Sam,
> But he cawn't do it you know.
> Tried to take the wind out of our yacht
> Puritan,
> But they cawn't do it you know.

Then he discusses the proximity of the United States to Canada and the numerous bank embezzlers who fled the United States to seek immunity up north:

> If Canada wants to annex the State of Maine,
> Why—she cawn't do it, ye know,
> For Maine wants a chance for the White House*
>   again,
> But she cawn't do it, ye know.
> If each bank cashier who from here emigrates,
> A permanent residence there contemplates,
> She will have to annex quite a number of States,
> But she cawn't do it, ye know.

James G. Blaine of Maine had just been defeated for the presidency by Grover Cleveland.

Songs about the German-Americans were more common (one or two have been mentioned in other chapters). In 1880, Charlie Collins, a man with many good songs to his credit, was assigned the task of writing five more for a drama entitled *Reward*, or *The German Volunteer*. Some were sentimental, but one or two were humorous, such as "Look Out for that Mother-in-Law" and "Jakey Jump der Baby." (See page 156.) In the latter Jakey thinks ruefully of the days when he was single and laments the woes of his married life. After a hard day's work, and as soon as he has been served supper, his wife instructs him:

> Oh! Jakey, shump der baby,
> Vont you shump de little dear?
> Ids getting vild, shoost blease der shild,
> Say, Jakey, do you hear?

He continues:

> I stard do read der baper,
> Und I get my pipe to smoke,
> But stumble on der cradle,
> Und I dinks my legs vas proke,
> Dot baby make some music
> Like a prass pand in full play,
> My vife she comes a flyin in
> And hollers right away.

> CHORUS: Oh, Jakey shump der baby, [etc.]

And then there is the Chinaman. As early as the 1880's he was an object of ridicule.

"The San Francisco Minstrels" troupe had a popular soloist named Charles Backus. He was a comedian, and was particularly adept at impersonating prominent actors. Widely traveled, he invaded Australia twice after organizing his own troupe, "Backus' Minstrels." In 1880, Backus had the opportunity to present for the San Francisco Minstrels a song entitled "All-a-Same" or "The Chinee Laundryman" (see page 157), which was written and composed by Frank Dumont. Dumont was reported to be one of the most intellectual men in the minstrel profession. He started in minstrelsy when he was fourteen years old, and was associated with half a dozen minstrel troupes before he joined the San Francisco group. In addition to writing innumerable songs, he was the author of a number of sketches and plays. His Chinese laundryman sang:

> Me comee from Hong Kong Chinee
> To workee for de Mellican man,
> Me no can talkee much english,
> Me speakee you de best I can.
> Me workee all day in laundry,

For ching chong dat's his name,
Me catchee de rats in de market,
Makee pot-pie all a same.

CHORUS: Oh ching chong opium, taffy on a stick,
No likee brass band, Makee very sick,
Mellican man listen, sing you littee song,
With a chinee fiddle, and a shanghai gong.

And this passed for humor, oriental style. Today, much of the material in this chapter would not be considered funny at all. Indeed, many people would regard it as being in very bad taste. But our nineteenth-century ancestors were proud to be Americans, and they saw nothing wrong in poking fun at their hyphenated countrymen.

2. I look to the East I look to the West
   And I see ole Kossuth a comin
   With four bay horses hitch'd up in front,
   To tote his money to de oder side ob Jordan.
   So take off, &c.

3. David and Goliath both had a fight
   A cullud man come up behind 'em.
   He hit Goliath on de head, wid a bar of soft soap
   And it sounded to de oder side ob Jordan.
   So take off, &c.

4. If I was de legislator ob dese United States
   I'd settle de fish question accordin.
   I'd give de British all de bones and de Yankees all de meat
   And stretch de boundary line to de oder side ob Jordan.
   So take off, &c.

5. Der's been excitin times for de last year or two
   About de great Presidential election
   Frank Pierce got elected and sent a hasty plate ob soup
   To his opponent on de oder side ob Jordan.
   So take off, &c.

6. Louis Napoleon after all is emperor of France
   And all Europe begins to tremble accordin.
   But the Yankees dont care for if with us he wants to fight
   He'll wish he'd staid on de oder side ob Jordan.
   So take off, &c.

Nancy Fat & My Polly Ann

TWO SONGS

Written and sung with the greatest success by

DAVE REED,

MUSIG BY

T Mc NALLY.

Nº1 Nancy Fat 4

Nº2 My Polly Ann 4

NEW YORK,
Published by Wᵐ A. POND & Cº 547 Broadway.

LITH OF MAJOR & KNAPP 449 BROADWAY N.Y.

BOSTON,
O. DITSON & Cº

MILWAUKEE,
H. N. HEMPSTED

CHICAGO,
ROOT & CADY.

PITTSBURG,
H. KLEBER & BRO.

Entered according to Act of Congress in the year 1864 by W.A. Pond & Cº in the Clerks Office of the District Court of the South. Distᵗ of New York

Nancy Fat

O Nan-cy Fat she was a gal, fair and tall and slen-der, the fair-est gal I ev-er saw, In all the fe-male gen-der; A love-ly foot I know she had, in-to a boot to thrust, Her an-kles small were made for use, to keep from it the dust. O Nan-cy Fat What are you at, I love you as no oth-er, O Nan-cy Fat get out of that, with sweet-ness me you'll smo-ther

2. O Nancy Fat she had a mouth,
   I cannot now describe it,
   It open'd like a safety valve,
   When she wish'd to divide it;
   And well I knows she had a nose,
   And ev'rybody knows it,
   The end of it just looks as if
   The Brandy bottle froze it.
   O Nancy Fat, &c.

3. O Nancy Fat had two such eyes,
   Like burnt holes in a blanket,
   The inspiration from her soul
   I took it in and drank it;
   She says this darkey am so sweet

   She loves me like molasses,
   Dat small machine she calls her heart,
   Goes pit pat as it passes.
   O Nancy Fat, &c.

4. If Nancy Fat does marry me,
   How nice we'll live together,
   She and I and all de bairns
   Like ducks in rainy weather;
   And as we march unto de church,
   And hear de bells a ringin,
   De joy will break dis Niggar's heart,
   To hear de darkies singin.
   O Nancy Fat, &c.

133

MY GAL IS A HIGH-BORN LADY.

BY
BARNEY
FAGAN.

M. WITMARK & SONS.

My Gal Is A High Born Lady

Thar' is gwine to be a fes-ti-val this eve-nin' and a gath-er-in of col-or migh-ty rare, Thar'll be

not-ed in-di-vid-u-als of prom-i-nent dis-tinc-tive-ness, to per-me-ate the col-ored at-mos-phere, Sun-ny

Af-ri-ca's Four Hun-dred's gwine to be thar, to do hon-or to my love-ly fi-an-cee, Thar will be a grand o-

va-tion, of es-pec-ial os-ten-ta-tion, when the par-son gives the dus-ky bride a-way! My gal is a high born

Chorus

la-dy, She's black, but not too sha-dy, Fea-thered like a pea-cock, just as gay, She is not col-oured, she was

born that way, I'm proud of my black Ve-nus, No coon can come be-tween us, 'Long the line they

can't out-shine, this high born gal of mine!

2. When the preacher man propounds the vital question,
   Does ye' take the gal' for better or for wuss?
   I will feel as if my soul had left my body, gone to glory,
   And I know my heart will make an awful fuss,
   I anticipates a very funny feelin'
   Nigger's eyeball, like a diamond sure to shine,
   But I'll bask in honeyed clover, when the ceremony's over,
   And I press the ruby lips of baby mine?
   My gal, &c.

135

What! Marry Dat Gal?

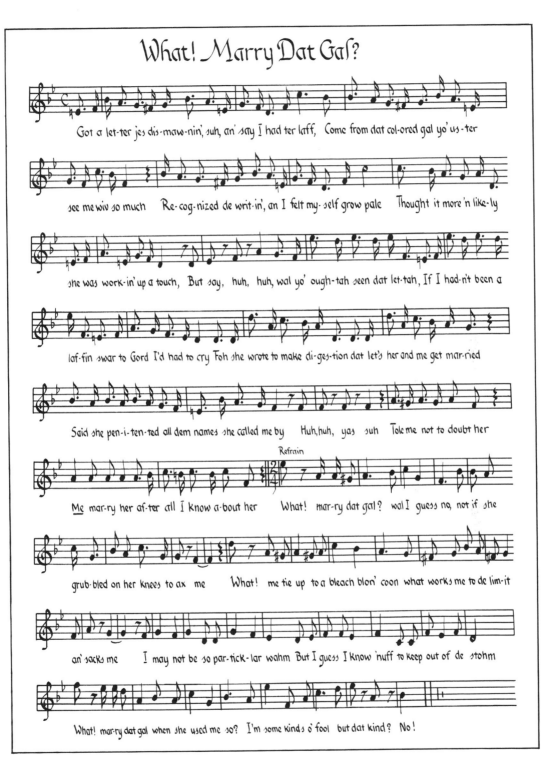

2. Say yo' oughtah saw de answer what I sent her in reply,
   Got de boss to write it in de reddes' kind o' ink
   Talk about sarkastical mos' burned de papah up
   Bet when she perused it, took her har all out o' kink,
   An' say, huh, huh, if yo' see a colored lady
   Havin' de hysterics an' a prancin' like a goat
   Yo' needn't ax her name, it is Phoebe Emma Jackson
   An' her ravins are de symptom ob de lettah what I wrote
   Huh, huh, yas suh Her career am checkered
   Me marry her when I know de lady's record.
   What! marry dat gal? &c.

THE FINE OULD

IRISH GINTLEMAN,

Written and Sung by

JOHN BROUGHAM,

AND BY HIM DEDICATED, TO HIS FRIEND

OLIVER C. WYMAN.

OF BOSTON.

Price 25 cts net

BOSTON.
Published by GEO. P. REED, 17 Tremont Row.
Entered according to act of Congress in the year 1843 by Geo P Reed in the clerks office of the District Court of Massachusetts.

The Fine Ould Irish Gintleman

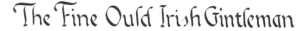

I'll sing you a fine ould song made by a fine ould Pad-dy's pate of a fine ould Irish gintleman who

had the devil a taste of an es-tate, ex-cept a fine old patch of pitaty's that he liked ex-ceed-ing-ly to ate,

For they were beef to him and mutton too and barring a red herring or a rusty rasher of bacon now

and thin almost ev'ry oth-er sort of mate Yet this fine ould Irish gin-tle-man was one of the rale ould stock

2. (*Spoken*) His cabin walls were cover'd o'er with
   (*Sung*) fine ould Irish mud, Be–
   (Spoken) cause he couldn't afford to have any paper hangings, and between you
   and me he wouldn't give a
   (*Sung*) pin for them if he could. And
   (*Spoken*) just as proud as Julius Sayzer or
   (*Sung*) Alexander the great, This
   (*Spoken*) independent ragamuffin stood with a glass of fine ould Irish whiskey
   in his fist which he's decidedly of opinion will do a
   (*Sung*) mighty dale of good,
   To this fine ould Irish Gintleman,
   All of the rale ould stock.

3. (*Sung*) Now this
   (*Spoken*) fine ould Irish gintleman wore
   (*Sung*) mighty curious clothes, Tho' for
   (*Spoken*) comfort I'll be bail that they'd bate any of your
   (*Sung*) fashionable beaux, For
   (*Spoken*) when the sun was very hot the gintle wind right through his ventilation
   garments most
   (*Sung*) beautifully blows.

(*Spoken*) And he's niver troubled with any corns and I'll tell you why, because
he despises the wakeness of waring anything as hard as
(*Sung*) leather on his toes,
Yet this fine ould Irish gintleman was one of the rale ould stock.

4. (*Sung*) Now this
(*Spoken*) fine ould Irish gintleman has a
(*Sung*) mighty curious knack, Of
(*Spoken*) flourishing a tremendous great shillaly in his hand and letting it
drop down with a most un–
(*Sung*) compromising whack
(*Spoken*) So of most superiour shindies you may take your oath if you ever
happen to be called upon for it he very nearly
(*Sung*) never had a lack, and it's
(*Spoken*) very natural and not at all surprising to suppose that the fine ould
Irish mud was well ac–
(*Sung*) quainted with the back of this Fine Ould Irish Gintleman,
All of the rale ould stock.

5. (*Sung*) This
(*Spoken*) fine ould Irish gintleman he was once
(*Sung*) out upon a spree, and as
(*Spoken*) many a fine ould Irish gintleman has done and more betoken will do
to the end of time he got about as
(*Sung*) dhrunk as he could be,
(*Spoken*) His senses was completely mulvathered and the consequence was that
he could
(*Sung*) neither hear nor see, So they
(*Spoken*) thought he was stone dead and gone intirely, So the best thing they
could do would be to have him waked and
(*Sung*) buried dacintly,
Like a Fine Ould Irish Gintleman
All of the rale ould stock.

6. (*Sung*) So this
(*Spoken*) fine ould Irish gintleman he was laid
(*Sung*) out upon a bed,
(*Spoken*) with half a dozen candles at his heels and two or three dozen more or
(*Sung*) less about his head,
(*Spoken*) But when the whiskey bottle was uncorked he couldn't stand it any
longer so he
(*Sung*) riz right up in bed,
(Spoken) and when sich mighty fine stuff as that is goin' about says he you
don't think I'd be such a soft headed
(*Sung*) fool as to be dead,
Oh this fine Ould Irish Gintleman it was mighty hard to kill.

Finnigan's Musketeers

Mike Fin-ni-gan a pa-tri-ot he swore that he would raise a might-y corps of mus-ket-eers that all the

world would daze And so he bought 'em guns and swords car-bines and dy-na-mite and

when they went up-on pa-rade it was a love-ly sight I was first to join the corps and thin came Jim McGee

who with Ma-hone was soon out-shone by Pat O' Fla-ri-tee To see us march as stiff as starch and lis-ten

to the cheers Foin-er boys yez niv-er saw than Fin-ni-gan's Mus-ket-eers. I joined Fin-ni-gan's Mus-ket-

eers One St. Pa-trick's day Said Fin-ni-gan "take the drum and blaze and blaze a-way

Strike out from the shoul-der and all the boys will come They'll ral-ly round Fin-ni-gan when they

hear his drum."

2. The corps it grew to such a stringth, the boys became quite gay
   Divil a bit for Finnigan they cared I heard thim say
   They smash'd the chairs, the tables and the sofas and the cribs

They broke the glass and then alas they broke each others ribs
"Commander," said young Patsy, "I'll be or else I'll die."
"Go and die," said Finnigan, "Commander in chafe am I."
Thin Patsy rose and shtruck two blows straight at Finnigan's head
But miss'd and lo! the deadly blow Mulligan got instead.

CHORUS

3. Rebellion came within the camp it was a sorry sight
   For all but one were slaughtered quite before they left that night
   Finnigan lay a corpse quite stiff upon the gory floor
   And poor O'Flynn it was a sin he fell to shpake no more
   The loiks of it you ne'er saw! the dying and the dead!
   'Twas not my doom as from that room twas I alone that fled
   So me friends if you will read in history it appears
   That I'm the sole survivor of Finnigan's Musketeers.

CHORUS

Is That Mr. Reilly?

I'm Ter-rence O'Reil-ly, I'm a man of re-nown, I'm a tho-rough-bred to the back-bone,—— I'm re-lat-ed to O'Con-nor, my mo-ther was Queen of Chi-na, ten miles from Ath-lone,—— But if they'd let me be I'd have Ire-land free, On the rail-roads you would pay no fare—— I'd have the U-nit-ed States un-der my thumb and I'd sleep in the Pres-i-dent's chair—— Is that Mis-ter Reil-ly, can an-y one tell? Is that Mis-ter Reil-ly? that owns the ho-tel? Well if that's Mis-ter Reil-ly, they speak of so high-ly, well up-on my soul Reil-ly you're do-ing quite well.

(*Spoken after 1st verse*) I was walking across the Atlantic Ocean the other day, and as I was coming in the dock a fellow says:

        CHORUS

2. I'd have nothing but Irishmen on the police,
   Patrick's Day will be the Fourth of July,
   I'd get me a thousand infernal machines to teach the Chinese how to die;
   I'll defend workingmen's cause,
   Manufacture the laws,
   New York would be swimming in wine.
   A hundred a day, will be very small pay, when the White-House and
      Capitol are mine.

(*Spoken*) As I was walking quietly along the Elevated Railroad the other day, a
      gang of people hollered up—

        CHORUS

Sung with Great Success by COLLINS & WELCH.

I've Worked Eight Hours This Day.

Written and Composed by

FELIX McGLENNON.

PUBLISHED BY

W. F. SHAW,
721 Vine Street, Philadelphia.

I've Worked Eight Hours This Day.

Have ye heard the rule, me boys, the lat-est rule, me boys? Ye must-n't work more than eight hours an-y day or else you're fined Eight hours work a day, then eight hours to play, ye must work on more d'ye mind. Pat had a hod of bricks to-night, 'twas strik-ing six, The top of the lad-der he was on but would-n't leave thim thin he would-n't work o-ver-time for that would be a crime, Says he, "I'll car-ry thim down a-gin." For I've worked eight hours this day, and I think I've earned my pay, Whin the clock struck six he tuk down the bricks, He would-n't work half a min-ute lon- ger.

2. Patsey Mulligan last night got full agin,
   He came home drunk at two o'clock a.m. and made a din;
   He kicked at the dur, he did, jumped on the flure, he did,
   Shouted, "Bridget, let me in."
   She heard the shindy and she opened the windy,
   And says she, "Is that you Pat?" Says he, "Sure, I'm wet to the skin."
   Says she, "I'm sorry, Pat, but till to-morroy, Pat,
   Me darling, I can't let ye in—

   CHORUS: "For I've worked eight hours this day
           And I think I've earned my pay,
           Ye can stop out there in the rain and swear,
           I wont work half a minute longer."

3. Barney Brockey was me fav'rite jockey,
   And whene'er he rode a horse I had me bottom dollar on.
   He was a flier and a good ould trier.
   Wan day I got ten to wan,
   Me puids I parted, and the horses started;
   They ran like the devil up to ten yards from the winning-post,
   Then he stopped; bedad I nearly dropped, bedad.
   Says he, "To-morrow I'll finish this race—

   Chorus: "For I've worked eight hours this day,
         And I think I've earned my pay,
         The others may pass, let my horse eat grass,
         I wont work half a minute longer."

4. Johnny Hooligan's been made a fool agin:
   He went to the barber's just to get a decent penny shave,
   He'd lovely whiskers on, Donegal whiskers on,
   But had that barber did behave.
   He soaped and lathered, then he jawed and blathered;
   He scraped wan side of Johnny's face so nice and clean all o'er,
   He went to the other jaw, then the clock he saw,
   Says he, "To-morrow I'll finish the shave—

   Chorus: "For I've worked eight hours this day,
         And I think I've earned my pay,
         Lave your whiskers on till the mornin', John,
         I wont work half a minute longer."

5. Now, I am quiet and I don't like riot,
   But last night at the corner of the street a man came up to me,
   Says he, "I'll batter ye, bedad, I'll scatter ye,"
   And then he smashed my nose, d'ye see?
   His fist was a whopper, so I called out, "Copper!"
   Then a P'liceman grabbed him, and says he, "Me boy I have ye tight."
   Then the clock did chime, says he, "Luk at the time,
   I can't lock this man up to-night—

   Chorus: "For I've worked eight hours this day
         And I think I've earned my pay,
         Fa la loo ting, ting, put yer nose in a sling,
         I won't work half a minute longer."

Thomas Q. Seabrooke's

GREAT SONG

"SWIM OUT, O'GRADY."

Words by
EDGAR SMITH,

Music by
GEO. LOWELL TRACY.

THE JOHN CHURCH COMPANY,

CINCINNATI. ✛ NEW YORK. ✛ CHICAGO.

Swim Out O'Grady

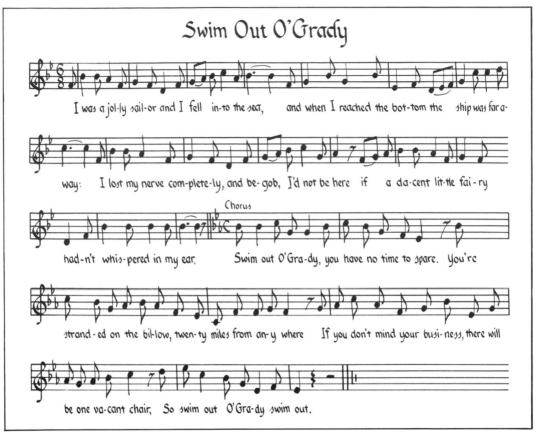

I was a jol-ly sail-or and I fell in-to the sea, and when I reached the bot-tom the ship was far a-way: I lost my nerve com-plete-ly, and be-gob, I'd not be here if a da-cent lit-tle fai-ry had-n't whis-pered in my ear. Swim out O'Gra-dy, you have no time to spare. You're strand-ed on the bil-low, twen-ty miles from an-y where If you don't mind your busi-ness, there will be one va-cant chair, So swim out O'Gra-dy swim out.

2. As downward I was sinking, to old Oceans coral caves,
   I spied some mermaids winking at me from behind the waves,
   I made a grab to catch one, and a codfish grabbed at me
   I meant no harm at all says I, then take my tip says he.

   CHORUS: Oh swim out O'Grady—before I run yer in
            For flirting with a mermaid, is a very heinous sin
            As you have no influence, it will surely cost you ten
            So swim out, O'Grady,—swim out!

   Repeat

3. I met a whale out walking, he was fat and full of fun
   And the two of us got talking about the yarn that Jonah spun,
   He said he'd never heard it, so I told it to him thin
   He smiled and said politely as he winked his other fin.

CHORUS: Oh swim out, O'Grady! you take me for a flat?
I've got a great big swallow, but I could'nt swallow that
Believe me Mr. Jonah was conversing thro' his hat
So swim out, O'Grady, swim out!

Repeat

4. Oh when I reached the bottom where the pearls were growing thick
What should loom up before me but another shipwrecked Mick
He was very old and feeble, and a tear was in his eye,
But when I reached a diamond, he had strength enough to cry:

CHORUS: Oh swim out, O'Grady, this is no place for ye,
I'm the first and only squatter at the bottom of the sea;
Begorra, I'm McGinty and the place belongs to me
So swim out, O'Grady,—swim out!

Repeat

5. I ran across a cable and was waiting for a car
And right forninst me was a seal, smoking a cigar
I was sympathizing with him, You must find it hard sez I,
Dodging mermaids after sealskins! listen now to his reply,

CHORUS: Oh swim out, O'Grady—try and get it thro' your wool,
That natures dispensations are exceeding merciful
You see I have the sealskin, but I have no leg to pull
So swim out, O'Grady,—swim out!

Repeat

Cawn't Do It Ye Know!

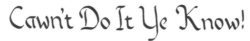

I have heard peo-ple say that they'd star-tle the world, but they cawn't do it you know   That they'd

nav-i-gate ships through the air to be whirled, but they cawn't do it you know,   And pi-ous Bob In-ger-soll's

lec-tures they tell you to go as you please and in hea-ven you'll dwell, that there are hon-est law-yers who

keep out of - (ahem) - well, but they cawn't do it ye know.   They cawn't do it ye know,   They cawn't do it ye

know; Let some clev-er man try In-ger-soll to re-ply, but he cawn't do it ye know.

2. They say that John Bull can outsail Uncle Sam,
   But he cawn't do it you know,
   Tried to take the wind out of our yacht Puritan,
   But they cawn't do it you know;
   Prove the Pall Mall Gazette is a very clean sheet,
   That old England will yet young America beat,
   That they won't have to come over here for their meat,
   But they cawn't do without it ye know.

   CHORUS: They cawn't do it ye know,
               They cawn't do it ye know;
               Mister Bismarck tried hard,
               Our pork to discard,
               But he cawn't do it ye know.

3. Just show me a country where women can vote,
   But ye cawn't do it ye know,
   Show a true Irishman who will wear a red coat,

152

TO
GEORGE C. BROTHERTON,
Manager "TEMPLE THEATRE," Phila.

The Great Original
Topical Song

"CAWN'T DO IT, YE KNOW!"

Composed and Sung by

Mr. R. E. GRAHAM,

In his Original Character Creation of General Knickerbocker,

In the First Successful

American Comic Opera,

"THE LITTLE TYCOON."

☞ This Song was first Written and Sung by Mr. Graham at Chicago, Illinois, in September, 1885,
and is his Original Work.

Waltz Simplified by Sep. Winner, 25 cents.
Violin and Piano arr. by   "   30 "
Cornet and Piano "   "   "   30 "
Violin Solo   "   "   "   20 "
Cornet Solo   "   "   "   20 "

Song, 40 cents.
Banjo, 40 cents.
Waltz, 35 cents.

"PHILADELPHIA:

PUBLISHED BY WM. H. BONER & CO., 1102 CHESTNUT STREET.

But ye cawn't do it ye know,
Prove a policeman never drinks beer on his beat,
That they'll drive all the rats from Chicago's main street,
Just show us a gal in this town with small feet,
But they cawn't do it ye know,
They cawn't do it ye know,
They cawn't do it ye know,
They often have tried their small anklets to hide,
But they cawn't do it ye know.

4. They say they can show us a dude that has brains,
But they cawn't do it ye know,
One who has sense enough to go in when it rains,
But they cawn't do it ye know,
The Schuylkill water to drink's very queer;
I'm afraid if they do not soon filter it clear,
Philadelphia Quakers will have to drink beer,
But they don't like it ye know,
They cawn't do it ye know,
They cawn't do it ye know,
'Twould be very sad news If they'd all take to booze,
For they cawn't stand it ye know.

5. Show a woman who has not the gift of the jaw,
But ye cawn't do it ye know,
Show a man who's in love with his mother-in-law,
But ye cawn't do it ye know,
A married man often looks like a gawk
Who comes home late at night with his coat full of chalk,
And thinks he can sleep when his wife wants to talk,
But he cawn't do it ye know,
He cawn't do it ye know,
He cawn't do it ye know,
When he tries loud to snore She will talk more and more,
And he cawn't do it ye know.

Jakey Jump Der Baby

Oh! vonce ven I vas sin-gle, den I haf such lods of fun, But now dot I vas mar-ried, all der

shol-ly dimes are done, Ven I come hime at efen-ing, af-ter vork-ing all der day, So quick I eats my

sup-per, den my vife to me vill say, Oh! Ja-ky, shump der ba-by, Vont you shump de lit-tle dear? Ids

get-ting vild, shoost blease der shild, Say, Ja-ky do you hear? Oh! Ja-ky shump der ba-by, Vont you

shump der little dear? Ids get-ting vild, shoost blease de shild, Say, Ja-ky, do you hear?

2. I stard do read der baper,
   Und I get my pipe to smoke,
   But stumble on der cradle,
   Und I dinks my legs vas proke,
   Dot baby make some music
   Like a prass pand in full play,
   My vife she comes a flyin in,
   And hollers right away,

   CHORUS

3. Of course I vas ids father,
   Und I'd be an awful goose,
   Of I should be so cruel
   As to gife id some abuse,
   Vat drives me nearly crazy,
   Is ad nighd to sleep away,
   Und haf my vife shust vake me ap
   Boud two o'clock, und say,

   CHORUS

156

DEDICATED TO ROBERT J. TIFFANY ESQ. OF SAN FRANCISCO, CAL.

"THE CHINEE LAUNDRYMAN"

"ALL—A—SAME."

Not Pretty but Good
Charley Backus

SUNG BY

CHARLES BACKUS

OF THE SAN FRANCISCO MINSTRELS
OPERA HOUSE, 29th ST. & BROADWAY

WORDS & MELODY BY FRANK DUMONT.

PHILADELPHIA,
PUBLISHED BY CHAS. F. ESCHER JR. 1242 GIRARD AVE.

The Chinee Laundryman

Me com-ee from Hong Kong Chin-ee to work-ee for de Mel-li-can man, Me no can talk-ee much eng-lish, Me speak-ee you de best I can Me work-ee all day in laun-dry, for ching chong dat's his name, Me catch-ee de rats in de mar-ket, Mak-ee pot-pie all a same All same! All same! All same!

Chorus

Oh ching chong o-pi-um, taf-fy on a stick, No lik-ee brass band, Mak-ee ve-ry sick, Mel-li-can man lis-ten, sing you lit-tee song, with a chi-nee fid-dle and a shang-hai gong.

2. Me no go backee to Chinee,
    Me doee welly well out here,
    Me cheatee all melican gambler,
    Me likee sour krout and beer,
    Me soon becomee citizen,
    And votee just like me please,
    By'm bye me gettee a good job,
    To workee on de Police
    All same! Police! All same!

    CHORUS

3. Me soon gettee money very plenty
    And wantee gettee nice littee wife,
    Me lovee her better dan chou chou
    Me likee her better dan life,
    Me feedee her rice and opium,
    Me buyee nice littee house,
    For dinnee me fixee de rat-trap,
    To catchee nice littee mouse
    Good mouse! All same! Nice mouse!

    CHORUS

158

Nonsense

4

IN NURSERY RHYMES AND FAIRY TALES, nonsense syllables have been as acceptable as words listed in Webster's dictionary. "Deedle deedle dumpling, my son John," "Fee fi fo fum, I smell the blood of an Englishman," and "Hi diddle diddle, the cat and the fiddle" were among the earliest phrases in the vocabulary of a small child. Such youthful conditioning enriches our conversations—and our songs, too, from time to time—with meaningless words and syllables.

To solemn grown-ups in whom the spark of youth has long been extinguished it may seem downright silly to mouth inanities like "Hut sut Ralson on the Rillera," or "A tisket, a tasket." But most of us, who like to relax completely when we can, enjoy an easy flow of gibberish set to a simple tune that anyone who isn't tone-deaf can pick up after he hears the melody once or twice.

Our nineteenth-century tunesmiths sensed the possibilities of attaining popularity with the aid of such nonsense syllables and phrases, and they put their talents to good use. Probably the best known, and one of the earliest, nonsense phrases was introduced by Stephen Foster in 1850 in "Gwine to Run All Night," more often referred to as "Camptown Races." The popular Christy and Campbell Minstrels promoted this song, and soon it became one of the most entertaining numbers in their repertoire. It started:

> De Camptown Ladies sing dis song,
> Doodah, doodah.

Nobody understood what "doodah" meant, but it was on everybody's

159

tongue, and no one felt self-conscious if he went around singing a word which served only to make lighter a light-hearted minstrel song.

"Camptown Races" was followed by a song with another dreamed-up phrase which caught the public fancy. "Keemo Kimo'" (see page 165) was one of the sensational new ditties introduced by Geo. Christy and Wood's minstrels in 1854. The author and the composer are unknown today. Christy himself, more than likely, was responsible for the words or the music or both:

> In South Car'lina de darkies go
> Sing song Kitty can't you ki me, oh!

The chorus is completely bereft of reason:

> Keemo ki'mo! Dar! Oh whar?
> Wid my hi, my ho, and in come Sally singing
> Some times penny winkle, lingtum, nip-cat—
> Sing song Kitty can't you ki'me oh.

But the decade in which the nonsense lyrics played their biggest role was the 1890's, when they made a sizeable contribution to the not-too-extensive vocabularies of the writers of most popular songs.

One of the first of this group carried words published originally in the *Harvard Lampoon*, of all places. Hubbard T. Smith, a composer who went on to prolific productivity in the popular sheet music field, wrote the music for "Wing Tee Wee, the Sweet Chinee." (See page 167.)

Wing Tee Wee, says the *Lampoon*, falls in love with Win Sil, who "wrote his love on a laundry bill," singing:

> Then ZIP, boom yah! Ev'rybody sing
> Ump-ha, Ump-ha, zing, zing, zing!
> Love is a hoky, poky, joky sort of thing,
> Hi-yah, Coom shaw, zing, zing, zing!
> Hi, yi, yi yi, zing! zing! zing!

Unfortunately this is apparently unintelligible to Wing Tee Wee, who probably never completed elementary school and could hardly be expected to qualify by responding to Harvard poetry—if such it may be called. So she elopes with a rich pirate named Tin Told, who takes her out to sea in a Chinese junk and never brings her back. Ah, me! Ah, Wing Tee Wee!

A writer named Frank Addis Kent could not resist the temptation to season his nonsense syllables with the most popular songs of the day. In "Um-Skit-a-Rat-Trap Si-si-do" (see page 169) he tells of a great musician, a cornetist who doubles as a pianist. When he rehearses, says Kent, it goes like this:

> Um-skit-a-rat-trap-si-si-do,
> There goes Casey
> After the ball is over,
> My sweetheart's the man in the moon!
> And for bonnie Annie Laurie
> I'd lay me down and Um-skit-a-rat-trap-si-si-do!

Senseless, to put it mildly, but he had sense enough to bring in a few bars from four of the best-known songs of the period.

Another well-known composer was Felix McGlennon, an Irishman, whose songs were so widely accepted in this country that most people assumed he was American-born. He was probably best known for "But Oh! What a Difference in the Morning," reprinted in one sell-out edition after the other.

Lottie Gilson, one of the cutest comediennes who ever captivated an audience, was a reigning favorite on the stage at that time, and McGlennon was fortunate enough to know her. Lottie was of the type called soubrette in those days. She was diminutive and not exceptionally pretty; in fact, when dressed in her street clothes, she could be taken for a little German *Hausfrau*. But in the late 1880's and early 1890's she was one of the most important song boosters in the business. When she set out to charm the people on the other side of the footlights, she was so appealing that almost any song she sang was enthusiastically received.

Lottie was most helpful in making a success of "But Oh! What a Difference," and she was McGlennon's little helper again when he introduced "Tol Lol Lol" (see page 171), for which he wrote the music and assisted the lyricist, Geo. Horncastle, with the words. The title page lists "Tol Lol Lol" as "Lottie Gilson's Big Hit." Miss Gilson always made a song sound good, even though the lyric was as inane as:

> Tol, lol, lol, tol, lol, lol, Isn't this a silly
>   chorus,
> There isn't much sense and there isn't much
>   rhyme,
> But I think it will suit the time.
> So we'll tol, lol, lol, tol, lol, lol, hip, hip,
>   hip, hooray,
> Sing this chorus all together tol, lol, lol, lol,
>   lay.

Lottie Gilson—sometimes known as "The Little Magnet"—was helpful to many hopeful song writers. Among them was C. M. Rodney, who wrote the music, and collaborated on the verses, of "La-Didily-Idily, Umti-Umti-Ay!" or "Jones' Wedding." (See page 174.) Jones decides to get married, but first he has to sow his last wild oats, which he does, with his friends, one of whom narrates:

> La-didily-idily, umti-umti-ay!
> La-didily-um, was all that we could say,
> We were out upon a spree, and felt a trifle gay,
> La-didily, idily, umti-umti-ay!

All of which sounds as if Jones and the boys were enjoying themselves thoroughly.

A different version of the nonsense verse is the stuttering song. One entertaining version of this approach to stage humor was written in 1894 by L. T. Gottschalk and L. B. Pemberton, Gottschalk composing the music also. It was sung by a comedian most famous for his roles as a tattered tramp, Walter Jones, who introduced his "Stuttering Song" (see page 176) in a musical show entitled "1492." Jones describes his deficiencies as a singer and explains:

> Oh I n-never could yodel and I n-never could
> t-trill
> But when it comes to stuttering, I can s-s-stutter
> to k-kill
> I s-s-stutter when I m-m-mutter, I s-s-stutter till
> I s-s-s-s-stop
> I s-s-stutter when I m-m-mutter, I s-s-stutter till
> I drop.

One of the neatest writing jobs of this sort was done by Karl Kennett, whose biggest success was called "Zizzy Ze Zum Zum Zum." (See page 179.) His composer was Lyn Udall, a big name of the late 1890's, and the two men were able to introduce the song in 1898 in a Koster and Bial production, *Cook's Tours*.

A happy little chappie writes a ditty, and soon his friends:

> All joined in and sang like sin . . . .
> Ze zizzy, ze zum, zum, zizzy, ze zum zum,
> That was the rag refrain.
> Zizzy, ze zum, zum, zizzy, ze zum,
> It drove them all insane,

From the yappy of the chappie to the deep bazoo,
Of the raggedy tag old bum,
The whole town rang with the rattlety bang,
Of ze zizzy, ze zum, zum, Zizzy, ze zum, zum,
Zizzy, ze zum, zum, zum.

But the nonsense song which attained more popularity than all others that had been written previously was "Ta-Ra-Ra Boom-De-Ay!" (See page 182.) In 1891, Henry J. Sayers, a writer with no previous important songs to his credit, turned out one with a nonsense chorus, called "Ta-Ra-Ra Boom-Der-E." It failed to stir up much interest, until, like many other popular songs of the period, it was introduced in London, where a leading comedienne, Lottie Collins, built it up into an overwhelming success. From there it came to America, destined to become one of the greatest hits—possibly the very greatest—on the American variety stage. New verses were written for it; a new composer's name appeared on thousands upon thousands of sheet-music copies.

As might be expected, this led to a copyright suit in the federal courts, where testimony was introduced to prove that the tune originated in a St. Louis "resort" of questionable fame, operated by one Babe Connors and stocked with colored female inmates. According to Edward B. Marks, a famous music publisher for two generations, Connors' place was frequented by traveling minstrels, who were always on the lookout for new material. When asked to describe the place run by Babe Connors, one witness replied, "Let's be polite and call it a cabaret!"

The "new" "Ta-Ra-Ra Boom-De-Ay!" listed as its composer Angelo A. Asher and as its lyricist Richard Morton. Morton wrote six sets of verses for ladies and five for gentlemen. For the ladies he starts out:

A smart and stylish girl you see,
Belle of good society;
Not too strict, but rather free,
Yet as right as right can be!
Never forward, never bold,
Not too hot, and not too cold,
But the very thing, I'm told,
That in your arms you'd like to hold!
Chorus: Ta-ra-ra Boom-de-ay,
(Repeat seven times—that's all there is to it.)

As for the gentlemen, most of the story concerns a young man who can't pay his bills; but the last verse becomes personal in the extreme:

163

Once I met a lady fair,
All in tears, with straggling hair,
She saw me, began to blare,—
I could only stand and stare!
A bundle in her arms was borne,
She held it out to me in scorn,—
Cried that female all forlorn:
"Take it, wretch, this parcel's your'n!"

CHORUS: Ta-ra-ra Boom-de-ay!

After all, what else would he say?

So the songs with the nonsense choruses had their distinct place in the entertainment world of the nineteenth century. Some appear stilted now, but many of us can still enjoy the Doo-dahs, the Keemo Kimos, and the Ta-ra-ra Boom-de-ays.

KEEMO KIMO

Geo. Christy Wood's

CELEBRATED

BANJO SONG

Hays N.Y.

Arranged by

SEDGWICK.

NEW YORK
Published by WILLIAM HALL & SON, 239 Broadway.

Entd. according to Act of Congress A.D. 1854 by W. Hall in the Clerks Office of the District Court of the Southern District of N.York.

Keemo Kimo

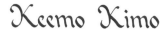

In South Car-li-na de dark-ies go Sing song Kit-ty cant you ki' me oh! Dats whar de

white folks plant de tow Sing song Kit-ty cant you ki' me, oh! Cov-er de ground all ov-er wid smoke

Sing song Kit-ty cant you ki' me oh! And up de dark-ies heads dey poke Sing song Kit-ty cant you

Chorus

ki' me oh! Kee-mo ki'mo!- Dar! oh whar? Wid my hi, my ho, and in come Sal-ly sing-ing

Some times pen-ny win-kle, ling-tum, nip-cat- Sing song Kit-ty cant you ki' me oh.

2. Milk in de dairy nine days old,
   Sing song Kitty cant you Ki' me oh.
   Frogs and de skeeters getting mighty bold—
   Sing song Kitty cant you Ki' me oh!
   Dey try for to sleep but it ain't no use
   Sing song Kitty cant you Ki' me oh
   Dere legs hang out for de chickens to roost
   Sing song Kitty cant you Ki' me, oh!

3. Dar was a frog lived in a pool,
   Sing song Kitty cant you Ki' me, oh!
   Sure he was de biggest fool—
   Sing song Kitty cant you Ki' me oh!
   For he could dance and he could sing
   Sing song Kitty cant you Ki' me, oh!
   And make de woods around him ring
   Sing song Kitty cant you Ki me oh.

TO
STERLING GALT, ESQ.
WASHINGTON, D.C.

WING TEE WEE
THE SWEET CHINEE

Words from
THE HARVARD LAMPOON

MUSIC BY
Hubbard T. Smith

Pr. 40 cts.

WASHINGTON, D.C.
PUBLISHED BY JOHN F. ELLIS & Co., 937 PENNA AVE.

Wing Tee Wee

Wing Tee Wee was a sweet Chi-nee and she lived in the town of Tac She had eyes of blue, and a

braid-ed cue hung dang-ling down her back. She fell in love with gay Win Sil, when he wrote his love

on a laun-dry bill! Then ZIP, boom, yah! Ev'-ry-bo-dy sing Ump-ha, ump-ha, zing, zing, zing!

Love is a ho-ky, po-ky, jo-ky sort of thing, Hi-yah, coom shaw, zing, zing, zing! Hi, yi, yi, yi,

zing! zing! zing!

2. And, old Tin Told
   Was a pirate bold,
   And he sailed in a Chinese junk,
   And he loved, ah, me,
   Sweet Wing Tee Wee,
   But his valiant heart had sunk;
   So he drowned his blues in sparkling fizz,
   And vowed the maid would yet be his.

   CHORUS

3. So bold Tin Told
   Showed all his gold
   To the maid in the town of Tac,
   And sweet Wing Wee
   Eloped to sea
   And never more came back,
   For in far Chinee the maids are fair,
   And the maids are false as ev'rywhere.

   CHORUS

The Latest Rage.

UM-SKIT-A-RAT-TRAP SI-SI-DO.

Comic Song & Chorus,

WRITTEN & COMPOSED

by

FRANK ADDIS KENT.

4

NEW YORK
PUBLISHED BY SPAULDING & GRAY, 16 WEST 27TH ST
HOWARD & CO. London, Eng.

Um-Skit-a-Rat-Trap-si-si-do!

I'll sing of a great mus-i-cian, who plays in a big brass band, He blows on a sil-ver cor-net, and trills with a mas-ter hand; His runs on a grand pi-an-o are ev-er a source of bliss, and when he re-hears-es, it sounds like this, "Um-skit-a-rat-trap-si-si-do," "There goes Cas-ey,""After the ball is o-ver," "My sweet-heart's the man in the moon!"—"And for bon-nie An-nie Lau-rie—I'd lay me down" and "Um-skit-a-rat-trap-si-si-do!

2. He plays all of Sousa's marches,
   On Wagner he loves to dwell,
   He studies the latest op'ra's
   And renders the music well;
   At times he will start to whistle,
   And sing all the tunes he knows,
   It's funny to hear him,
   This way he goes,—

   Chorus

3. I think he is going crazy,
   On music and instruments,
   His fam'ly is getting worried,
   They say he has lost all sense;
   He plays from the morn 'till ev'ning,
   And sometimes his meals he'll miss,
   He won't cease from playing,
   His tune's like this,—

   Chorus

TOL LOL LOL

Comic Song and Chorus

WRITTEN BY
Geo. Horncastle

MUSIC BY
Felix McGlennon

4

New York:
Published by M. WITMARK & SONS, 51 West 28th Street,
LONDON: CHAS. SHEARD & CO.

Tol, Lol, Lol

There once was a man, a ver-y trick-y man, A ver-y trick-y man was he, And he wrote a song, a ver-y sil-ly song, A ver-y sil-ly song wrote he, He'd tried for suc-cess with some sen-si-ble songs But his ef-forts were in vain, So he thought he'd write some silly rhymes, and this was his re-frain.

Chorus

Tol, lol, lol, tol, lol, lol, Is-n't this a silly chor-us, There is-n't much sense and there is-n't much rhyme, But I think it will suit the time. So we'll tol, lol, lol, tol, lol, lol, hip, hip, hip, hoo-ray, Sing this chor-us all to-geth-er tol, lol, lol, lol, lay.

2. There once was a girl, a very tricky girl,
   A very tricky girl was she,
   And she bought this song, this very silly song,
   This very silly song bought she
   She went on the stage and she sang this song
   Said the audience, "What a bore,"
   But the chorus caught their fancy, and,
   They shouted out, "Encore!"

   CHORUS

172

3. There once was a man, a muchly married man,
   A muchly married man was he,
   And he had a way, a very artful way,
   Of going out upon the spree
   But on one night oh he got so tight
   That he couldn't get home to bed
   When his wife next day said where have you been
   He hic-coughed thus and said

   Chorus

4. There once was a mash, a yummy sort of mash,
   As yummy as a mash could be,
   And with a girl a very pretty girl,
   Oh! he went one day to tea
   But her pa was there as cross as a bear
   He sat and wagged his head
   And the masher looked so meek and mild,
   Until pa went to bed.

   Chorus

An International Success.

"La-Didily-Idily-Umti-Umti-Ay"

OR Jones' Wedding.

Comic Song

Song...40
Lancers...60

Words by Richard Morton and C. M. Rodney.

Music by C. M. Rodney.

LOTTIE GILSON.

Sung by Miss Lottie Gilson, - (The Little Magnet.)

New York.

Published by Spaulding & Gray, 16 W. 27th Street.

HOWARD & CO., LONDON, ENGLAND.

La-Didily-idily, Umti-umti Ay!

On the day that Jones made up his mind that he would wed a gal, We re-solved we'd paint the city red in hon-or of our pal Then we hired a band, a coach and six, and formed a live-ly gang What-ev-er hap-pened, we cared "nix", and this is the song we sang La did-i-ly-id-i-ly, um-ti-um-ti-ay! La did-i-ly um, was all that we could say We were out up-on a spree, and felt a tri-fle gay, La- did-i-ly id-i-ly Um-ti-um-ti-ay!

2. When we reached the parsons residence 'twas twelve o'clock at night,
   And to get his reverence out of bed we tried with all our might.
   Then we pulled the knob, but found the bell was broke and wouldn't ring.
   But he arose and donned his clothes, as soon as he heard us sing:

CHORUS

3. When the preacher tied the marriage knot each heart was light and free,
   Until I asked Missus Jones to name the first boy after me,
   But the party said the child would be a "hoo-doo" if she did
   Then Jones said if the first's a boy I'm going to name the kid:

CHORUS

175

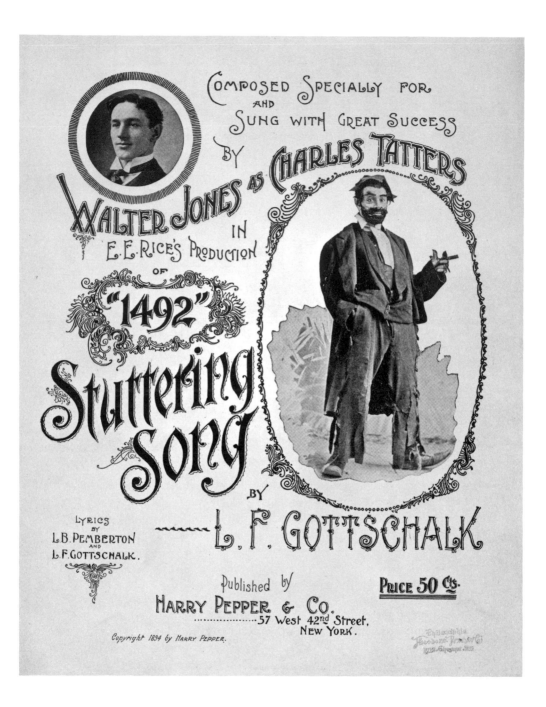

COMPOSED SPECIALLY FOR
AND
SUNG WITH GREAT SUCCESS
BY

WALTER JONES AS CHARLES TATTERS

IN
E. E. RICE'S PRODUCTION
OF

"1492"
Stuttering Song

LYRICS
BY
L. B. PEMBERTON
AND
L. F. GOTTSCHALK.

BY
L. F. GOTTSCHALK

Published by
HARRY PEPPER & CO.
57 West 42nd Street,
NEW YORK.

PRICE 50 Cts.

Copyright 1894 by Harry Pepper.

176

Stuttering Song

2. Last week I asked Ed. Rice for a job
And he said, "There is a hindrance in your speech."
I told him that I knew it, and would have it taken out,
But he said, "Young man, you're quite beyond my reach."
I then tried to yodel
I then tried to trill
He simply turned his back and said,
"You wont fill the bill."
But I snook in and I sneaked in
When no one was around
I wish to show and I want to show
That Charley Tatters owns the ground.

3. Mitchell is the greatest fighter I don't think
   With his mouth he can only fight
   It took just three rounds to lay him out flat
   And Corbett did it with his awful right
   Maybe Mitchell can yodel
   Maybe Mitchell can trill
   But when it comes to fighting
   It takes Corbett to kill
   Mitchell stuttered and he muttered
   "Don't hit so hard, Jim, please stop."
   Mitchell stuttered and he muttered
   This refrain until he dropped.

4. Some one asked me once to sing of "Sweet Marie"
   I did so and made quite a hit
   But I got stuck on the line of "I love thee,
   "Sweet Marie, I love thee, Sweet Marie."
   Then I tried to yodel
   Then I tried to trill
   But the more I tried to sing it
   The more they wanted me—to kill
   I stuttered and I muttered
   Till they yelled for me to stop
   I kept on stuttering, I kept on muttering
   Sweet Marie until I dropped.

5. As the tariff bill has now become a law
   We can all wear seal skin sacques and diamond rings
   But the fun Congress had in getting it passed
   The "monk and parrot" were there all the time
   Oh! the Senate it yodeled
   The house it did trill
   But all did want their sugar free
   Including Davy Hill
   Wilson stuttered, Gormon muttered
   Grover swore and he did yell,
   "If they dont pass it by thunder
   They can all go to h—l."

ZIZZY ZE ZUM ZUM ZUM

A "RAG-TIME" NIGHTMARE.

SUNG WITH GREAT SUCCESS BY JOSIE HALL IN "COOK'S TOURS" AT KOSTER & BIAL'S N.Y.

WORDS BY KARL KENNETT

MUSIC BY LYN UDALL

COMPOSER OF "YOU WONT NEED TO SHOW ME HOW." "I SAY FLOSSIE." ETC. ETC.

5

PUBLISHED BY

NEW YORK

M. WITMARK & SONS.

CHICAGO.

SUCCESS IS WORK

CHAS. SHEARD & CO LONDON. ENG — WHALEY ROYCE & CO TORONTO. CAN.
COPYRIGHTED FOR GREAT BRITAIN & ALL BRITISH COLONIES & POSSESSIONS

Zizzy, Ze Zum, Zum!

2. The neatest little, sweetest little maiden gay,
   With a little wooly dog on a chain,
   Was skipping and a tripping on her homeward way,
   And caught the rag refrain.
   And she sang it to the spieler of the belfry chimes,
   And he to his belfry clumb,

And the chime he chome, in the glimm'ring gloam,
Was ze zizzy, ze zum, zum, zum.

Chorus

3. The happy little chappie got a dreadful jolt,
   When he thought of this awful crime,
   So he took his little ditty and he tried to bolt,
   They caught him just in time.
   He is tenting and repenting on a red hot stove,
   Where the little red devils come,
   And they don't do a thing, but make him sing,
   Zezizzy, ze zum, zum, zum.

Chorus

TA-RA-RA BOOM-DE-AY!

Comic Character Song

Music by ANGELO A. ASHER.

MARCH by J.J. FREEMAN.

③ x

SONG ④ x

NEW YORK
HAMILTON S. GORDON 13 EAST 14TH ST.

Ta-Ra-Ra Boom-De-Ay!

A smart and styl-ish girl you see, belle of good so-ci-e-ty; not too strict but rath-er free, yet as right as right can be! nev-er for-ward, nev-er bold, not too hot, and not too cold, but the ve-ry thing I'm told, that in your arms you'd like to hold!

Ta-ra-ra Boom-de-ay Ta-ra-ra Boom-de-ay Ta-ra-ra Boom-de-ay, Ta-ra-ra Boom-de-ay; Ta-ra-ra Boom-de-ay, Ta-ra-ra Boom-de-ay, Ta-ra-ra Boom-de-ay, Ta-ra-ra Boom-de-ay!

2. I'm not extravagantly shy,
And when a nice young man is nigh,
For his heart I have a try—
And faint away with tearful cry!
When the good young man in haste,
Will support me round the waist;
I don't come to, while thus embraced,
Till of my lips he steals a taste!

CHORUS

3. I'm a timid flower of innocence—
Pa says that I have no sense—
I'm one eternal big expense;
But men say that I'm just "immense!"
Ere my verses I conclude,
I'd like it known and understood,
Though free as air, I'm never rude,—
I'm not too bad, and not too good!

CHORUS

History with a Smile

5

IT HAS ALWAYS been taken for granted that the proper way for school children to acquire a knowledge of American history is through textbooks. That is all very well if the child likes to study and has a serious turn of mind; but a large percentage of youngsters do not fit into this category. Many are easy going and fun loving, with an innate aversion to tackling dry accounts of historical facts. For children of such temperament, and for their elders too, a solution to drudgery of this sort can be found, from time to time, in comic songs. To the song writer, no personality and no event of national importance is too sacred to be reduced to a level of popular appeal which a topical ballad represents. In this chapter, a few examples will be presented, in historical order. Most of these songs were written almost immediately following the event described; a few were produced long afterwards.

The first example was written four hundred years after the event occurred. In 1893, the year of the World's Columbian Exposition in Chicago, a song writer named Francis J. Bryant composed a ditty about Christopher Columbus. (See page 192.) On the first page he describes it, modestly, as "The World's Fair Novelty and Historical Song Sensation, written up to suit the times." It was "written up" in considerable detail—sixteen verses in all—the finale stating that one of the new series of 1893 postage stamps bears the likeness of Columbus. The puns in verse after verse are terrible, and those *aficionados* who plowed through them all had to wind up sixteen times with this chorus:

> He knew the Earth was round, ho!
> That land it could be found, ho!
> This geographic, hard and hoary

Navigator, gyratory
Christofo Columbo.

The melody was extremely simple; once you heard it, the words fitted in with ease. And its popularity hung on and on, even though during the ensuing twenty-five years college students coarsened the verses and chorus to such an extent that it became a song suitable only for stag parties.

The story of the Boston Tea Party, which occurred in 1773, was not set to music until sixty years later. The composition, entitled "The Tea Tax" (see page 195), and described as "a Yankee comic song" had words by a modest fellow who described himself, simply and mysteriously, as "A gentleman of Boston." The music was arranged by T. Comer, who, the piece noted, was "Composer and Director of the Music to the Tremont Theatre."

The music bears a startling resemblance to "Christofo Columbo," which followed it sixty years later, but there is no indication of musical piracy involved. The verses are presented in a singsong Yankee style, with Yankee phrases, such as "I snum," "a plaguy sight," a "tarnel curse." The tale recounts:

> T'other day we yankee folks were mad about the taxes,
> And so we went, like Indians dress'd, to split Tea
>   chests with axes,
> I mean, 'twas done in seventy-five,* an' we were real
>   gritty,
> The Mayor he would have led the gang, but Boston warn't
>   a City.

A prolific song writer of the mid-nineteenth century who contributed a popular piece on American history was Pete Morris. Morris was one of the best-known composers of his day, writing both for comic actors and for minstrel shows. In addition to writing songs, Morris was well known for his renditions of his own compositions; in fact, from his first appearance as a twenty-year-old youth in 1841 in Barnum's Museum, he had wide appeal onstage.

For more than fifteen years he played the music halls in New York and Brooklyn. In 1845 he could be seen at Barnum's American Museum, Peale's New York Museum, and the Vauxhall Gardens, where he was billed as "the best comic vocalist now living"; in 1848 at the Odeon and the Melo-

* *The author missed the date by two years.*

deon, along with the Hippoferaean Arena in Brooklyn; in 1857 at the Musical Hall on the Bowery and White's Opera House, which advertised him as "our old, old friend." The old, old friend was thirty-six at the time and apparently quite healthy and at the height of his song-writing powers, as the song sheets of the period indicate.

A title page, used on half a dozen of his favorites, has a picture of the affable Mr. Morris surrounded by sketches illustrating several of his biggest hits. Above the portrait is a vignette of the Lexington Monument, to point up what was probably Morris' best-known number, "Revolutionary Times." (See page 199.) Written in 1857, it is addressed to the symbolic Englishman, and reminds him of bygone days:

> John Bull don't you remember now,
> Some eighty years ago,
> When we were very young, sir,
> Your head was white as snow;
> You did not count us much, John,
> But thought to make us run,
> Yet found out your mistake, John,
> One day at Lexington.

Like other comic writers of his day, Morris made frequent, and pretty awful, use of puns, but he kept at it for seven verses and wound up with Washington and Yorktown, subjects which, on their own, could insure a song's acceptance by the public.

The so-called War of 1812 with England continued till near the close of 1814. In fact, a fierce battle took place at New Orleans in 1815, apparently because no news had reached the combatants there that the war was over. A number of the important battles in this war were naval engagements, one of the fiercest of which took place between the fleets of American Commodore Oliver Hazard Perry and British Admiral Robert Heriot Barclay on a warm September day in 1813, off Amherstburg on Lake Erie. Perry's flotilla consisted of one brig, six schooners, and a sloop; Barclay's was comparable in size. Perry maneuvered his fleet to the greater advantage, closing in to deliver his most effective blows at close range. The superiority of the American sailors was clearly demonstrated, and the British admiral was soundly defeated.

So delighted were the American people when they learned the result of the battle that several musical compositions were published promptly, hailing Perry as the great American hero. Among them was "Commodore

Perry's March," by the prolific Charles Meineke, and "Perry's Victory," by Joseph Hutton, another well-known musician whose inspiring verses and stirring melody found great favor with the public.

A second "Perry's Victory" (see page 201), with the subtitle "September the Tenth in the Morning," was written by Andrew C. Mitchell to a rollicking melody in 6/8 time. The song commences with a deliberate taunt aimed at the widow of King George III, who enjoys her pear cider, or "perry," the morning of the battle, thereby giving the author an opportunity for an obvious pun:

> As old queen Charlotte a worthless old varlet,
> Our brave naval forces was scorning,
> She wish'd to be merry so called for some Perry,
> September the tenth in the morning.

After Perry's victory, we are enjoined to remember the tenth of September:

> When Yankees gave Britons a warming,
> When our foes on Lake Erie, were beaten and weary,
> So full of conceit in the morning.

It cannot be said that the United States won the War of 1812, but the American sailors gave a superb account of themselves in battles like the one off Amherstburg.

In 1854 a popular composer named Van der Weyde put to music a set of verses, by an unknown lyricist, entitled "Fillibustering." "Filibuster" is an English derivation of the Dutch word "Vrijbuiter," which means "freebooter." It was first applied to seventeenth-century English buccaneers who made their living plundering Spanish ships and settlements in the Caribbean.

In the middle of the nineteenth century the term came to be applied to American adventurers who were engaged in armed expeditions against defenseless countries which had been friends of the United States. At that time many Americans were convinced that it was this country's "manifest destiny" to assume benevolent jurisdiction over the entire Western Hemisphere. A few hardy souls set out to implement these convictions by "filibustering," or taking over friendly nations by force. Two of the boldest attempts were made by a small band under the leadership of William Walker, a California lawyer and editor. They were doomed to failure, although Walker had been intrepid enough first to try to seize the Mexican state of Sonora, and then, when that move was thwarted, to stage a wild coup which brought the country of Nicaragua under his control, and indeed under his presidency. Almost a year elapsed before the power of the United States Navy forced Walker to surrender and to withdraw his filibusterers from the country.

The stage was now set for a sardonic song (see page 202) describing the vicious practice, and commencing:

> Says Captain Robb to Farmer Cobb,
> "Your Farm is very fine, Sir;
> Please give me up your title deeds;
> I claim it all as mine, Sir."
> "Pray, how can it be thine?" says Cobb;...
> 'Twas left me by my father, Sir.

But Robb is not to be swayed:

> "Nay, Cobb; the march of destiny—
> 'Tis strange you don't perceive it—
> Is sure to make it mine, some day;
> I solemnly believe it."

And eventually:

> Poor Cobb can only grind his teeth,
> And grumble protestations
> That *might* should be the rule of *right*,
> Among *enlightened nations*.

If Cobb were around today, he might find reasons for similar protests.

For a three-year period in the 1850's, it seemed that a powerful new party was about to become a permanent part of the American political scene. It was made up of three classes, and members of the third class were pledged to reply, "I do not know," to all questions about the party. Its official name, adopted in 1855, was the American party, but its adherents became known popularly as the "Know-Nothings." The members were nicknamed "Sams." Sam was antiforeign (in fact, the Know-Nothings swore death and destruction to all foreigners) and anti-Catholic.

To "see Sam" was to become impressed with the merits or the popularity of the Know-Nothing party. Its activities stirred the fancies of the popular song writers, who welcomed the new contestant into the political arena. Songs entitled "Have You Seen Sam" (see page 204) and "Sam" appeared. The latter had a handsome title page on which was a portrait of a stern-visaged young man framed by the stars and stripes. "Sam" brooked no foolishness:

189

Let young America be seen
True to the old thirteen . . . .
The Union that our fathers won
Must ne'er be ruled by a traitor son.
Go in boys for Sam!
Wide awake, boys, for Sam.

"Have You Seen Sam," like "Sam," was published in 1855, but its author was much more disposed to use a light, rather than a serious, tone when writing about the Know-Nothings. The narrator of the verses is a country boy from upstate New York, who is not aware of the newest political movement. He has come down the Hudson to the big city,

A very verdant man;
I gather'd up my baggage In a shocking crowd and jam,
When a fellow jump'd before me saying, "Have you seen Sam?"

CHORUS: I don't know Sam, I don't know Sam,
Confound this noise and bother
Who is this fellow Sam?

The poor man, bewildered, makes his way to the advertised spots in New York that he most wants to see—the Astor Hotel, Barnum's great poultry and baby shows, and his side shows too, including the "woolly horse" and the "mermaid." Everywhere the stranger wanders he gets but one comment from the people he meets—"Have you seen Sam?" He travels to Albany, then to Washington, where the senators ask him the same question. Finally he gives up:

I'm going up the river,
My purse is running down;
No matter whom I chance to meet,
They ask if Sam's in town

By the end of 1855, the promising new party had run out of steam and was unable to put up a presidential candidate for the 1856 election.

Little of contemporary importance escaped the popular composers. A number of the sights of New York were deemed worthy of musical tributes, among them the places visited by the man from upstate. The Astor Hotel was the subject of a waltz; Barnum's great baby and poultry shows had polkas written about them. But there seems to have been no song about the "woolly horse," although this animal had an amusing, if short, history as a Barnum acquisition.

190

It had fast become one of his most popular exhibits, until it got him into trouble. Having seen a Cincinnati advertisement describing the Indiana-foaled horse, Barnum purchased it for five hundred dollars and sent it to his Bridgeport, Connecticut, headquarters. The animal was a freak; it had a mat of heavy hair all over its body, but none on its tail, and it had no mane. Barnum set it up as a special exhibition, announcing that it had been captured in the passes of the Rocky Mountains by the party of the famous explorer John C. Frémont. And his description of the odd creature was stupefying. "Colonel Fremont's Nondescript or Woolly Horse," read the advertisement, "is extremely complex and made up of the Elephant, Deer, Horse, Buffalo, Camel, and Sheep. It is the full size of a horse, has the haunches of the deer, the tail of the elephant, a fine curled wool of camel's hair color, and easily bounds twelve or fifteen feet high. Admission 25 cents; children half price."

Unfortunately for Barnum, one of the visitors to this miraculous exhibit was Senator Thomas H. Benton of Missouri, Frémont's father-in-law, who smelled a rat. He had Barnum's agent arrested for extracting twenty-five cents from him under false pretenses, stating that Frémont had never mentioned to him anything about the capture of the animal. Barnum managed to get the case dismissed, but decided that discretion was the better part of valor, and retired his woolly equine to private life in Bridgeport.

The Hit of the Day!
Sung by Leading Comedians.

Christofo Columbo

(CHRISTOPHER COLUMBUS)

A HISTORICAL SUBJECT

WRITTEN UP TO SUIT THE TIMES

BY FRANCIS BRYANT

He knew the Earth was round ho!
That land it could be found ho!
This geographic, hard & hoary
Navigator Gyratory
Christofo Columbo

NEW YORK
Published by M. WITMARK & SONS 51 West 28th Street.
LONDON   Chas. Sheard & Co.

Christofo Columbo

I'll sing to you a-bout a man whose name you'll find in hist'ry He solved a prob-lem ve-ry deep, which long had been a myst'ry, Na-vi-ga-tors young and old gave way to him quite fit-ly, His name it was Co-lum-bus, and he came from sun-ny It-'ly.

Chorus

He knew the earth was round, ho! That land it could be found, ho! This ge-o-graph-ic, hard and hoar-y na-vi-ga-tor, gy-ra-to-ry Chris-to-fo Co-lum-bo

Finale (after last verse)

Did he sail to the North? No, no, no, no, Did he sail to the South? No, no, no, no, Did he sail to the East? No, no, no, no, Did he sail to the West? Yes, yes, yes, yes, To Co-lum-bia, to Co-lum-bia to Co-lum-bia's glo-rious shore

2. To the Kings and Queens of Europe, Columbus told his theory,
   They simply thought him crazy, and asked him this here query,
   How could the earth stand up if round? It surely would suspend,
   For answer, C'lumbus took an egg and stood it on its end.

   CHORUS

3. In Fourteen Hundred and Ninety-two, 'twas then Columbus started,
From Palos on the coast of Spain to the westward he departed,
His object was to find a route, a short one to East India,
Columbus wore no whiskers, and the wind it blew quite windy.

CHORUS

4. When Sixty days away from land, upon the broad Atlantic,
The sailors they went on a strike which nearly caused a panic,
They all demanded eggs to eat for each man in the crew,
Columbus had no eggs aboard, but he made the ship lay too.

CHORUS

5. The hungry crew impatient grew, and beef-steak they demanded,
Equal to the emergency, Columbus then commanded
That ev'ry sailor who proves true, and his duty never shirks,
Can have a juicy porterhouse, "I'll get it from the bulwarks."

CHORUS

6. Not satisfied with steak and eggs, the crew they yelled for chicken,
Columbus seemed at a loss for once, and the plot it seemed to thicken,
The men threatened to jump overboard, Columbus blocked their pathway,
And cried: "If chicken you must have, I'll get it from the hatchway."

CHORUS

7. The sailors now so long from home with fear became imbued,
On the twelfth day of October their fears were all subdued,
For after Ninety days at sea, they discovered America's shores,
And quickly made a landing on the Isle of Salvador.

CHORUS

THE TEA TAX

A Yankee Comic Song

Sung with Unbounded Applause

BY

Mr. Andrews,

at the Federal Street Theatre.

The Words by a Gentleman of Boston;

The Music newly arranged with an
Accompaniment for the Piano Forte,

BY

T. COMER.

Composer and Director of the Music to the Tremont Theatre.

BOSTON, Published by C. BRADLEE Nº 164 Washington St.

Entered according to Act of Congress

The Tea Tax

I snum I am a Yank-ee lad, and I guess I'll sing a dit-ty, and if you do not re-lish it, the more will

be the pi-ty, That is, I think I should have been a pla-guy sight more fin-ish'd man, if I'd been born

in Bos-ton Town, but I warn't cause I'm a coun-try man. Tol lol de ra Ri tol de rid-dle id-dle

right tol de da.

2. And t'other day we yankee folks, were mad about the taxes,
   And so we went, like Indians dress'd, to split Tea chests with axes,
   I mean, 'twas done in seventy-five, an' we were real gritty,
   The Mayor he would have led the gang, but Boston warn't a City.

3. Ye see we yankees didn't care, a pin for wealth or booty,
   And so in State street we agreed we'd never pay the duty,
   That is, in State street 'twould have been, but 'twas King street, they call'd it then,
   And tax on Tea, it was so bad, the women wouldn't scald it then.

4. To Charlestown Bridge we all went down to see the thing corrected,
   That is, we *would* have gone there, but the Bridge it warn't erected;
   The Tea perhaps was very good, Bohea, Shouchong or Hyson,
   But drinking Tea it warn't the rage, the duty made it poison.

5. And then we went aboard the ships, our vengeance to administer,
   And didn't care a tarnal curse, for any King or minister;
   We made a plaguy mess o' Tea, in one of the biggest dishes,
   I mean, we steeped it in the Sea, and treated all the fishes.

196

6. And then you see, we were all found out, a thing we hadn't dreaded,
   The leaders were to London sent and instantly beheaded,
   That is, I mean, they *would* have been if ever they'd been taken,
   But the leaders they were never cotch'd, and so they saved their bacon.

7. Now Heaven bless the President and all this goodly nation,
   And doubly bless our Boston Mayor and all the corporation;
   And may all those who are our foes, or at our praise have falter'd,
   Soon have a *change*, that is, I mean may all of 'em get *haltered*.

THE
COMIC
AMERICAN MELODIES.

Pete Morris

"TO THE MANOR BORN"

AS SUNG BY
PETE MORRIS.

Nº 1. *Revolutionary Times*.   Nº 3. *Newspaper Song*.   Nº 5. *Crinoline Song*.
" 2. *I'm off to the Diggins*   " 4. *Pete Morris' Bird Song*   " 6. *My Mary's Nose*.

NEW YORK
PUBLISHED BY FIRTH, POND & Cº

ALBANY   WORCESTER   BUFFALO   CHICAGO   ST LOUIS
J.H RIDLEY.   J P SHAW   H.N KEMP TED   B. K MOULD   H PILCHER & SONS

Revolutionary Times

John Bull don't you re-mem-ber now some eight-y years a-go, When we were ve-ry young,sir,

your head was white as snow; You did not count us much, John, but thought to make us run, Yet

Chorus

found out your mis-take, John, one day at Lex-ing-ton. Ha, ha, ha, Ha, ha, ha, In-deed you

did, Pon my soul you did one day at Lex-ing-ton.

2. Then we invite you in, John,
   To take a cup of tea
   In Boston harbor made Sir,
   The teapot of the free;
   You didn't like the party, boy,
   It was'nt quite select,
   There were some aboriginies
   You did'nt quite expect.
   Indeed you did,
   Pon my soul you did,
   You did'nt quite expect.

3. Then another much loved spot, John,
   Such sweet associations
   The day you marched down to York
   To see your rich relations
   The Dutchmen of the Mohawk, sir,
   Wishing to entertain
   Put up some Gates that stopped you
   On Saratoga's plain.

Indeed you did,
Pon my soul you did,
On Saratoga's plain.

4. Oh! no we never mention it,
   You never thought it lucky
   The day you charged the cotton bags,
   And got into Kentucky;
   Why I thought you knew geography,
   For misses in their teens,
   Would told you that Kentucky lay
   Why just below Orleans.
   Indeed you did
   Pon my soul you did
   Why just below Orleans.

5. You say we are great braggers, John,
   But you know it is our wont,
   We gave some Bragg in Mexico,
   Likewise in old Vermont;

At Bennington you must confess
That you really felt quite sad
The Green Mountain boys I swow did
    think
You were actually Stark mad.
Indeed you did,
Pon my soul you did,
You were actually Stark mad.

6. The mistress of the ocean, John,
   She could not rule the lakes,
   You had some *ganders* in your fleet,
   But John you had no *Drakes*!
   Your choicest *spirits*, too, were there,
   Why you took your hock and sherry,
   But John you could not stand our fare,
   You could not take our Perry.

Indeed you did
Pon my soul you did
You could not take our Perry.

7. You had some corns upon your toes,
   Cornwallis, that was one,
   And at the siege of Yorktown,
   Why then you could not run;
   You tried quite hard you must admit
   And threw away your gun,
   Gave up your sword, fie John for
      shame,
   To the immortal WASHINGTON
   Indeed you did,
   Pon my soul you did,
   To the immortal WASHINGTON.

Perry's Victory

As old queen Charlotte a worthless old varlet, our brave naval forces was scorning; She wish'd to be merry so called for some Perry, September the tenth in the morning; When brisk Perry came, she found him true game, To her cost too, he gave her a warming, When brisk Perry came, she found him true game, To her cost too he gave her a warming, To her cost too he gave her a warming, So let her be merry and remember Perry, September the tenth in the morning.

2. It was on Lake Erie—when all hands were cheary,
   A fleet was descried in morning,
   'Twas Queen Charlott's fleet, so handsome and neat,
   In bold line of battle were forming;
   But when evening came—though the fleet were the same,
   That our brave naval forces were scorning,
   They were beat—so complete—that they yielded the fleet,
   To the one they despis'd in the morning.

3. Now let us remember the tenth of September,
   When Yankees gave Britons a warming,
   When our foes on Lake Erie, were beaten and weary,
   So full of conceit in the morning;
   To the skilful, and brave, who our country did save,
   Our gratitude ought to be warming,
   So let us be merry, in toasting of Perry,
   September the tenth in the morning.

Filliebustering

A Comic Song

Composed & Arranged by

Van Der Weyde.

New York
PUBLISHED BY BERRY & GORDON 297 BROADWAY.

Phil.ª
J.E.GOULD.

Boston.
O.DITSON.

Cincinnati.
D.A.TRUAX.

Entered according to Act of Congress AD 1858 by Berry & Gordon in the Clerk's Office of the Dis.t Court of the South.n Dist.t N.Y.

Fillibustering

Says Cap-tain Robb to Farm-er Cobb, "Your farm is ve-ry fine, Sir; Please give me up your

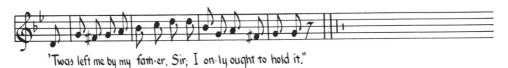

ti-tle deeds; I claim it all as mine, Sir." "Pray how can it be thine?" says Cobb; I'm sure I never sold it;

'Twas left me by my fath-er, Sir; I on-ly ought to hold it."

2. "Nay, Cobb; the march of destiny—
'Tis strange you don't perceive it—
Is sure to make it mine, some day;
I solemnly believe it."
"But have you not already got
More land than you can till, Sir?
More rocks than you can ever blast?
More weeds than you can kill, Sir?"

3. "Aye, Cobb, but something whispers
me—
A sort of inspiration—
That I've a *right* to ev'ry farm
Not under cultivation.
I'm of the Anglo Saxon race,
A people known to fame, Sir;
But you—what right have you to land?
Whoever heard your name, Sir?

4. "I deem you, Cobb, a lazy lout,
Poor, trodden-down, and blind, Sir;
And if I take your useless land,
You ought to think it kind, Sir!
And with my scientific skill,
I set it down as true, Sir,
That I can gather from the farm
Full twice as much as you, Sir."

5. "To be explicit: 'Tis an age
Of freedom and progression;
No longer, dog-in-manger-like,
Can you retain possession.
The farm long since you forfeited,
Because you failed to till it;
To me it clearly now belongs,
Simply because—*I will it.*"

6. "My logic if you disapprove,
Or fail of comprehending,
Or do not feel convinc'd that I
Your welfare am intending,
I've plenty more of arguments
To which I can resort, Sir;
Six-shooters, rifles, bowie knives,
Will indicate the sort, Sir."

7. "So, prithee, Cobb, take my advice
Make over your domains, Sir;
Or, sure as I am Captain Robb,
Will I blow out your brains, Sir."
Poor Cobb can only grind his teeth,
And grumble protestations
That *might* should be the rule of *right*,
Among *enlightened nations.*

203

Have You Seen Sam

I float-ed down the riv-er on the schoon-er Pol-ly Ann; I land-ed on York Is-land,   a

ve-ry ver-dant man; I gath-er'd up my bag-gage in a shock-ing crowd and jam, when a fel-low

Chorus

jump-ed be-fore me say-ing "Have you seen Sam?"   I don't know Sam, I don't know Sam, Con-

found this noise and bo-ther   who is this fel-low Sam?

2. I thought the fellow crazy,
   And fled before the wind:
   The Astor rose before me,
   My coat tail stream'd behind:
   Soon up the steps I scrambled,
   And shouted, "Here I am."
   Another fellow tapp'd me
   And asked, "Have you seen Sam?"

   CHORUS

3. I then went straight to Barnum's
   To see the mighty show;
   The Shanghais and the Babies,
   How loudly they did crow!
   I stood and gaz'd about me,
   To see if 'twas a sham:
   I smooth'd the bearded lady's cheek,
   She sigh'd, "Have you seen Sam?"

   CHORUS

4. I hunted through each corner,
   Till nearly out of breath;
   I ask'd about the wooly horse,
   The mermaid and Joice Heth;
   Men laugh'd, the Shanghais cackled,
   I left old Captain Sham:
   And as I turn'd to leave the place,
   The monkey's chatter'd Sam!

   CHORUS

5. I went up to Albany,
   To see the wires at play;
   'Twas pulling here 'twas bawling there
   Has Sam been here to day?
   To Washington I went to see,
   The Senatorial jam:
   I told them of the war in York,
   They ask'd if I'd seen Sam?

   CHORUS

6. I told them horns and bugles blew
   A fearful warlike blast:
   That crotchets, quavers, fiddles flew
   In bloodless conflict past:
   The fifers scream'd their piercing notes,
   The drummer's beat their flam
   While high above the noise and din,
   The cry was, "Where is Sam?"

Chorus

7. I'm going up the river,
   My purse is running down:
   No matter whom I chance to meet,
   They ask if Sam's in town:
   It's Sam around above me,
   In Croton or in dram:
   With luck, I'm off tomorrow,
   Who is this fellow Sam?

Chorus

More History

6

IN EVERY PRESIDENTIAL CONTEST since 1840 there has been an outcropping of campaign songs. Most of them have been laudatory, emphasizing the leadership qualities of the contender—"Honest Old Abe" (1860), "Horace and No Relations" (1872), "Hurrah for Hayes and Honest Ways" (1876), "Harrison and Protection" (1888), "Gold Is the Standard to Win" (1896), "On the Right Road with Roosevelt" (1932). But sometimes the punches were below the belt—"Van is a Used Up Man" (1840), "Polk is a Used Up Joke" (same vintage); other foul blows were struck as the years and the campaigns went on.

In 1864, the year Lincoln ran for a second term, dirty politics, on both sides, was accepted campaign procedure. The President had a large number of enemies composed of many elements—disappointed seekers of appointments, demoted men of the military establishment, potential devaluers of the country's currency, and others such as the Copperheads, who were demanding an end to the war and peace with and concessions to the South.

The Copperheads, Democratic critics of the Lincoln administration who resisted any changes in policy that the President proposed, had adopted as their slogan "The Constitution As It Is. The Union As It Was." Their opponents viewed them as men "whose hearts were black, whose blood was yellow, and whose minds were blank."

So it was not unexpected to find campaign songs that year casting aspersions at Lincoln's enemies. One song which sought to cover the widest territory in the art of castigation was written by J. William Pope and was entitled "Uncle Sam's Menagerie." (See page 216.) On the title page is this quotation from Pennsylvania Congressman J. K. Moorhead, to whom the song is dedicated:

So wide spread was treason, so faithless the President, that all hope was exhausted except the single one that his term would expire before all was lost. Thank God! Abraham Lincoln became President before the cause of the Union was totally ruined, and then the work of rescue began.

Pope's first volley is aimed at George B. McClellan, who, after serving as head of the Union forces, was coerced into opposing Lincoln for the presidency. He is reviled with:

> I'll have that man of wondrous fame,
> George B., George B.
> George Blunder I would call his name.

Then the author goes after a leader of the Copperhead movement, Clement Laird Vallandigham. Vallandigham's family had originated in the South, to which he remained devoted even after moving to Ohio and being elected to Congress as a representative of that state. He had been an advocate of states' rights, and his fellow Republicans in the House were cold to him, particularly since he opposed violently every defense measure proposed in Congress. Defeated in the election of 1862, he was thereafter regarded as a leader of the Copperheads, the peace demonstrators. In fact, in January, 1863, before his term in Congress ended, he delivered a speech in the House in which he demanded a cessation of hostilities and a negotiated peace.

In May of that year he was arrested and tried for expressing "treasonable sympathy." He was remanded to confinement in Fort Warren, Ohio, but President Lincoln released him, and he moved to the South for a short while, then to Canada. Back in Ohio the following year, he denounced "King Lincoln" in an address in Hamilton.

A fiery orator, he brought other legislators into his camp, among them Alexander Long of Ohio, Fernando Wood, former mayor of New York, and Benjamin G. Harris, Peace Democrat from Maryland, all of whom wished to recognize the Confederacy.

So virulent did Long become in his emotional demands for a compromise settlement of the conflict, that the Speaker of the House of Representatives, Schuyler Colfax, left his seat, descended to the floor, excoriated Long, and demanded that he be expelled from the House. When Harris and Wood rallied to Long's defense, Congressman Elihu B. Washburn of Illinois moved for their expulsion also. The two-thirds vote needed for this drastic punishment could not be obtained, so the Republicans were obliged to settle for a vote of censure for the dissidents. This required only a majority vote, which was secured handily.

Our song writer was disgusted with the efforts of these defectors. Of Vallandigham he writes:

> I'll have that cunning little fox
> From O-hi-O . . . .
> He has a serpent's tongue and eye;*
> But I'll take care he does not bite,
> For well I know he'll try.
>
> *[An allusion, of course, to the Copperhead.]

He covers the other rascals in the next verse:

> I'll also have his great colleague,
> A. Long, A. Long,
> Who with the De'il had form'd a league
> Quite strong, quite strong,
> Till Colfax drove the De'il away,
> And Long, dishonor'd, left to stay,
> To see the great Fernando Wood
> And Harris go marching home.

Pope winds up with a prediction that he will be going to Washington to

> . . . leave old Father Abraham
> To manage for four years.

A prediction which sadly was shattered a month after the inauguration.

In 1870 there was published in Louisville, Kentucky, a song with words by "Henry," melody by "Ward," and arrangement by "Beecher," with the title "Shoo Purp, Dont Bodder Me." (See page 218.) The title was, of course, a parody on "Shew Fly, Don't Bother Me," a popular minstrel song and "walk-around," which had been composed in 1869 by Billy Reeves, with words by Frank Campbell, and which even today is heard from time to time.

The title page of "Shoo Purp" bears a small vignette of a sad-looking animal of indeterminate breed, his tail between his legs, slinking away from the Capitol. Under the picture is the inscription "A true likeness of the 'Purp' Expressed from Cleveland, O. Jan. 27, and refused audience to the President." After such a cruel reception, who wouldn't feel crushed and mortified? All our little fellow had to show for his tribulation was the song which, proclaims the title page, is "Dorgonically Dedicated to the Rejected Purp."

The song wastes no time in getting to the point. It starts:

> Ho Sergeant kick that nasty purp
> From off the White-house door.
> No Spanish dorg from Ohio shall trod upon my floor,
> I've got a fifteenth in the house,
> A wolly [*sic*] dog at that,
> No Strait hair cropp'd and foreign purp
> Off me shall e'er get fat.

With a one-line, no-nonsense chorus:

> Shoo purp, Shoo purp, Buck-eye purp,
> don't bodder me.

The allusion to a Spanish dog raises the question, was the newcomer a spaniel? Possibly so. But President Grant, the villain—or antivillain, depending on one's point of view—had not been known to turn back gifts from his constituents, whatever the connotation. In this particular case the President may have had a point. Spain had recognized the Confederacy during the Civil War, and this probably influenced Grant to approve Cuba's belligerency against Spain shortly after his installation as President in 1869. Spain continued to demand that its entire army be sent to Cuba to suppress the revolt, while public meetings were held in Madrid and elsewhere expressing defiance of the United States and condemning its pro-Cuban attitude. Grant might well have bridled if anyone had tried to foist on him a gift which reminded him of a country so distasteful.

When the lyricist of the song states that there were already fifteen dogs in the White House, he may have been indulging in flights of fancy. One of Grant's biographers, Hamlin Garland, refers to cartoons which depict the President strolling on his grounds followed by two sullen bull pups. In such cartoons Grant is called a "dog-fancier," whereas, asserts Garland, Grant never owned a dog in his life, and could not bear to have them around him.

On February 1, 1870, a lengthy editorial appeared in the Louisville *Courier Journal* under the headline "The Rejected Pup." Referring to the "dozens who . . . laid their precious offerings in the open palm of the President," it laments the reversal of his attitude about accepting tributes: "By what motive could General Grant have been impelled in taking a step so utterly at variance with the former course of his administration? . . . What has Ohio done—what has Cleveland done—what has the original owner of the dog done—that Ohio and Cleveland and the original owner of the dog . . . should thus be blasted in a single blow? . . . Why was this canine of Western loyalty denied admission to the White House, and forbidden the inestimable position of reposing upon the executive hearth-rug and inhaling the political wisdom and cigar smoke which flow in such perennial streams from the lips of the great American statesman? Dare we venture to suggest that because the gift was Spanish—that the President feared that an acceptance of the offering might disturb the serene repose of his evenly-balanced policy toward the Spanish cause and that of the Ever Faithful Isle?" (Enter the delicate problem of Cuban belligerency.)

On February 2, the Cleveland *Plain Dealer* reprinted the *Courier-Journal*'s editorial in full and drew an immediate response from the other great Cleveland paper, the *Daily Herald*, which put forth its own conclusions succinctly: "We have interviewed the express managers at this point and have become satisfied that no dog has been sent from this city to the president. Neither of the express companies in this city have received a dog for conveyance to Washington. The whole thing is a put-up job. Some copper-headed scamp has attached a tag from an express package and put it on the Spanish dog and snuck it into the express car."

Back came the *Plain Dealer* two days later stating its conviction that the tale of the dog was fact and not fiction: "Nobody sends purps, or plugged hats, or fighting cocks, to Grant unless they hold an office, and what office could this Cleveland pup be after. Was it the Post Office?"

And there, unfortunately, the strange story runs into the ground. Nothing has come to light to indicate who wanted to present President Grant with a dog, or what favors the would-be donor had hoped to receive in exchange, or whether the little puppy ever existed.

If it did not exist, "Shoo Purp" may be the only song ever published about an imaginary incident in American history.

In 1875 two of the most popular men in the field of entertainment, Sol Smith Russell and Howard Paul, joined forces to present a new comic song, "Upside Down."

Born in the late 1840's, Russell had tried at the outbreak of the Civil War to enlist as a fighting man in the Union Army, but could not do so because he was only fourteen and his parents would not give their consent. Nevertheless, he left home to serve for several months as a drummer boy.

After leaving his regiment, he commenced a professional stage career, singing in stock companies and gaining such rapid recognition that, by the time he was twenty, the concert troupe with which he was associated included his name in their title. Show business was in his blood throughout his lifetime. Tall, slender, and deliberate, he had a delightful comedy approach, and his delineations of quaint, lovable characters won the affection of his audiences. He loved to recite the poems of James Whitcomb Riley, who was one of his closest friends.

Howard Paul, a great character actor himself, enjoyed writing much of his own material. Born in Philadelphia, he married an English girl with a beautiful contralto voice. Paul and his wife performed as a team in London, Edinburgh, Dublin, and other important cities in Great Britain. After ten successful years, they left England in 1866 and opened at Irving Hall in New York. Paul sang in a buffo-lyric style, with vim and a robust sense of humor. His wife's approach was strictly dramatic. Their American audiences were enthusiastic.

For several years Paul's interpretations of his own songs were among the most popular performances on the variety stage. A quaintly illustrated title page portrayed him in half a dozen of his comic impersonations.

In the mid–1870's, however, he permitted the successful Sol Smith Russell to share his personal spotlight. A nearly full-size likeness of Russell's face adorns the title page of Paul's "Upside Down." (See page 220.) The title page, which gives Paul modest credit for the song, proclaims that it is "sung with great success by Sol. Smith Russell" in enormous letters, and then, in tiny type, almost as an afterthought, adds "and the author."

"Upside Down" describes the wild dreams of the lyricist, who had eaten pickled salmon before going to bed, with the result that

> The world seem'd topsy turvy, and people of renown
> Were doing the most outrageous things, When the
> world turn'd upside down!

And what were some such "outrageous things"? Well, first of all, Paul envisioned people on the stage:

> The Pope was dressed as harlequin, and danced a
> Highland fling;
> Queen Victoria came from England a comic song to
> sing;
> Old Barnum acted Hamlet, and Booth was playing Clown,
> And Bismarck was an acrobat—when the world turned
> upside down.

Jay Gould, continues the song, was a Quaker. In real life, as people then knew, he had concocted gigantic nefarious schemes which shook the American economy.

It goes on:

> Mr. Tilton was an Emperor, and wore a golden crown,
> And Beecher danced the Can can—when the world turned
>   upside down.

These two important men were the central figures in one of the most publicized scandals of the early 1870's. Theodore Tilton, Henry G. Bowen, and the Reverend Henry Ward Beecher were actively involved in an important sectarian weekly paper called the *Independent*.

In 1860, Bowen, treasurer and a founder of the large and powerful Congregationalist Plymouth Church in Brooklyn, had acquired control of the paper, and the following year he induced Beecher, Plymouth Church's spiritual leader, to assume the editorship of the *Independent*. At Beecher's request, the thirty-year-old Tilton was engaged as his assistant, taking over as editor when Beecher resigned shortly thereafter.

Tilton, whose close friends included such powerful figures as Charles Sumner, the senator from Massachusetts, and Horace Greeley, editor of the New York *Tribune*, developed the *Independent* into a family magazine, which was at the same time an organ of political power, espousing the Radicals, the right wing Republicans.

Tilton's wife, a Sunday-school teacher Beecher had known since childhood, edited a paper of her own, *Revolution*, a journal of the suffragists, whose cause Beecher championed vigorously.

In 1870, Mrs. Tilton astounded her husband by confessing that she had had intimate relations with Beecher. Horribly distressed, Tilton tried to keep the revelation a secret, but it was not long before members of the women's rights group, then others in Plymouth Church, learned of it. The news reached Henry Bowen shortly after he had called Tilton "bold, uncompromising, a master of men." It is probably because of this accolade that Paul's song refers to him as an emperor—or possibly the "Upside Down" title was used because, following the disclosure of the startling affair, Bowen decided to dissociate himself from Tilton, dismissing him as the paper's editor.

Tilton sued Beecher for $100,000 for "criminal conversations," but a four-month trial ended with a hung jury. Public opinion was divided; Tilton left the country and never returned.

213

Later verses disclose further weird imaginings of the dreamer, who envisions Brigham Young as a bachelor, and John Gough, a nationally famous temperance lecturer, as the proprietor of a "Sample Room" serving gin and beer. Then Boss Tweed comes in for a bit of a dig; he is pictured at his "Island Home."

Tweed, the biggest sachem in Tammany Hall, had been disclosed as the leader of a multi-million-dollar swindling ring. In 1871 the *New York Times* published proof of the gigantic embezzlement, and Tweed was arrested and charged with swindling the city. He was convicted and sentenced to a $12,750 fine and twelve years in prison, but the court of appeals reduced the fine to $250 and the prison term to one year. Tweed's island home was the prison on Blackwell's Island, where he was treated like a distinguished visitor, given a daily carriage ride, and permitted frequent visits to his own home in New York City.

Russell and his audience must have had a capital time with the many sly digs in the song.

The brief war with Spain in 1898 made a national hero out of Theodore Roosevelt, but he did not emerge as the conflict's most exalted fighting man. That honor must be given unequivocally to Commodore—later Admiral— George Dewey, commander of the American naval forces in the Far East, a squadron consisting of four small cruisers and two gunboats.

President McKinley sent his war message to Congress in April, 1898, following the sinking of the battleship *Maine* in Havana harbor. Prior to the declaration of war, however, Dewey had been told what to do in case hostilities were to start—the orders coming from none other than Theodore Roosevelt, at that time assistant secretary of the navy.

Dewey got his message to go into action immediately after the war was declared, and he steamed, with his "six pack," out of Hong Kong, reaching the Manila area and the Spanish fleet there early on the morning of May 1. Sighting the Spaniards from the bridge of his flagship, the *Olympia*, he turned to the vessel's captain and said, "You may fire when you are ready, Gridley." The salvos of shells that were loosed crushed the sorry fleet of Spanish Admiral Montejo, and in hardly more time than it takes to relate it, the Battle of Manila was over. One English historian called it "a military execution rather than a real contest."

American song writers had a new giant to acclaim, and they went at it immediately and with gusto. There were Dewey marches and Dewey songs galore. The commodore's name lent itself to a series of outrageous puns; one of the most popular songs bore the title, "Come Home Dewey, We Won't Do a Thing to You." Another, reproduced here, was "What Did Dewey Do to Them?" (See page 222.) It was described by the composers, R. H. Brennen and Grant W. Barnett, as a "Patriotic Query." Like every other Dewey song, it showed a likeness of the hero on the title page. The chorus admitted to a play on words, an unusual kind of modesty for song writers:

> What did Dewey do to them
> What did Dewey do?
> He did them up so thoroughly
> He only left a few.
> It wasn't to the Queen's taste,
> That's a pun and very true,
> He didn't do a thing to them.
> *What didn't Dewey do?*

And the sixth verse of the song, written fifty years before Castro, winds up:

> And poor Cuba's cry for freedom,
> Will ring out strong and true;
> And Uncle Sam will sing and dance,
> *What didn't Dewey do?*

Uncle Sam's Menagerie;

A

UNION CAMPAIGN SONG AND CHORUS,

WORDS AND MUSIC COMPOSED AND RESPECTFULLY DEDICATED TO

HON. J. K. MOORHEAD, M. C.

BY

J. WILLIAM POPE.

"So wide spread was treason, so faithless the President, that all hope was exhausted except the single one that his term would expire before all was lost. Thank God! Abraham Lincoln became President before the cause of the Union was totally ruined, and then the work of rescue began."—*Moorhead.*

(3.)

Published by CHARLES C. MELLOR, No. 81 Wood Street, Pittsburgh, Pa.

Uncle Sam's Menagerie

I'd like to have you all to know that I, that I am going to have a lit-tle show and try, and try

to raise some cash in shape of votes, to buy my quad-ru-peds some oats, and you'll all get a peep at

them, when next No-vem-ber comes. Then come with your cash ev'-ry one, but don't bring Con-fed-er-ate

notes, For Green-backs you'll see lots of fun, but I much pre-fer loy-al votes.

2. I'll have the man who caught the ass,
   They say, they say,
   While grazing on the mountain pass,
   One day, one day:
   He brings him here to show his wool,
   And try it o'er your eyes to pull,
   But you will all have a good time,
   When I bring out my show.

CHORUS

3. I'll have that man of wondrous fame,
   George B., George B.
   George Blunder I would call his name,
   Would ye? would ye?
   Before Yorktown he beat his drums,
   But was afraid of wooden guns;
   But still, upon a dress-parade,
   He was a splendid man.

CHORUS

4. I'll have that little cunning fox
   From O-hi-o,
   I'll keep him in a dry goods box,
   You know, you know.
   He stands, I think, just four feet high,

He has a serpent's tongue and eye;
But I'll take care he does not bite,
For well I know he'll try.

CHORUS

5. I'll also have his great colleague,
   A. Long, A. Long,
   Who with the De'il had form'd a league
   Quite strong, quite strong,
   Till Colfax drove the De'il away,
   And Long, dishonor'd, left to stay,
   To see the great Fernando Wood
   And Harris go marching home.

CHORUS

6. To manage all I have the man
   Of rails, of rails,
   To make them shake (I know he can)
   Their tails, their tails.
   And when you all have seen my show,
   To Washington I'm bound to go,
   And leave old Father Abraham
   To manage for four years.

CHORUS

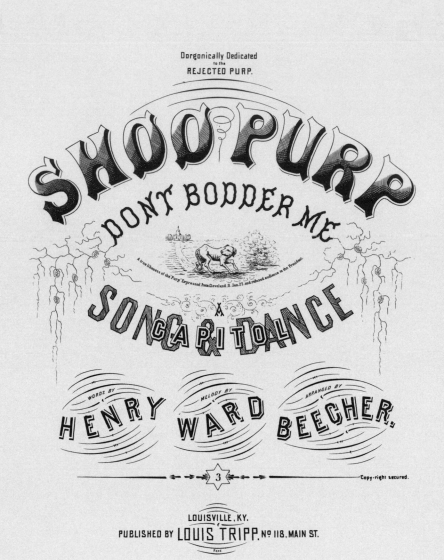

Shoo Purp Don't Bodder Me

Ho Ser-gant kick that nas-ty purp from off the white house door, No Span-ish dorg from

O-hi-o shall trod up-on my floor, I've got a fif-teenth in the house, a wol-ly dog at that   No

Strait hair cropp'd cur for-eign purp off me shall e'er get fat.   Shoo purp, Shoo purp, Buck-eye purp,

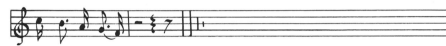

don't bod-der me —

2. Of all the purps I dread the most;
   A french or one from Spain,
   They snarl and whine, off me they dine,
   And often cause me pain.
   That Alabama Rebel dorg,
   Once did commit a breach,
   He tore my seat of government pants,
   And loudly made me screech.

   CHORUS

3. I've dogs enough around me now,
   Curly black and tan,
   No Buckeye Purp with Spanish blood
   Can mix with white house Clan.
   So no more purps sent by Express,
   Shall to the white house reach,
   My Bull Fice Butlers in his pen,
   A whining o'er his speech.

   CHORUS

219

UPSIDE DOWN.

COMIC SONG Sung with great Success by

WRITTEN AND COMPOSED by HOWARD PAUL.

SOL SMITH RUSSELL, AND THE AUTHOR.

NEW YORK
PUBLISHED BY Wm. A. POND & Co. 547 BROADWAY
AND 39 UNION SQUARE.

MILWAUKEE.   SAN FRANCISCO,   BOSTON,   CINCINNATI,   NEW ORLEANS.
H.N. HEMPSTED.   M. GRAY.   CARL PRÜFER.   C.Y. FONDA.   L. GRUNEWALD.

Henry A. Thomas Lith? 50 Bleecker St. N.Y.

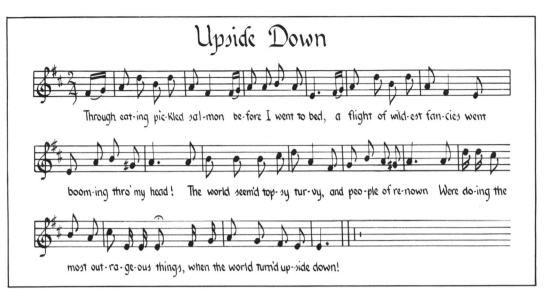

Upside Down

Through eat-ing pic-kled sal-mon be-fore I went to bed, a flight of wild-est fan-cies went boom-ing thro' my head! The world seem'd top-sy tur-vy, and peo-ple of re-nown Were do-ing the most out-ra-ge-ous things, when the world turn'd up-side down!

2. The Pope was dressed as harlequin, and danced a Highland fling;
   Queen Victoria came from England, a comic song to sing;
   Old Barnum acted Hamlet, and Booth was playing Clown,
   And Bismarck was an acrobat—when the world turned upside down.

3. Jay Gould he was a Quaker, and "bossed" a spelling match;
   Vanderbilt had a railway scheme he somehow couldn't hatch;
   Mr. Tilton was an Emperor, and wore a golden crown,
   And Beecher danced the Can can—when the world turned upside down.

4. Brigham Young was a bachelor who wished a wife to win;
   John Gough opened a "Sample room" and served out beer and gin;
   Old Tweed was at his Island home dressed in a suit of brown;
   Ben Butler had joined the Shakers—when the world turned upside down.

5. The shining Truth gleamed o'er the land, and Virtue—more or less—
   And womankind gave no more thought to vanity or dress;
   All husbands were like angels, wives never wore a frown,
   And U.S. Grant said "No third term, or the States are upside down!"

6. Brooklyn had changed into a sort of Paradise on earth,
   For it had had some Trials, and one heard no ribald [mirth]
   The people of this mighty globe were all just what they seem;
   There was an end to "Rings" and "Jobs"—when I woke, and 'twas a dream!

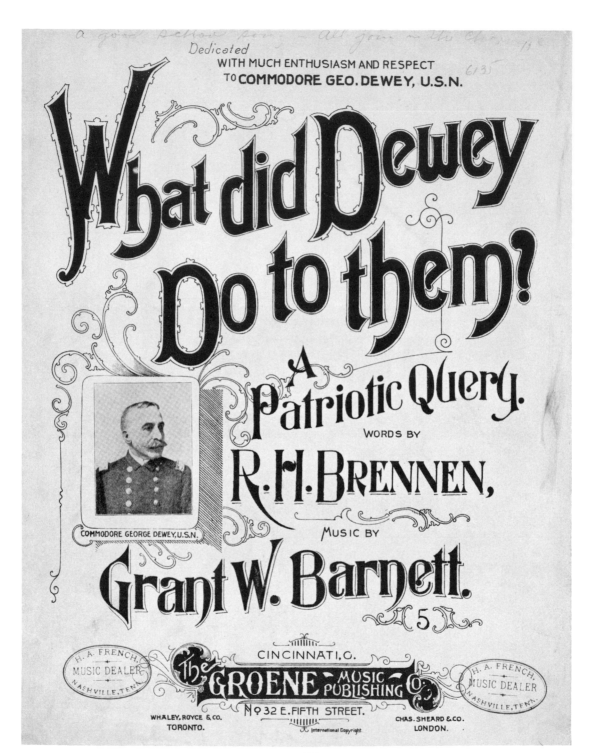

What Did Dewey Do To Them?

Oh when the war with Spain broke out, the Span-iards cheered with vim When Dew-ey left Hong Kong to fight they swore they'd set-tle him But Dew-ey mere-ly smiled at them and whis-pered "When I'm through You'll hear the Span-iards weep and howl," What did-n't Dew-ey do? What did Dew-ey do to them What did Dew-ey do He did them up so tho-rough-ly He on-ly left a few It was-n't to the Queen's taste That's a pun and ve-ry true He did-n't do a thing to them What did-n't Dew-ey do?

2. The Spaniards ran away like curs,
   They couldn't fight us Yanks.
   Manilla's Gov'nor Gen'ral said,
   "Come take our town with thanks";
   The town's now ours but in old Spain,
   The very air is blue
   While every organ grinder plays,
   What didn't Dewey do?

3. The English are amazed at us,
   Oh they admire our pluck;
   They say us Yanks are up to date,
   And always play in luck.
   It isn't luck, its Yankee nerve,
   That carries us straight through;

And all the world yells out to-day—
What didn't Dewey Do?

4. In years to come the Spanish Dons,
   Will tell in whispers low;
   How Dewey ruined the Spanish fleet,
   And did it at one blow.
   They'll tell their children in the schools
   Of the Red, White and Blue;
   While Cuba's bands will sweetly play,
   What didn't Dewey do?

5. In all the towns in this broad land,
   Our flag is waving high;
   The finest flag that's ever waved,

Beneath a brave blue sky.
And all the foreign nations know,
That we are brave and true.
While every paper headlines it—
What didn't Dewey do?

6. When this cruel war is over,

And war's black curtain falls;
You will see our grand old banner
Wave over Spanish walls.
And poor Cuba's cry for freedom,
Will ring out strong and true;
And Uncle Sam will sing and dance,
What didn't Dewey do?

The Animal Fair

7

WHAT'S SO FUNNY ABOUT ANIMALS? Not much these days, it seems; anyway, not enough to write popular song about them. Oh, every few years such a song attracts national attention and holds its position near the top of the heap for a short while. Most of us remember "Who's Afraid of the Big Bad Wolf?" written in 1933 by Frank E. Churchill and Ann Ronell, and "The Donkey Serenade," made popular by Rudolf Friml in 1937, when he revived one of his melodies which had failed to arouse interest fifteen years earlier. And, "Three Little Fishes," a "sleeper" by a near-unknown, Saxie Dowell, and foisted on the public by bandleader Kay Kyser, in 1941, whereupon over one million records of the juvenile jingle were sold. And, twelve years later, "How Much is that Doggie in the Window," written by Bob Merrill and sung by Patti Page for another million and more record buyers.

Throughout the nineteenth century, many popular American composers felt that comic songs, and even instrumental numbers, about animals would appeal to the American sense of humor. Dancers whirled around the floor merrily to the strains of "The Giraffe Waltz," "The Hippopotamus Polka," "The Grasshopper Waltz," "Pussy's Polka" (by "Kitty"), "The Tiger Quickstep," and "The Butterflies' Ball."

Some of the airs which were whistled and sung over one hundred years ago are still familiar. Take for example, "The Monkey's Wedding." (See page 231.) Its origin remains a mystery; the sheet music of the 1830's gives no clue to author or composer. But children today still hear, at times, a version with the original words:

> The Monkey married the Baboons sister,
> Smack'd his lips and then he kiss'd her;
> He kiss'd so hard he raised a blister.
>
> · · · · ·

225

What do you think the bride was dressed in?
White gauze veil and a green glass breast-pin
Red kid shoes—she was quite interesting,
She was quite a belle.

In this same period an Englishman, William Clifton, introduced his American public to cat songs. In 1836 his offerings were published by Endicott of New York, who, incidentally, was also a lithographer and illustrated the title pages of much of the music he published. Thus the covers of two of Clifton's compositions—"The Cat's Grand Concert" or "Grimalkin's First Appearance" (see page 233), and "Our Old Tom Cat," or "The Cats March Out of the Ash Hole" (see page 235)—are the work of Endicott, who had a proclivity for designing comic subject matter.

Endicott particularly enjoyed designing covers for songs about the Negro or for the Negro minstrel, and some of the most entertaining title pages of such songs, through the period of the 1830's and early 1840's, bear striking testimony to both his wit and his draftsmanship.

Although the verses of "Our Old Tom Cat" are ascribed to Clifton, it is not known who composed the melody. Credit is given to Jupiter Zeus (!) Hesser, who "arranged with symphonies and accompaniments" the music of "Our Old Tom Cat." As for the ash hole:

It was Tom's place of birth, he said,
And ev'ry night it was Tom's bed;
For rats and mice were banished hence,
Done by our Old Tom Cat.
Meough, meough, meough,
When he march'd out of the Ash Hole.

"The Cat's Grand Concert" starts:

Come let us meet when day light sets,
Grimalkin he can bawl;
Thou slick skinn'd Tom Cat, Prince of pets,
Can teach us how to squall.

Then comes a plethora of meoughing for a half dozen verses, and at last:

In chorus let us all conclude,
To finish this night's sport;
Let's swell our notes in magnitude,
Till we begin to snort.

Followed by a grand finale of meoughs.

Nearly sixty years later another cat was the hero of a popular ballad, "The Cat Came Back." (See page 238.) The words and music were by Harry S. Miller, who had several other hits to his credit. Many an old-time songfest, conducted in the privacy of somebody's parlor, would at some period during the evening dissolve into the rousing shout of "The Cat Came Back." The cat's owner, Mr. Johnson, is a gentleman of color who decides it is necessary to dissociate himself from his pet and goes to considerable trouble to accomplish the desired result. But:

> De cat came back, couldn't stay no longer,
> Yes, de cat came back de very next day;
> De cat came back—thought she was a goner,
> But de cat came back for it wouldn't stay away.

Probably the most popular and the longest remembered of the "dog" songs was one written by Septimus Winner, which he called "Der Deitcher's Dog," but which is familiar to us as "Oh Where, Oh Where, Has My Little Dog Gone?"

Winner, a Philadelphian, was one of the most popular song writers of the 1850's and 1860's. Millions of copies of Winner's songs were printed. His gushy "Listen To the Mocking Bird," written under the pseudonym Alice Hawthorne (his mother's maiden name), was republished a dozen times. But he liked comic songs. Some of the best humorous songs to come out of the Civil War (the soldiers couldn't sing about the flag, home, and mother *all* the time) were written by Winner.

His "Little Wee Dog" (see page 241), written in 1864, was a favorite stage number, altered a bit at times in the presentation, but never made unrecognizable. One actor to mold it to his own particular style was A. W. Young, who affected a ridiculous Dutch attire, with large white ruff and knickerbockers, and who puffed an enormous meerschaum as he sang:

> Oh where, and oh where, is my leetel wee dog?
> Oh where, oh where can he be?—
> Mit his ears cut short and his tail cut long,
> Oh where, oh where is he?
> Sausage is good, and Bologna also,
> Oh where! oh where can he be?
> Dey makes dem of horse, and dey makes dem of dog,
> And I fear dat dey makes dem of he.

To square dancers, the most familiar animal tune is undoubtedly "Pop Goes the Weasel" (spelled with a "z" on the title pages of some early musical publications). (See page 244.) These days "weasel," at least as a verb, comes close to being a derogatory word, but in the middle of the last century the "weazel" song was a leader in the field of entertainment, building up from a stealthy beginning through a dozen verses that the populace sang with gusto:

> When de night walks in, as black as a sheep,
> And de hen and her eggs am fast asleep
> Den into her nest with a sarpent's creep,
> Pop goes de weasel!

> CHORUS: All around the Cobblers house
> The Monkey chased the people,
> The Minister kiss'd the Deacons wife,
> Pop went the Weasel.

And more and more verses, some of which described the dances which the song inspired:

> Ob all de dance dat ebber was plann'd
> To galvanize de heel and de hand,
> Dar's none dat moves so gay and gra[n]d
> As "Pop goes de Weasel!"

> Den form two lines as straight as a string,
> Dance in and out, den three in a ring—
> Dive under like de duck and sing
> "Pop goes the Weasel."

One of the great comediennes of the 1890's was May Irwin. She secured her first professional billing at the age of thirteen in Buffalo, New York, teaming up with her sister Georgia. Within two years the great Tony Pastor had signed them as members of his New York company. Eventually May went on to tour the country in many vaudeville sketches. In her floor-shaking, window-rattling "Bully" song, she introduced a Negro style in which she outshouted the late Sophie Tucker.

To describe Miss Irwin as buxom would be putting it mildly; and her voice was even bigger than her body. She could belt out a song with such high-spirited power that eardrums would throb as their owners relished the shouts and the struts that were the signatures of May's stage personality. Her audiences were widespread. In later years, they even included President Wilson; the story goes that once he offered her the portfolio of Secretary of Laughter.

Her two most successful presentations were the work of one writer,

Charles E. Trevathan, who supplied her with her "Bully" song and her "Frog" song. (See page 247.) Trevathan was an easygoing but brilliant newspaper writer and song composer. He liked to work with a tiny Negro associate named Cooley, who could visit various dives where catchy numbers had their origin. Cooley would memorize the tunes and the words and bring them back to Trevathan, who would then arrange them for May's publishers. Miss Irwin was called the "stage mother of ragtime," and Trevathan the "father of ragtime."

May Irwin's "Frog" song, introduced in 1896, goes like this:

> Away down a-yonder in Yankety Yank,
> A bull-frog jumped from bank to bank,
> 'Cause there wasn't nothin' else to do.
> He stubbed his toe an' in he fell,
> An' de neighbors all say dat he went to—well,
> 'Cause he hadn't nothin' else to do.

And it winds up with a brief sermon:

> Now all uv yo' people dat heah dis song,
> Yo' knows why dis po' frog went wrong,
> 'Cause he hadn't nothin' else to do.
> You'd bettah keep busy on any kind of pay,
> Till de big horn blow on de judgement day,
> Den you will hab somethin' else to do.

In the early 1890's, Billy Emerson, one of the greatest minstrels of all time, was a member of W. S. Cleveland's troupe. His specialty, in this most popular minstrel organization, was "Could I Only Back the Winner" (see page 249), which relates poor Billy's misfortunes at the track. He laments:

> I've studied sporting papers till they nearly
>   drove me wild,
> I've watch'd each horses pedigree, since I
>   was but a child.
> I've tried all sorts of dodges, I've committed
>   many a sin;
> Misfortune's been my fortune, for my fortune
>   I can't win.

It may be stretching a point to include along with "animal" music a song about insects and arachnids, but "The Spider and the Fly" (see page 252), is too well-known a story to be left out. The old morality tale has a flavor combining sly humor and common sense, which gave it good circulation around 1850. The spider is a supersalesman; the fly resists his blandishments as long as he can, but is at last trapped in the web. And the song concludes:

> Now all young men take warning by this foolish
> little Fly,
> Pleasure is the spider that to catch you fast
> will try;
> For although you may think my advice is quite
> a bore,
> You're lost if you stand parleying outside of
> Pleasure's door.
> Remember, oh! remember, the foolish little
> Fly.

Nearly 150 years ago a German entrepreneur named Isaac Van Amburgh brought to America an impressive animal show—with lions, camels, monkeys, a rhinoceros, and a huge elephant—and took to the road. For a quarter of a century he was the hub around which his big show revolved. Dressed picturesquely in a Roman toga and sandals, he would mingle with the wild beasts.

According to his flamboyant publicity, he would enter several cages, one after the other, containing lions, lionesses, leopards, "leopardesses" (he seems to have been a word-coiner), royal tigers, and tigresses. Fixing the beasts with his baleful eye, without the use of whip or stick, he would compel them to act to suit his will, and would fondle them as if they were kittens.

His most terrifying stunt was to thrust his head into the lion's mouth. At least once each season a newspaper would carry an account with the sickening news that poor Van Amburgh had lost his head while performing this maneuver, but despite these horrible reports, the gentleman would be on hand at the beginning of the following season, with an unqualifiedly sound head on his shoulders, ready to repeat the same daredevil acts as before.

After a while he died a natural death and the show began a slow process of disintegration. Near the circus's wintering ground in New York State, the animals were put up at auction, and were "knocked down," one by one, not by a club or stick wielded by a trainer, but by a hammer pounded by an auctioneer.

Van Amburgh himself had already passed from this mortal scene when a Dr. A. J. Wetmore produced a song (see page 254), published in 1865, whose words remained familiar for many years:

Old Van Amburgh is the man that runs all
      these ere shows,
He goes into the lion's den and shows you
      all he knows.
He sticks his head in the lion's mouth and
      holds it there awhile,
Then he pulls it out again and turns around
      and smiles.

CHORUS: The elephant now moves round, the music begins
            to play,
        Them boys around the monkey's cage had better
            keep away.

An entertaining story, written and sung in 1904, was "The Tale of a Shirt." (See page 256.) Billy Brackett, an amusing vaudevillian, who billed himself as "The Man with Red Hair," wrote the words and popularized his own song on the stage.

A man named Burke—goes the tale—had four beautiful red shirts on his clothesline. They had a strong appeal for Burke's goat, who made a meal of them. This so infuriated Burke that he decided to do away with the goat. He tied him securely to a railroad track, sure that a train would soon bear down on the animal and finish him off. But the goat had no wish to perish:

Say au revoir, but not good-bye,
This goat was wise, and too smart to die.
He struggled and tugged with might and main,
Coughed up a red shirt, and flagged the train.

MONKEYS   WEDDING

For   *The*

PIANO   FORTE

Firth & Hall 1 Franklin Sq N York

231

Monkeys Wedding

The mon-key mar-ried the ba-boon's sis-ter smack'd his lips and then he kiss'd her He

kiss'd so hard he rais'd a blis-ter, she set up a yell. The bride's maid stuck on some court plais-

ter; It stuck so fast it cou'dn't stick fast-er, sure-ly 'twas a sad dis-as-ter, but it soon got

well.

2. What do you think the bride was dress'd in?
   White gauze veil and a green glass breast pin
   Red kid shoes—she was quite interesting.
   She was quite a belle.
   The bridegroom swell'd with a blue shirt collar—
   Black silk stock that cost a dollar—
   Large false whiskers the fashion to follow;
   He cut a monstrous swell.

3. What do you think they had for supper?
   Black eye'd peas and bread and butter—
   Ducks in the duck-house all in a flutter—
   Pick'led oysters too.
   Chestnuts raw and boil'd and roasted.
   Apples sliced and Onions toasted.
   Music in the corner posted,
   Waiting for the cue.

4. What do you think was the tune they danced to?
   "The drunken Sailor" sometimes "Jim Crow"
   Tails in the way and some got pinch'd too,
   'Cause they were to long.
   What do you think they had for a fiddle?
   An old Banjo with a hole in the middle—
   A Tamborine made out of a riddle.
   And that's the end of my song.

THE CAT'S GRAND CONCERT.

or

CRIMALKINS FIRST APPEARANCE.

a Favorite

Song & Trio,

arranged for

THE PIANO FORTE

NEW YORK.

Published by ENDICOTT. 359 Broadway.

SOLD BY
FIOT. MEIGNEN & Cº
217 Chesnut Street
Philad.

The Cat's Grand Concert

Come let us meet when day light sets, Gri-mal-kin he can bawl; Thou slick skinn'd Tom Cat, Prince of pets, can teach us how to squall Thou slick skinn'd Tom Cat, Prince of pets can teach us how to squall —— We'll sing in har-mo-ny a glee, Me-ough, me-ough, me-ough;— This is the cats' first ju-bi-lee, Me-ough, me-ough, me-ough — me-ough, me-ough, me-ough — me-ough, me-ough, me-ough.—

2. We'll give a first rate concert now,
Grimalkin take the lead;
Don't let them Tom Cats make a row,
Our harmony impede.
We'll sing, &c.

3. For now's the hour for loving Cats,
In harmony to meet;
Secure from noisy dogs and rats,
Let each Cat take her seat.
We'll sing, &c.

4. Grimalkin hear our dulcet squall
That rolls along in piles;
It takes us young Cats, thus to bawl,
The old ones they may smile.
We'll sing, &c.

5. That Cat there sings quite out of tune,
Grimalkin close her jaws;
We have no place for such a lune,
Nor those with dirty paws.
We'll sing, &c.

6. But oh Grimalkin should they still,
Not mind their P's and Q's;
Expell them from the place they fill,
And let them take a snoose.
We'll sing, &c.

7. In chorus let us all conclude,
To finish this night's sport;
Let's swell our notes in magnitude,
Till we begin to snort.
We'll sing, &c.

234

OUR OLD TOM CAT

Lith. of Endicott.

THE CATS MARCH OUT OF THE ASH HOLE

A Favorite comic Song or Duett

Written by

W. CLIFTON

arranged with Symphonies and accompaniments by

Jupiter Zeus Hesser.

NEW YORK,

Published by **G. ENDICOTT**, 359 Broadway.

Entered according to act of Congress in the Year 1836 by George Endicott in the Clerk's Office of the District Court of the Southern district of New York.

Our Old Tom Cat

It oft was told me by my Dad, when I was young and but a lad, how ma-ny won- drous things he saw, done by our old Tom Cat Me-ough, me-ough, me-ough, When he march'd out of the ash hole. He march'd out me-ough, me-ough, Our old Tom Cat me-ough'd when he march'd out of the ash hole

2. It was Tom's place of birth, he said,
   And ev'ry night it was Tom's bed;
   For rats and mice were banish'd hence,
   Done by our Old Tom Cat. When he march'd out, &c.

3. Tom thought he would not live alone,
   So a kitten he stole and brought it home;
   A beautiful creature it was, I say,
   Just like our Old Tom Cat. When he march'd out, &c.

4. This kitten grew up under Old Tom's care,
   And many a Kitten he had to spare;
   For twelve generations he liv'd to see,
   Just like our Old Tom Cat. When he march'd out, &c.

5. Tom was a musician, and taught the same,
   If they did'nt learn, he was not to blame;
   For all kind of Instruments they did play,
   Made by our Old Tom Cat. When he march'd out, &c.

6. In his merry mood, great concerts he gave,
   I've oft been delighted with voices so grave;
   With Cymbals, and Trumpets, and Double Brass Drums,
   Play'd by our Old Tom Cat. When he march'd out, &c.

7. Now Tom was Col. of a rigement brave,
   He'd march out his soldiers, his Ash Hole to save;
   With a Brass Band, superior to all in the town,
   Made by our Old Tom Cat. When he march'd out, &c.

8. In Battle Tom always was head of his Clan,
   He fought like a Hero, and died like a man;
   They retreated in order into the Ash Hole,
   To mourn over our Tom Cat. When he march'd out, &c.

9. Now poor Old Tom is dead and gone,
   He lay in the Ash Hole there till morn;
   His will was made, and legacies left,
   Done by our Old Tom Cat. When he march'd out, &c.

10. They burried Old Tom, with honors of war,
    Then return'd to the Ash Hole, their sorrows to pour;
    When lo, in a moment a voice was heard,
    Done by our Old Tom Cat. When he march'd out, &c.

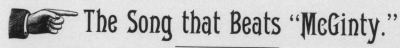

The Song that Beats "McGinty."

"THE CAT CAME BACK"

WORDS AND MUSIC BY **HARRY S. MILLER,** AUTHOR OF

"I'm 17 To-day," "Not on Your Life, Says Dolan," "Keep Your Eye on Duffy," his latest big "Hit" being

"HE'S GOT FEATHERS IN HIS HAT," "WHEN YOU'RE SINGLE," &c., &c.

{ 4 }

PUBLISHED BY

WILL ROSSITER,

THE POPULAR SONG PUBLISHER,

MAIN OFFICES, 56 FIFTH AVE., CHICAGO.   Branch, 377 Sixth Ave., New York.

The Cat Came Back

Dar was ole Mis-ter John-son, he had trou-ble of his own, He had an ole yal-ler cat that would-

n't leave its home; He tried eb-ry-thing he knew to keep de cat a-way Eb-en send it to the preach-er

Chorus

an he tole it for to stay, But the cat came back, could-n't stay no long-er, Yes, the cat came back the

ver-y next day, The cat came back, thought he was a gon-er, but the cat came back for it would-n't

stay a-way.

2. De cat did hab some company one night out in de yard,
   Some one frowed a boot-jack, an' dey frowed it mighty hard,
   Caught de cat behind de ear, she thought it rather slight,
   When along dar comes a brick-bat an' it knocked it out ob sight.

   CHORUS

3. Away across de ocean dey did send de cat at last,
   Vessel only out a day and making water fast;
   People all begin to pray, de boat begin to toss,
   When a nodder vessel came along and took de people off.

   CHORUS

4. On a telegraph wire sparrows sitting in a bunch;
   Cat a feeling hungry, thought she'd like 'em for a lunch,
   Climbing softly up de pole, an' when she reached de top
   Put her foot upon de 'lectric wire, which tied her in a knot.

   CHORUS

239

5. One time did gib de cat away to man in a balloon
   An' tole him for to gib it to de man in de moon;
   But de b'loon it busted, sho, an' eb'rybody sed
   It wer seben miles away or more dey picked de man up dead.

   CHORUS

6. De cat was a possessor ob a fam'ly ob its own
   Wid seben little kittens till dar comes a cyclone,
   Blowed de houses all apart and tossed de cat around;
   While de air was full ob kittens not a one was eber found.

   CHORUS

7. De cat it were a terror and dey said it wer de best
   To gib it to a nigger who was going out West.
   De train going 'round de curve struck a broken rail,
   Not a blessed soul aboard de train wer left to tell de tale.

   CHORUS

8. A man down on de corner swore to kill de cat at sight,
   Loaded up a musket full ob nails and dynamite,
   Waited in de garden for de cat to come around;
   Half-a-dozen little pieces ob de man was all dey found.

   CHORUS

9. Little boy took de cat away, he got a dollar note,
   Took it down de ribber in a little open boat,
   Tied a brick around its neck an' stone about a pound;
   Now dey're grappling in de ribber for a little boy that's drowned.

   CHORUS

10. While de cat lay a-sleeping an' a resting one day,
    'Round came an organ grinder an' he began to play;
    De cat look'd around awhile an' kinder raised her head
    When he played Ta-rah-dah-boom-da-rah, an' de cat dropped dead.

    CHORUS: But its ghost came back to tell you all about it;
            Yes, its ghost came back, between you and I.
            Its ghost came back, may be you will doubt it,
            But its ghost came back just to bid 'em all good-bye.

THE LITTLE WEE DOG.

As sung in "LA BELLE SAUVAGE" by

MR A. W. YOUNG.

AT THE ST JAMES'S THEATRE.

WORDS BY

BARTON HILL.

Philadelphia **LEE & WALKER** 922 Chestnut St

O. Ditson & Co. Boston   W. H. Boner & Co. 1102 Chestnut St.   Chas. W. Harris N. York

ENTERED ACCORDING TO ACT OF CONGRESS IN THE YEAR 1876 BY LEE & WALKER IN THE OFFICE OF THE LIBRARIAN OF CONGRESS AT WASHINGTON.

241

Little Wee Dog

Oh where, and oh where, is my leet-el wee dog? Oh where! oh where can he be? Mit his ears cut short

and his tail cut long, Oh where, oh where is he? Sau-sage is good and Bo-lo-gna al-so Oh where!

oh where can he be? Dey makes dem of horse, and dey makes dem of dog, and I fear dat dey makes

da capo al Fine

dem of he.

2. Whenever I see a Bologna I shtop,
   And I whistle dis bootiful air,
   But the sausages never run out of the shop
   So I don't think my leetel dog's there.
   Oh where, and oh where, &c.

3. But either in Camden or Manayunk, or New York
   Or else in my own Amsterdam,
   My leetel dog's made into beef, or to pork,—
   Unless he is chicken und ham!
   Oh where, and oh where, &c.

4. De reason I tink my leetel wee dog
   To sausages must have been mince;—
   I had a Bologna for dinner last week,
   And by dam, I have growled ever since!
   Oh where, and oh where, &c.

5. MORAL (adorning a tail):
   My leetel dog waggles his stump of a tail,
   Whenever he wishes for prog;

242

If the tail was the strongest, I makes no doubt,
The tail would waggle the dog.
Oh where, and oh where, &c.

ENCORE VERSES:
Well, perhaps I have tasted my little wee dog
And swallowed his last vital spark;
His flesh it was sausage, his skin it is gloves,
But what have they done mit his *bark*?
Oh where, and oh where, &c.

My little dog's spirits, that never would flag,
Are turned into "spirits of *whine*";
His tail is preserved as the last of a *wag*,
And his *bark* is "sulphate of *canine*."
Oh where, and oh where, &c.

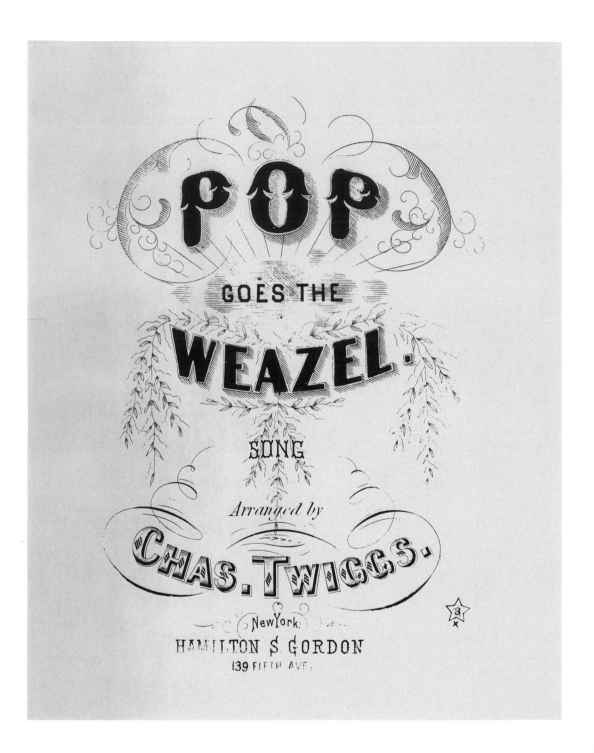

Pop Goes De Weasel

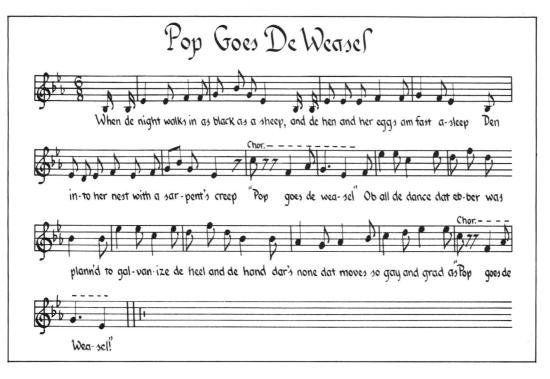

When de night walks in as black as a sheep, and de hen and her eggs am fast a-sleep Den
in-to her nest with a sar-pent's creep "Pop goes de wea-sel" Ob all de dance dat eb-ber was
plann'd to gal-van-ize de heel and de hand dar's none dat moves so gay and grad as Pop goes de
Wea-sel!

2. John Bull tells, in de ole cows hum,
   How Uncle Sam used Uncle Tom,
   While he makes some white slaves at home,
       By "Pop goes de Weasel!"
   He talks about a friendly trip
   To Cuba in a steam war-ship,
   But Uncle Sam may make him skip
       By "Pop goes the Weasel!"
   He's sending forth his iron hounds
   To bark us off de fishin'-ground's—
   He'd best beware of Freedom's sounds
       Oh "Pop goes the Weasel!"

3. My wife she is very sick,
   The baby's got the measles,
   Sally's got the whooping cough,
       Pop goes the Weasel,
   Forward two and balansay,
   Cross hand with Sally Teazle,
   Oh gracious what a time I had
       Singing pop goes the Weasel.

245

All around the Cobblers house,
The Monkey chased the people,
The Minister kiss'd the Deacons wife,
    Pop went the Weasel.

4. De Temperance folks from Souf to Main,
   Against all liquor spout and strain,
   But when dey feels an ugly pain
       Den "Pop goes the Weasel!"
   All New York in rush now whirls
   Whar de World's Fair its flag unfurls
   But de best World's Fair am when our girls
       Dance "Pop goes de Weasel."
   Den form two lines as straight as a string,
   Dance in and out, den three in a ring—
   Dive under like de duck, and sing
       "Pop goes the Weasel."

May Irwin's "Frog" Song

A-way down a-yon-der in Yank-e-ty Yank, a bull-frog jumped from bank to bank, Cause there was-n't noth-in' else to do —— He stubbed his toe and in he fell, an' de neigh-bors all say dat he went to _ well, Cause he had-n't noth'in else to do ——

Chorus

An' jus' lots uv folks is like dis fool-ish frog uv mine —— A' run-nin' in-to trou-ble jus' to pass de time, An' de dev-il's al-lus loaf'in round heah jus' to grab de kind dat nev-ah has-n't noth'in else to do ——

2.

When dey buried dat frog, de preacher said,
"De reason why dis young frog is dead,
"'Cause there wasn't nothin' else to do."
An' all you frogs jus' a listen to me,
Yo' bettah stay at home wid yo' family,
When you hav'nt nothin' else to do.

CHORUS

3.

Some frogs I know is pow'ful fond
Uv spendin' dey time in 'nother frog's pond,
'Cause dey hasn't nothin' else to do.
But dis consolation, de good book brings,

De frog uv dem habits won't wear no wings,
'Cause he hasn't nothin' else to do.

CHORUS

4.

Now all uv yo' people dat heah dis song,
Yo' knows why dis po' frog went wrong,
'Cause he hadn't nothin' else to do.
You'd bettah keep busy on any kind of pay,
Till de big horn blow on de judgement day,
Den you will hab somethin' else to do.

CHORUS

BILLY EMERSON'S LATEST SONG

"COULD I ONLY BACK THE WINNER"

AS SUNG IN
W. S. Cleveland's Minstrels.

NEW YORK
Wm A. POND & CO.
25 Union Square.
Copyright 1890.

Could I Only Back The Winner

Be-hold in me a man who's lost a for-tune on the field, But still my great pro-pen-si-ties to nev-er, nev-er yield! I've "made a book," I've tak-en "tips," I've squared the jocks when cross'd; But when I bal-anced my ac-count, I found that I had lost. Could I on-ly back the win-ner— what a dif-f'rent man I'd be! — I'd spare e-nough to share e-nough to show my char-i-ty! I'd be like Plung-er Wal-ton,— and I'd give a cham-pagne din-ner— to ev-'ry friend that's here to-night, could I on-ly back the win-ner!—

2. I've studied sporting papers till they nearly drove me wild,
I've watch'd each horses pedigree, since I was but a child.
I've tried all sort of dodges, I've committed many a sin;
Misfortune's been my fortune, for my fortune I can't win.

CHORUS: Could I only back the winner,
What a diff'rent man I'd be!
I'd spare enough to share enough
To show my charity!
No more I'd tackle pork and beans
By the gaslight's brightest glimmer!
I'd have a darling double team,
Could I only back the winner!

3. "Faint heart ne'er won fair lady," so I'll have another try;
   And as long as I have got my health, I never will say die!
   I know my luck will change some day, so I'll not throw up the sponge;
   And long as I've a dollar, boys, you bet yer life I'll "plunge!"

   CHORUS: Could I only back the winner,
   What a diff'rent man I'd be!
   I'd spare enough to share enough
   To show my charity!
   I'd be another Pittsburgh Phil!
   I'd give the books a skinner!
   I'd have a girl upon each arm,
   Could I only back the winner!

The Spider And The Fly

"Will you walk in-to my par-lour," said a spi-der to a fly, "'Tis the pret-tiest lit-tle par-lour that

ev-er you did spy: You've on-ly got to pop your head with-in side of the door, You'll see so ma-ny cur-ious

things you nev-er saw be-fore.   Will you, will you, will you, will you walk in pret-ty fly?

Will you, will you, will you, will you walk in pret-ty fly?"

2. "My house is always open," said the Spider to the Fly,
"I'm glad to have the company of all I see go by";
"They go in, but don't come out again, I've heard of you before,"
"Oh yes they do, I always let them out at my back door."
"Will you, will you," &c.

3. "Will you grant me one sweet kiss, then," says the Spider to the Fly,
"To taste your charming lips, I've a curiosity."
Said the Fly, "If once our lips did meet, a wager I would lay,
Of ten to one you would not, after, let them come away."
"Will you, will you," &c.

4. "If you wont kiss will you shake hands," says the Spider to the Fly,
"Before you leave me to myself, with sorrow and to sigh."
Says the fly, "There's nothing handsome unto you belongs,
I declare you should not touch me, even with a pair of tongs."
"Will you, will you," &c.

5. "What handsome wings you've got," says the Spider to the Fly,
"If I had only such a pair, I in the air would fly;
But 'tis useless, all my wishing, and only idle talk,
You can fly up in the air, while I'm obliged to walk."
"Will you, will you," &c.

6. "For the last time now I ask you, will you walk in Mr. Fly,"
   "No, if I do may I be shot, I'm off, so now good bye."
   Then up he springs, but both his wings were in the web caught fast;
   The Spider laughed, "Ah ha, my boy, I have you safe at last."
   "Will you walk out pretty Fly."

7. "And pray how are you now," says the Spider to the Fly,
   You fools will never wisdom get, unless you dearly buy;
   'Tis vanity that ever makes repentance come too late,
   And you who into cobwebs run, surely deserve your fate."
   "Listen to me, listen to me, foolish little Fly."

8. Now all young men take warning by this foolish little Fly,
   Pleasure is the Spider that to catch you fast will try;
   For although you may think my advice is quite a bore,
   You're lost if you stand parleying outside of Pleasure's door.
   Remember, oh! remember, the foolish little Fly.

VAN AMBURGHS MENAGERIE

A

COMIC SONG

BY

Dr. W. J. WETMORE

BROOKLYN. E. D.,
Published by D. S. HOLMES. 67 Fourth St

3

Entered according to Act of Congress A. D. 1865 by D. S. Holmes in the Clerks Office of the District Court of the Eastern District of New York.

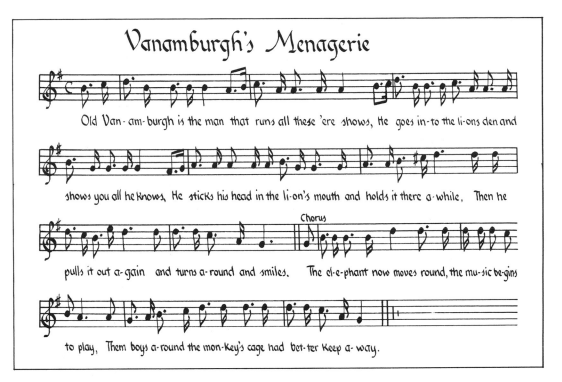

Vanamburgh's Menagerie

Old Van-am-burgh is the man that runs all these 'ere shows, He goes in-to the li-ons den and shows you all he knows, He sticks his head in the li-on's mouth and holds it there a-while, Then he pulls it out a-gain and turns a-round and smiles.

Chorus

The el-e-phant now moves round, the mu-sic be-gins to play, Them boys a-round the mon-key's cage had bet-ter keep a-way.

2. There's the polar bear we sometimes call the iceberg's daughter,
   He'll eat six tons of ice a day, and frolics in the water,
   He wades the deepest rivers, which scarcely wet his knees,
   And he never catches cold, for you never hear him sneeze.

   CHORUS

3. The peacock is a pretty bird, his tail is wondrous fine,
   The jay bird and the jackdaw are mad to see it shine,
   The kangaroos are jumping, and rattling the cage door,
   Look out ye little boys, for the lion's going to roar.

   CHORUS

4. The monkey in the next cage, is cuffing his little brother,
   He's not to blame for doing that, for he learned it of his mother;
   The skin of his face is drawn so tight, and cover'd o'er with kinks,
   And when he winks, he's sure to gape, and when he gapes he winks.

   CHORUS

5. The last is the eagle, from the highest mountain tops,
   He's been known to eat up little birds, and here his history stops;
   The performance can't go on, there is too much noise and confusion,
   If the ladies give them monkeys fruit, it will injure their constitution.

   CHORUS

255

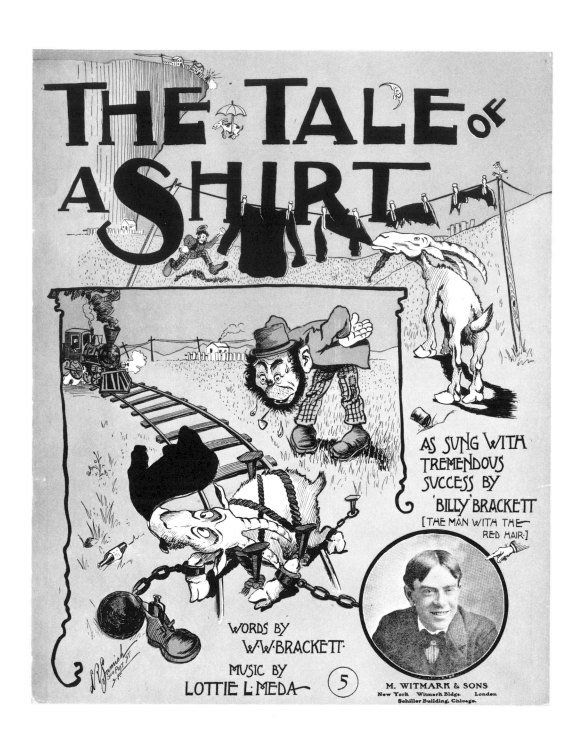

The Tale Of A Shirt

There was a man, his name was Burke, He was a friend of mine; He had four love-ly bright red shirts,

that hung on his clothes-line. Not sat-is-fied with all his wealth, what do you think Burke did —— He

took a trip to Butch-er-town, bought a goat just for a kid; He tied him up in his back-yard where the

shirts were hung in line; The goat got loose and ate them all, just as the clock struck nine——— This

made my friend Burke good and mad, To kill him then he swore, So he tied the goat to a rail-road track, sat-is-

Chorus

fied he'd be no more. Say au re-voir, but not good-bye, This goat was wise, and too smart to

die, He strug-gled and tugged with might and main, coughed up a red shirt, and flagged the

train.

2. Now when Burke saw the goat's cute
           trick,
   He quick said, "I'll forgive;
   I'll take that goat right home again,
   For he deserves to live."
   Burke had a silk umbrella,
   'Twas the apple of his eye,
   This goat thought it was good to eat,
   So he ate it on the sly;
   Burke found it out and swore again
   It was time to make him stop.
   Says he, "I'll take him to some place
   Where I have got the drop";
   So he pushed him off the Call Café,
   'Twas eighteen stories high;
   Then left the place with smiling face,
   Says, "This time it is good-bye."

CHORUS: Say au revoir, but not good-bye,
This goat was wise, though he could not
        fly,
He gave one cry, it was a beaut,
Coughed up the umbrella, made a para-
        chute.

3. Once more to dear old home, sweet home,
   Burke took this goat again;
   Two times he'd tried to kill the beast,
   His efforts were in vain.
   He ate the paint from Burke's front door,
   From his bed he drank the spring,
   And ate Burke out of house and home,
   He did not leave a thing;
   Burke fed him tons of paris green,
   Six sticks of dynamite;
   He threw him in the ocean deep;
   But goat returned all right;
   The fatal day at last came round,
   Though that goat knew a lot;
   He wandered out on Market street,
   And looked into the slot.

CHORUS: Say au revoir, this time good-
        bye,
His time was up, he was doomed to die;
The grip-man yelled, and rang the bell
Car hit the poor goat,—now he's
        in———.

Drink

8

THE EIGHTEENTH AMENDMENT to the Constitution of the United States did not completely shut off distribution of alcoholic beverages in this country, but it did signal an end to the numerous musical tributes to men who enjoyed their liquor legally. It started the song writers off on a new tack; lamentations on the subject of the enactment of the Volstead Act broke out in the form of popular sheet music, such as "The Alcoholic Blues," "America Never Took Water and America Never Will," and others equally distressing. At the same time Bert Williams, one of the great comedians of the first quarter of the twentieth century, recorded for posterity a sly description of a new, illicit, but highly popular pastime, the distribution of bootleg whiskey, in a song called "The Moon Shines On the Moonshine."

But prior to the grim day in the winter of 1918–19 which closed the bars and eliminated legitimate traffic in the American "spirit" world for nearly fifteen years, we used to sing about liquor with gusto. Many of the songs had their serious side. Our national anthem, as is well known, was written to the tune of an English drinking song of nearly two hundred years ago, "To Anacreon in Heaven." England, and later America, published hundreds of such songs, most of them mildly festive; indeed, some could be called almost sober. Occasionally, one or another would attain overwhelming popularity, such as "Auld Lang Syne," Robert Burns's famous verses written in the early 1800's and sung on both sides of the Atlantic, and fifty years later a rollicking Harrigan and Hart number, "Salvation Army, Oh," which proclaimed, "Away, away with rum and gum! . . . As we join'd the army, oh!" (Today the words sung are "away, away with rum, by gum!")

There are many more, most of them long forgotten, but some that have retained an amazing vigor over the decades. One of these is a real old-timer from 1853. In that year a writer named Julien Carle offered to the public a "Spirited Ballad" entitled "Brandy and Water." (See page 266.) Even before hearing the notes on the piano, anyone who glances at the words will be ready to join in a musical rendition, for they commence:

> O Here's success to Brandy,
> Drink it down, Drink it down.

and go on to:

> Here's success to Brandy,
> For it always comes so handy.
> [Etc.]

The toasts continue to flow: success to "Whiskey," to "Lager" ("For it seldom makes you stagger"), to Sherry, Wine, Punch, and finally even to Water. ("O it never makes you frisky . . . like a toddy made of Whiskey.") Until another Volstead rides again, Julien Carle should remain an honored name among toastmasters.

Certain groups of active imbibers formed clubs engaged primarily in the rite of heavy drinking, at least according to some song writers. A writer and performer named Chas. J. Miers produced in 1869 a song called "The Rollicking Rams." (See page 268.) The title page depicts a gay blade, with foot-long side whiskers, slick double-breasted coat, and high hat, who, with monocle swinging freely, is waving his cane in the air wildly. The gentleman sings:

> Button up your waistcoat, button up your shoes,
> Have another liquor and throw away the blues.
> Be like me, and good for a spree
> From now till the day is dawning.
>
> · · · · ·
>
> We scorn such drink as Lemonade, Soda, Seltzer, Beer,
> The liquors of our Club I'd tell to you but I can't
> for there's ladies here.

CHORUS: For I am a member of the Rollicking Rams,
Come and be a member of the Rollicking Rams,
Out all night till broad daylight,
And never go home till morning.

What a life! According to the Rollicker, he has no worries at home, for he sings:

We don't care, we're single men, not hampered with a wife.

Other later songs indicate that those who left the single state had some explaining to do in emergencies. Joseph P. Skelly was one of the most prolific song writers of the seventies and eighties, writing all kinds of songs —sentimental, serious, and humorous. One of his more entertaining efforts describes experiences of a husband who enjoyed "bending the elbow." As Skelly tells it in "I've Only Been Down to the Club" (see page 271):

> Last night I was out rather late,
> 'Twas only an innocent spree,
> My wife for my coming did wait,
> When sleeping I thought she would be.
> I found her in temper and tears
> Oh! she cried, it's a sin and a shame,
> And she scratch'd both my eyes and my ears.
> But I told her I soon would explain.

> CHORUS: The "Club" had a meeting tonight, love,
> Of business we had a great sight, love,
> Don't think for a moment I'm tight, love,
> I've only been down to the "Club."

It takes our hero three verses, with the promise of a new dress, before he wins his way back into his wife's graces.

As we had done so many times before in search of musical material, we turned to our friends in England for songs about drinking. Around 1870, two very popular English writers, Alfred Lee and George Leybourne, who were responsible for a number of other hit songs which crossed the Atlantic, wrote a song about a gentleman they called "Champagne Charlie." (See page 273.) This song ran through several editions here; its music was gay and animated. "Charlie" sang:

> The way I gain'd my title's by a hobby
> which I've got,
> Of never letting others pay, however long
> the shot,
> Whoever drinks at my expense are treated
> all the same;
> From Dukes and Lords to Cabmen down, I make
> them drink Champagne. For

> CHORUS: Champagne Charlie is my name, Champagne
> Charlie is my name.

Good for any game at night, my boys, good for
any game at night, my boys,

. . . . .

Good for any game at night, boys, Who'll come
and join me in a spree.

For over fifteen years, from the early seventies until the late eighties, two
writer-performers held the center of the American stage. They were Edward Harrigan and Tony Hart. Hart was a gifted comic, a graceful dancer,
a delightful mimic. Harrigan was a born showman, a playwright who was
always *en rapport* with his audiences, a lyricist with a particular gift for the
light humorous touch which marked his many musical plays. His composer
was David Braham, who wrote the tunes for some two hundred of Harrigan's lyrics and whose daughter eventually became Mrs. Harrigan.

The most popular of Harrigan's plays were cast in Irish-American set-
tings. In the seventies and eighties the great masses of Irish immigrants were
struggling to achieve a standing of sorts, a situation on which Harrigan
capitalized with comical digs which convulsed the crowds that packed
Tony Pastor's theater on the Bowery. He wrote a number of songs on the
Irishman's weakness for the bottle, and one of his earliest and best known
was "I'll Never Get Drunk Any More." (See page 276.) To a merry tune by
Braham, Harrigan wrote:

> My father he was a great drinker,
> He never was sober a day,
> And when he'd Roll in, in the morning
> Oh these are the words he would say.

CHORUS: I'll never get drunk any more
I'll never get drunk any more.
The pledge I will take, the whiskey I'll shake,
Oh, I'll never get drunk any more.

Then he goes on to sing, "Well of course you know I took after my dad,"
and, after discoursing about his weakness, winds up:

> And when I lay down in me coffin
> These are the words that I say.
> CHORUS: I'll never get drunk any more [etc.].

A few years after this song had scored, Harrigan and Braham had another
good one in a new play of Harrigan's, *The McSorleys*. This was a bar-
tender's song, called "I Never Drink Behind the Bar" (see page 279), with
a chorus composed for two voices, a tenor and a baritone.

I used to own a fine saloon with mirrors
    on the wall,
The finest class would never pass but just
    drop in and call.

But when his customers would ask him to join them in a drink he would declare in a nonwhisky tenor:

I never drink [*baritone obbligato*]: "He never drinks"
Behind the bar, [*baritone*]: "before the bar,"
But I will take [*baritone*]: "But he will take"
A Mild cigar, [*baritone*]: "a mild cigar,"
I'll take a sip [*baritone*]: "He'll take a sip"
Of polinar,* [*baritone*]: "of polinar,"
I never drink [*baritone*]: "He never drinks"
Behind the bar. [*baritone*]: "before the bar."

In the 1880's, Felix McGlennon wrote a tune which he christened "But Oh! What a Difference in the Morning." It appeared in many editions, with lyrics by several authors, each of whom felt that he could improve on the verses of his predecessors. But all commence with the tale of the young man, who overindulges at the bar with unfortunate results. The chorus starts "But oh, what a difference in the morning!" (see page 281), and goes on:

Then comes repentance with the dawning!
With elegant black eyes,
And a head just twice its size.

Came the turn of the century, but there was no surcease of musical drinking material. However, the writers now were finding that they were more successful promoting songs about beer than about hard liquor.

At that time the most successful of them all was Harry von Tilzer. Von Tilzer once claimed that he had written eight thousand songs, of which two thousand had been published. Whether or not that was a figment of von Tilzer's imagination, he was probably as prolific a song writer as ever lived.

The name with which he started out in life was Harry Gumm, hardly one that would lend appeal to the title page of a song. Harry was born in Detroit. He joined a circus troupe at fourteen and was soon writing songs and performing on the piano, occasionally playing juvenile parts with a traveling repertory company. Feeling that "Gumm" was unsuitable for the stage,

*Appolinaris water.

he took his mother's maiden name, Tilzer, prefacing it with a "von" to make it more imposing. After a brief turn at burlesque he was induced to go to New York and to try song writing. He struggled for half a dozen years; then, with an up-and-coming young lyricist named Andrew B. Sterling, he had two enormous hits in 1898 and 1899, "My Old New Hampshire Home" and "I'd Leave My Happy Home for You." Total sheet-music sales of the two songs ran over three million copies, and the von Tilzer name was on the map. Another two million copies of a third song composed by von Tilzer, "A Bird in a Gilded Cage," were sold the following year.

Von Tilzer's great beer song, "Down Where the Wurzburger Flows," appeared in 1902, and the star who put it across was Nora Bayes. Nora Bayes has been called the aristocrat of lady vaudevillians, and possessed the art of showmanship to a degree equaled by few other popular artists of her time. When she selected a new song for her repertoire, its composers could be sure of a solid hit.

Nora took on "Down Where the Wurzburger Flows" (see page 284) and so delighted her audience with it that after her successful rendition she became known as the "Wurzburger girl." Here's what she sang:

> The Rhine by moonlight's a beautiful sight,
> When the wind whispers low thro' the vines,
> But give me some good old Rathskellar at night
> Where the brilliant electric light shines.
> The poets may think it's delightful to hear
> The nightingale piping his lay.
> Give me a piano a cold stein of beer
> And a fellow who knows how to play.

CHORUS: Take me down, down, down where the Wurzburger flows,
> flows, flows.
> It goes down, down, down but nobody knows where it goes.
> Just order two seidels of lager, or three.
> If I don't want to drink it, please force it on me,
> The Rhine may be fine but a cold stein for mine,
> Down where the Wurzburger flows.

The following year von Tilzer scored again with his second tribute to beer, "Under the Anheuser Bush" (see page 286), the chorus of which goes:

> Come, Come, Come and make eyes with me,
> Under the Anheuser Bush,
> Come, Come, drink some "Budwise" with me
> Under the Anheuser Bush.

> Hear the old German band [*the piano plays the*
> *strain of* "Ach Du Lieber Augustin"]
> Just let me hold your hand, Yah!
> Do, Do, Come and have a stein or two,
> Under the Anheuser Bush.

Von Tilzer was not only prolific—he was terrific!

Not so famous, but entertaining nevertheless, was a song written in 1903 by Dan McAvoy. McAvoy introduced it in *Mr. Bluebeard*, a musical produced by Klaw and Erlanger, a well-known pair of early twentieth-century theatrical entrepreneurs. The song was "The Beer that Made Milwaukee Famous." (See page 288.) Although the title was lifted bodily from the trademark of the Schlitz Brewing Company, no brand name is mentioned by the lyricist. He writes about a retired policeman who became a saloon-keeper.

> He invited all of the city sports,
> And all from the City Hall.
> The Mayor he was there,
> The judge was in the chair,
> And some aldermen from St. Paul.

> CHORUS: The big Dutch band, the finest in the land,
> Played 'till five o'clock,
> Mary Ann Breen, she kicked the tamborine,
> She woke the entire block.
> Marty McGee threw away the key
> That belonged to Murphy's trunk,
> And the beer that made Milwaukee famous
> Made all New York drunk.

Some writers recognized that a price had to be paid for overindulgence. Among them was a team of collaborators in the first decade of the twentieth century, Paul West and John W. Bratton. They seized the opportunity to describe the reform of a habitual drinker, as portrayed by a great comic actor of his day, Frank Daniels, who in a production presented by the "Frank Daniels Opera Company," scored a solid hit with West and Bratton's "I'm On the Water Wagon Now." (See page 290.)

> One night I met a college chum I hadn't seen for years.
> We razzle-dazzled 'round the town, and gave the college
> cheers
> Until the sun was shining; then for home we thought we'd
> start.

But to our great dismay, we couldn't tell ourselves apart.
At least we went to his address—or mine—we didn't know.
We pulled the bell, and waited for his wife—or mine—
    to show.
And when a voice called, "Well, who's there?" we cried in
    accents dim,
"Your husband's here. Come down and see which one
    of us is him!"

CHORUS: But I'm on the water wagon now.
              I never get a jag on now.
              Ginger ale or sars'parilla
              Is sufficient of a thriller,
              For I'm on the water wagon now.

With this plaintive ending, let us leave those who have made such a satisfactory habit of relying on the cup that cheers.

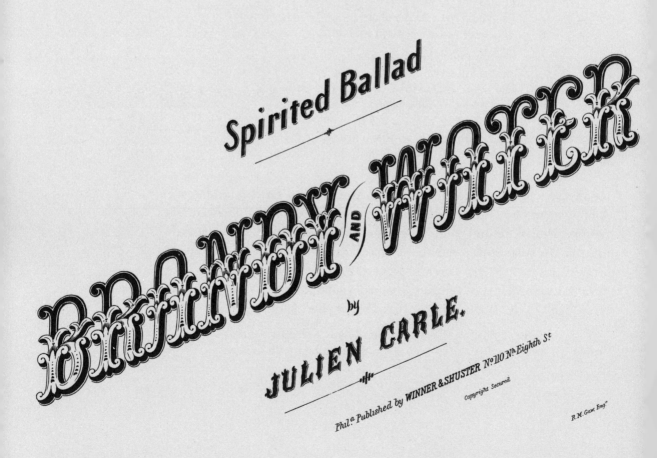

Spirited Ballad

BRANDY and WATER

by

JULIEN CARLE.

Phil.ª Published by WINNER & SHUSTER Nº 110 Nth Eighth St

Copyright Secured

R. M. Gaw, Engʳ

Brandy & Water

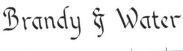

O here's suc-cess to Brandy, drink it down,— O here's suc-cess to Brandy

Chorus

drink it down— Here's suc-cess to Brandy, for it always comes so handy,

drink it down, drink it down, drink it down—

LIQUOR

2. O Here's success to "Whiskey"
Drink it down, Drink it down. O
Here's success to Whiskey
Drink it down, drink it down.
Here's success to Whiskey,
For it always makes you frisky,
Drink it down,
  Drink it down,
    Drink it down.

3. O Here's success to "Lager."
Drink it down, Drink it down,
For it seldom makes you stagger,
Drink it down, drink it down.

4. O Here's success to "Sherry"
Drink it down, Drink it down,
For it makes you feel so merry,
Drink it down, drink it down.

5. O Here's success to "Wine"
Drink it down, drink it down,
For it makes you feel so fine,
Drink it down, drink it down.

6. O Here's success to "Punch"
Drink it down drink it down
When you take it with a lunch
Drink it down, Drink it down.

WATER

2. O it always comes so handy,
Drink it down, Drink it down.
And it never costs like "Brandy"
Drink it down, drink it down.

3. O it never makes you frisky
Drink it down, Drink it down.
Like a "toddy" made of "Whiskey"
Drink it down, Drink it down.

4. O it never makes you stagger
Drink it down, Drink it down.
Like a mug of "German Lager"
Drink it down, Drink it down.

5. O it never makes you grum,
Drink it down, Drink it down.
Like a glass of "Gin" or "Rum"
Drink it down, Drink it down.

THE ROLLICKING RAMS.

WRITTEN COMPOSED & SUNG BY

CHAS. J. MIERS.

Philadelphia, **LEE & WALKER,** 722 Chestnut St.

L. B. POWELL   W. H. BONER & Cᵒ 1102 Chestnut   CHAS. W. HARRIS,
Scranton Pa.   A & S NORDHEIMER   Troy, New York.
                                         TORONTO, CA.

Rollicking Rams

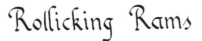

Button up your waistcoat, button up your shoes, have an-oth-er li-quor and

throw a-way the blues.   Be like me, and good for a spree from now till the

day is dawn-ing. For I am a mem-ber of the Rol-lick-ing Rams.   Come and be a mem-ber

of the Rol-lick-ing Rams, The only boys to make a noise from now till the day is dawning:

We scorn such drink as le-mon-ade,   soda seltzer beer, The liquors of our club I'd

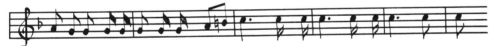

tell to you but I can't for there's ladies here.   Come a-long,   come a-long,   come, come,

come, come, come a-long.

2. When once you're a member of the Rollicking Rams,
   All things are real we have no shams,
   Except Champagne, good Champagne,
   We drink till the day is dawning:
   In all the pockets of the Rollicking Rams,
   Each one puts a bottle of Cham,
   And on some doorstep sit and drink,
   Till daylight in the morning:

With a pocket full of money, the Police make right
To what we do they're blind,
Such as pulling down bells and breaking lamps,
For which we should be fined.
Come along, come along, come, come.

Chorus

3. The Milkman in the morning, he knows us Rams,
We follow up behind and empty the cans,
Which down the Area he has put, for breakfast in the morning:
Upset a coffee stall, as we go home;
With us our Landladies pick a bone,
And get kicked out of house and home,
Without a moments warning;
But we don't care we're single men,
Not hampere[d] with a wife,
So now my friends, if you like the style,
Come and spend a noisy life.
Come along, come along, come, come.

Chorus

I've Only Been Down To The Club

Last night I was out rather late,— 'Twas on-ly an in-no-cent spree,— My

wife for my coming did wait,— When sleep-ing I thought she would be,— I

found her in tem-per and tears— Oh! she cried, it's a sin and a shame— And she

scratch'd both my eyes and my ears, but I told her I soon would explain——

Chorus

The "Club" had a meeting to-night, love, Of busi-ness we had a great sight,

love; Don't think for a moment I'm tight, love, I've on-ly been down to the Club.

2. My boots I left down in the hall,
   And softly I crept up the stairs;
   I kept rather close to the wall,
   And thought to ascend unawares.
   But, just as I got to the door,
   I seemed to get lost in the dark,
   I stumbled and fell on the floor,
   And just then I could only remark:

CHORUS

271

3. She sobbed and she wept and she screamed,
   And said she'd go back to her ma;
   While I on the mantel-piece leaned,
   And tried to enjoy my cigar,
   I promised to buy her a dress,
   If she'd let me alone for awhile;
   Then I gave her a sweet little kiss,
   And I saw her beginning to smile.

   (*Spoken*) So I thought it a favorable opportunity to assure her, once more, as a
   positive fact, that,

CHORUS

CHAMPAGNE CHARLIE.

COMIC SONG

FOR CHAMPAGNE CHARLIE IS MY NAME, CHAMPAGNE CHARLIE IS MY NAME. CHAMPAGNE CHARLIE IS MY NAME, CHAMPAGNE CHARLIE IS MY NAME. GOOD FOR ANY GAME AT NIGHT, MY BOYS, GOOD FOR ANY GAME AT NIGHT, MY BOYS. GOOD FOR ANY GAME AT NIGHT, MY BOYS, WHO'LL COME AND JOIN ME IN A SPREE.

PIANO SONG

MUSIC BY

Champagne Charlie

I've seen a deal of gai-e-ty through-out my noisy life. With all my grand ac-complish-
ments I ne'er could get a wife. The thing I most ex-cel in is the P. R. F. G. game, A
noise all night, in bed all day, and swimming in Cham-pagne. For Champagne
Char-lie is my name, Champagne Char-lie is my name. Good for an-y game at
night my boys, good for an-y game at night my boys, Champagne Char-lie is my
name, Champagne Char-lie is my name. Good for an-y game at night, boys,
who'll come and join me in a spree.

2. The way I gain'd my title's by a hobby which I've got,
Of never letting others pay, however long the shot,
Whoever drinks at my expense are treated all the same;
From Dukes and Lords to Cabmen down, I make them drink Champagne. For

CHORUS

274

3. From Coffee and from supper rooms, from Poplar to Pall Mall,
   The girls on seeing me exclaim, "Oh! what a Champagne swell!"
   The notion 'tis of ev'ry one, if 'twere not for my name,
   And causing so much to be drunk, they'd never make Champagne. For

CHORUS

4. Some epicures like Burgundy, Hock, Claret, and Moselle,
   But Moet's Vintage only satisfies this Champagne swell;
   What matter if to bed I go, and head is muddled thick,
   A bottle in the morning sets me right then very quick. For

CHORUS

5. Perhaps you fancy what I say is nothing else but chaff,
   And only done, like other songs, to merely raise a laugh;
   To prove that I am not in jest each man a bottle of Cham—
   I'll stand fizz round—yes that I will, and stand it—like a lamb.

CHORUS

I'll NEVER GET DRUNK ANY MORE

As sung by Harrigan AND Hart.

Words by
Ned Harrigan.

Music by
Prof. Dave Braham.

BOSTON
White, Smith & Company
298 300 Washington St

Chicago
G. F. Root & Sons.

N. York
J. L. Peters.

San Francisco
M. Gray.

Entered according to act of Congress in the year 1874 by White Smith & Co in the office of the Librarian of Congress at Washington

I'll Never Get Drunk Any More

I re-mem-ber when a bit of a boy, the lesson they taught me at home. If I want-ed to be a great man I must leave all the li-quor a-lone — My fa-ther he was a great drink-er He nev-er was so-ber a day — And when he'd roll in, in the morn-ing Oh these are the words he would say — I'll nev-er get drunk an-y more I'll nev-er get drunk an-y more — the pledge I will take, the whis-key I'll shake, Oh, I'll nev-er get drunk an-y more. —

2. Well of course you know I took after my dad
   And I got so I'd take a wee drop
   But a little it goes a great way
   It's the divels own job for to stop
   Whin I married my wife I was sober
   I drank nothing but coffee and tay
   I was drunk the night of the wedding
   Thin to her these words I did say.

   CHORUS

3. Whinever I get a dose of the blues
   I sind for a bottle and bowl
   Of the rale ould stuff in the closet
   Thin into me bed shure I roll,
   When I wake me head it is swimmin
   Pulverized wid the liquor I lay,
   Then I take a cocktail in the morning
   And these are the words that I say.

   Chorus

4. If I had the pluck of Napoleleon
   Wid the good since of General Grant
   Like a sober old judge I'd lave off the budge
   On my word and my honor I cant—
   You might try for to take Giberalter
   And talk till my hair it was gray,
   And when I lay down in me coffin
   These are the words that I say.

   Chorus

I NEVER DRINK BEHIND THE BAR

AS SUNG IN

ED. HARRIGAN'S

NEW PLAY,

"THE McSORLEYS,"

EMBRACING

I never drink behind the bar.	McNally's Row of Flats.
The Old Feather Bed.	The Charleston Blues. *March and Chorus.*
The Market on Saturday Night.	

WORDS BY

ED. HARRIGAN,

MUSIC BY

DAVE BRAHAM.

NEW YORK:
Published by WM. A. POND & CO., 25 Union Square,
(Broadway, bet. 15th & 16th Sts.)
Chicago: CHICAGO MUSIC CO., 152 State St.

I Never Drink Behind The Bar

I used to have a fine sa-loon with mir-rors on the wall. The fin-est class would
nev-er pass but just drop in and call; Good morn-ing, Pete, they'd say to me, you're
look-ing slick ta-ta, Oh, will you jine? I must de-cline while I'm be-hind the bar.

Chorus

I nev-er drink be-hind the bar but I will take a mild ci-gar I'll take a
sip of pol-i-nar I nev-er drink be-hind the bar.

2. Oh, like a pink I mix a drink and toss the glass in style;
This round on you a dollar due, I whisper with a smile;
Oh, don't go home, I'm quite alone, you've time to catch a car,
Try one with me, oh, don't you see that I'm behind the bar.

CHORUS

3. Oh, I could mix a lemonade, a cocktail, or gin fiz,
'Twas given out that none about could beat me at my biz;
Oh, your a lally cooler, Pete, a reg'lar la-di-da,
They'd wink at me, and bet a "V" I'd drink behind the bar.

CHORUS

4. I'd stand a lot of coaxing, and take taffy, too, you bet,
But if they'd try to hang me up, the house was not to let;
You know me, Pete, they'd say to me, you also know my pa,
I'm good for all, come, take a ball! 'Twas cash behind the bar.

CHORUS

But OH!
WHAT A DIFFERENCE
IN THE MORNING.

Another
great Hit
"Lilly Lally Dilly Dally
Oh! My Head"
Price 40 ¢

Comic Song.

WORDS BY
HARRY MILLER.
MUSIC BY
FELIX McGLENNON.

40 ¢

Published by

S. Brainard's Sons Co.
CHICAGO.

Oh, What A Difference In The Morning

How fun-ny the various sights that ap-pear, at night, at night! We seem to in-hab-it a different sphere, at night, at night! We see a young fellow go 'round with "the boys," He o-pens cham-pagne, a-mid rack-et and noise, and he spends his last cent while the spree he enjoys, at night, at night! But oh, what a diff'rence in the morn-ing! Then comes re-pen-tance at the dawn-ing! With e-le-gant black eyes, and a head just twice its size, he in-ter-views Judge Duf-fy, in the morning!

2. You see, at a ball, a fair girl you admire,
   At night, at night!
   To gaze on her beauty you never could tire,
   At night, at night!
   Her face is perfection, her form is divine!
   Her eyes are twin diamonds like gold her locks shine
   And you'd kneel at her feet to say, "Dearest be mine!"
   At night, at night!
   But oh, what a diff'rence in the morning!
   What alterations at the dawning!
   The locks you thought so fair,
   They are dangling o'er a chair,
   Her form is like a hat-rack, in the morning!

3. And then there's the frivolous gay married man,
   At night, at night!
   To tell what he gets at is part of my plan,
   At night, at night!
   With plenty of money, he goes on the booze,
   He meets some old pals, and they have a carouse,
   And when he gets home on the door-step he'll snooze,
   At night, at night!
   But oh, what a diff'rence in the morning!
   Then comes repentance with the dawning!
   Tho' he's very very dry,
   For a drink he'll vainly cry,
   For his wife's been thro' his pockets, in the morning!

4. A young man went courting his sweetheart, so dear,
   At night, at night!
   He never imagin'd her old man was near,
   At night, at night!
   He thought he was safely upstairs in his bed,
   He sat by her side, that young lover, 'tis said,
   Till he heard a loud voice which o'er-came him with dread,
   At night, at night!
   But oh, what a diff'rence in the morning!
   Hurt were his "panties" at the dawning!
   A number eleven boot,
   With his feelings didn't suit,
   And he took his breakfast standing, in the morning!

Down Where The Wurzburger Flows

Now po-ets may sing of the dear Fa-ther land and the soft flow-ing dream-y old

Rhine   Be-side the Blue Dan-ube in fan-cy they stand   and they rave of its

beau-ties di-vine   But there is a spot, where the sun nev-er shines, where

mirth and good fel-low-ship reign   For dear old Bo-hem-ia my lone-ly heart

pines   and I long to be there once a-gain   Take me down, down, down

where the Wurz-burg-er flows, flows, flows   It goes down, down, down but no-

bod-y knows where it goes   Just or-der two seid-els of la-ger or three   If I

don't want to drink it please force it on me, The Rhine may be fine but a cold stein for

mine,   down where the Wurz-burg-er flows

2. The Rhine by moonlight's a beautiful sight,
   When the wind whispers low thro' the vines,
   But give me some good old Rathskellar at night
   Where the brilliant electric light shines.
   The poets may think it's delightful to hear
   The nightingale piping his lay.
   Give me a piano a cold stein of beer
   And a fellow who knows how to play.

CHORUS

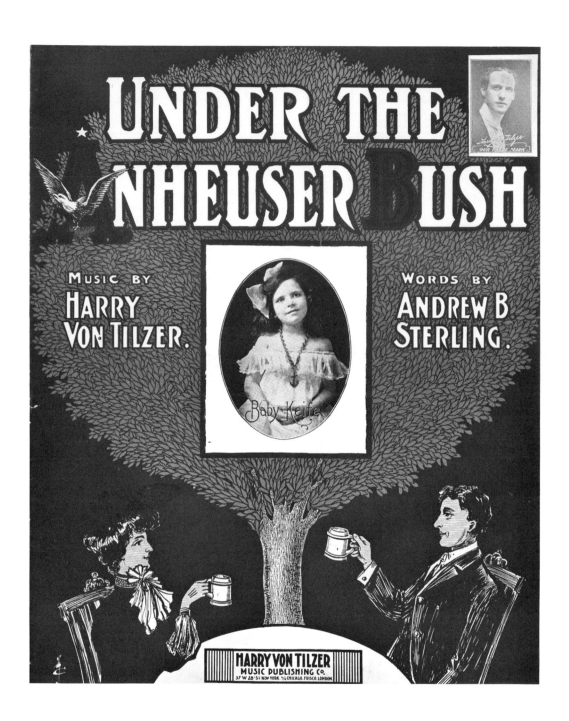

286

Under The Anheuser Bush

Tempo di Valse

Talk a-bout the shade of the shel-ter-ing palms Praise the bam-boo tree and its wide spread-ing

charms, There's a lit-tle bush that grows right here in town, You know its name, it has won such re-

nown; Of-ten with my sweet-heart just af-ter the play, To this lit-tle place then my foot-steps will stray

If she hes-i-tates when she looks at the sign, Soft-ly I whis-per, "Now Sue don't de-cline."

Chorus

Come, Come, Come and make eyes with me, un-der the An-heus-er Bush Come, Come,

drink some "Bud-wise" with me un-der the An-heus-er Bush, Hear the old Ger-man band,

Just let me hold your hand Yah! Do, Do, Come and have a stein or two, un-der the An-heus-

er Bush.

2. Rave about the place where your swells go to dine,
Picture Sue and me with our sandwich and stein,
Underneath the bush where the good fellows meet,
Life seems worth living, our joy is complete;
If you're sad at heart, take a trip there tonight,
You'll forget your woe and your eyes will grow bright,
There you'll surely find me with my sweetheart Sue,
Come down this ev'ning I'll introduce you.

CHORUS

The Beer that Made Milwaukee Famous

DAN McAVOY'S
BIG SONG HIT
in KLAW & ERLANGER'S
PRODUCTION
OF
Mr BLUEBEARD

WORDS AND
MUSIC BY

Dan McAvoy

PUBLISHED BY
SOL-BLOOM
NEW ZEALAND BLDG.
37th & BROADWAY.
NEW YORK

The Beer That Made Milwaukee Famous

When Ro-ger Mc Nal-ly re-tired from the force, he opened up a fine sa-loon —

His daugh-ter Nellie was the head cashier, The waiter was a big black coon —

He in-vit-ed all of the ci-ty sports & all from the City Hall. The May-or he was there,

the judge was in the chair, and some al-der-men from St. Paul.— The

big Dutch band, the fin-est in the land, played till five o'-clock, Ma-ry Anne Breen,

she kicked the tam-bo-rine, she woke the en-tire block. Mar-ty Mc-Gee threw a-way the

Key that be-longed to Murphy's trunk, and the beer that made Mil-wau-kee famous made all

New York drunk.

2. When Michael McClusky got up to make a speech,
   Somebody yelled, "Sit down."
   Gilhooly the plumber says, "Mac, you're it!"
   You could hear him 'way down town.
   They started to playing Kilkinny for me,
   Killarney's Lakes and Hills,
   They turned out the lights,
   Had half a dozen fights,
   As you know the Irish will.

CHORUS

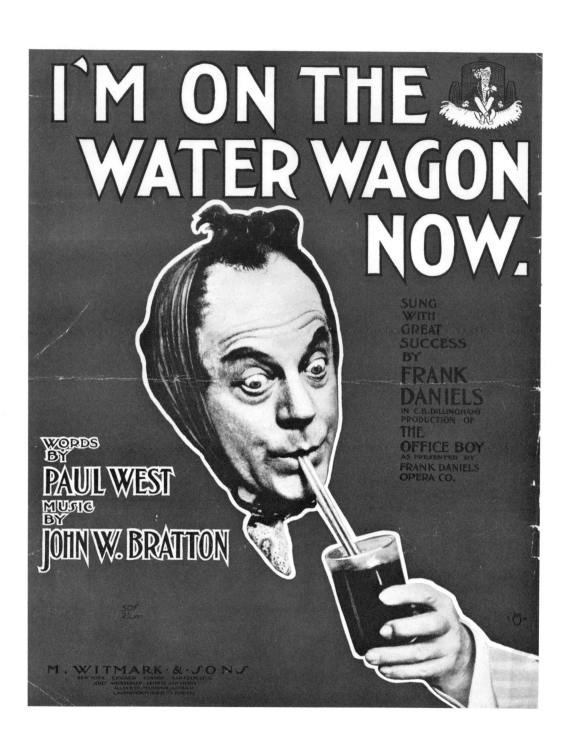

I'm On The Water Wagon Now

Of all the sport-y, sport-y boys who sport a-round the town, I used to be the sport-i-est and wore the King sport's crown, 'Twas John-ny-set-em-up a-gain, when a-ny one I'd meet I drank most a-ny-thing that was-n't thick e-nough to eat, The brew-'ries all worked o-ver-time to sat-is-fy my thirst, Of all the hu-man res-er-voirs I must have been the worst. I bought an au-to-mo-bile, but I ru-ined the ma-chine, For ev-'ry time I start-ed out I'd drink the gas-o-line.

Refrain

But I'm on the wa-ter wag-on now I nev-er get a jag on now I am rid-ing smooth and light-ly, To my seat I am strapp'd tight-ly, For I'm on the wa-ter wag-on now.

2. I don't know how it happened 'twas an accident, that's all,
   I went home sober by mistake and entered my front hall,
   The watch dog saw me coming, and he grabbed my trousers tight,
   The children did not know me, and they ran away in fright,
   My wife scream'd thieves and burglars, you'd have thought I was a mouse.
   She called police, and said there is a strange man in the house.
   They took me to the station and my finish I could see
   I had to get a bundle on to prove that I was me.

But I'm on the water wagon now.
I never get a jag on now.
No more coppers that are torrid,
No cold tow'ls upon my forehead,
For I'm on the water wagon now.

3. One night I went home very late and pretty well lit up.
I hunted 'round for one more drink, found something in a cup.
I drank it, though it tasted queer, then tumbled into bed.
Next morn my wife awakened me, "Get up, we're robbed," she said.
She'd put two point lace tidies in a cup to soak, said she,
She couldn't find them anywhere, wherever could they be?
I acted very innocent, but had to own my sin
When Irish point lace whiskers started sprouting on my chin.
But I'm on the water wagon now.
I never get a jag on now.
Ginger ale or sars'parilla
Is sufficient of a thriller,
For I'm on the water wagon now.

4. The fateful day that I swore off I never shall forget.
The papers printed extras, 'twas exciting, you can bet.
Bartenders begged me not to quit. They cried with bated breath
That if I did their families would surely starve to death.
Cab drivers wept to think that they would drive me home no more.
Distilleries and brew'ries have "To Let" upon the door.
And eighty-two drink chemists who had places on my beat,
Have had to quit their bus'ness and are working in the street.
For I'm on the water wagon now.
I never get a jag on now.
Keeley Cures and Carrie Nation
Point to me with admiration,
For I'm on the water wagon now.

N. Currier (Pre-Ives)

9

IF YOU WERE TO ASK a few acquaintances to name one famous American team, you would naturally receive an assortment of replies. The youngster of the 1960's, sophisticated, with a leaning toward popular music, would suggest Simon and Garfunkel. His father, remembering the movies of his childhood, would venture Laurel and Hardy. The father's banker would probably come up with Dun and Bradstreet. And the owner of the antique shop around the corner would be almost certain to nominate Currier and Ives.

Currier and Ives—the lithographers of a century ago—whose artistry, when contemplated today, brings on a wave of nostalgia for the U.S.A. that was. A team in a million!

But it was a team that started as a one-man performance. This pair did not emerge fully formed, like Athena from the brow of Zeus, nor did they find immediate kinship, one with the other, like Romulus and Remus. In fact, Mr. Ives was a Johnny-come-lately for the considerably older Mr. Currier, who worked alone for over fifteen years before taking young Ives into his establishment.

Nathaniel Currier was born in 1813 in Roxbury, Massachusetts. At fifteen he was apprenticed to the lithography firm of William and John Pendleton, whose business had been established in Boston in 1824. After five years, he left the Pendleton firm to work for M. E. D. Brown, a Philadelphia lithographer.

The following year he and John Pendleton decided to go into business together in New York. Pendleton preceded Nathaniel to that city, and upon his arrival received another offer so attractive that he decided to accept it; the Pendleton-Currier alliance was dissolved forthwith. Currier, now seeking a new associate, met a man named Adam Stodart and in 1834 formed a partnership with him under the firm name of Stodart and Currier.

Like other lithographers of the first half of the nineteenth century, Nathaniel Currier had a predilection for designing the title pages of popular sheet music. Stodart, who had been in partnership with a Frenchman named William Dubois, a New York music publisher on lower Broadway (there was no upper Broadway then), was now determined to venture into the field of lithography, a sideline not at all unusual for music publishers to assay. How he met with Nathaniel Currier is not known, but they set up a small plant at 7 Wall Street and began to turn out run-of-the-mill lithographs. The firm did not last long; Stodart quickly lost his taste for lithography and retired to devote his entire efforts to music publishing with his old sidekick Dubois. Currier continued alone, and in 1835 was operating at 1 Wall Street, moving later to other parts of downtown New York.

Currier's lithographs, in the 1830's and 1840's, were not sought after avidly, but were acquired in what was probably a perfunctory way for the time, just as the casual buyer of a framed print would make his selection depending more on the subject matter than on the skill of the artist or artisan.

Currier's early work included some eighty sheet-music covers. He seemed particularly fond of illustrating *comic* songs. Not all his designs for these were original; he was never averse to copying or redesigning a cover which someone else had developed. But when he did this, his own title pages were cleaner or more subtly sensitive, as a rule, than those which gave him his ideas.

One of his earliest covers is on "My Long Tail Blue" (see page 299), published in New York in the middle 1830's. It depicts a Negro in a cutaway coat with long tails, wearing a stovepipe hat. The lithograph bears the name of Stodart and Currier; and the subject of the song is indeed a dandy, proud as punch of his costume and eager to talk about it.

> Some Niggers they have but one coat,
> But you see I've got two;
> I wears a jacket all the week,
> And Sunday my long tail blue.

After exhibiting confidence in his self-satisfying appearance, for seven verses, he concludes:

Now all you chaps that wantsa wife,
And don't know how to do;
Just look at me and I'll show you how,
For to swing your long tail blue.

One of Currier's most amusing covers adorns "The Table D'Hote" (see page 301), an English composition first sung at the Theatre Royal Covent Garden in London, then published around 1840 in New York. The verses are interspersed with sharp repartee.

It starts mildly enough:

Hail to the hour when the circling bowl,
And the laugh and the festal chorus,
Fills with delight each jovial soul,
And drives dull care before us.

Then the conversational part of the piece takes over. For example:

SNUFFLING GENT: "Waiter, hand my plate to the Chairman, and ask him for the Parson's nose, if you please." OLD GENT: "I wish, Mr. Snuffle, you'd blow your nose, it's very unpleasant." SNUFFLE: "Blow it yourself, Sir,—it's quite as near to you as it is to me."

Then back to "Hail to the hour when the circling bowl," etc.

Other examples of his best work adorned the title pages of English songs which were imported and sung by Americans. So much in demand were they that American music publishers reissued them, commissioning Nathaniel Currier to lithograph title pages to enhance the sales.

One popular piece was "All the World Is Scheming" (see page 304), written by J. E. Carpenter, who had other hits to his credit. A Mr. Fitzwilliam was the performing artist who introduced it to an American audience. The singer contemplates:

Oh! times are really very hard,
There's little cash about now;
Tho' 'tis not that that I regard,
If I could make it out now.
What causes such a panic, I,
To think of have been dreaming,
And would you guess the reason why?
'Tis all mankind are scheming.

CHORUS: With plans your purse to renovate,
The Papers they are teeming,

295

So now's your time to Speculate
For all the world are scheming.

Another Englishman, Jonathan Blewitt, composed a song called "The
Handsome Man" (see page 307), which was popular in England and soon
traveled across the Atlantic. Blewitt was a Londoner by birth who spent
part of his life in Ireland and served as the grand organist of the Masonic
Church there. He achieved considerable prominence, too, as a conductor
in Dublin, later becoming director of music at London's Sadler's Wells
Theatre. Although he wrote many operas in Ireland and England, he was
best known for his songs. In all he composed two thousand pieces of vocal
music, which must certainly have made him the Harry von Tilzer of early
nineteenth-century Great Britain. Most were comic songs, and "The Hand-
some Man" was one of the best.

Currier and his artist, E. Brown, copied the English title page closely.
The figure of the "Handsome Man" is a masterpiece of caricature. As for
the song itself, the author, John Francis, proclaims:

> My nose is very aquiline,
> My eyes are very Grand,
> My teeth are very beautiful,
> And five feet eight I stand.
> My whiskers black, Mustachio's too,
> My waist a child could span,
> My dark hair curls, My foot is small,
> I am a handsome Man.

Also, you might have gathered, a conceited ass.

Blewitt wrote another song which Currier illustrated. This one was
"Tarnation Strange" or "Yankee Wonders" (see page 309), and Currier's
title page, a series of small vignettes, pictures some of the queer things that
Yankees do.

Henry Coleman, known as The American "Boz" (Dickens) wrote verses
like this:

> A waggoner dreaming of loads,
> With his harness himself put his dray in,
> And trotting along o'er the roads,
> Never stopp'd till he found himself neighing.

And again:

> Then a Rifleman there's such a shot
> The birds when they see him a loading

Come down and fall dead on the spot
They can't bear the noise of exploding.

Another English import, a lively waltz entitled "John Strauss! John Strauss! The Girls are All Mad" (see page 312) was illustrated by Currier with five lively little sketches depicting couples cavorting through the steps of the waltz.

The Strauss who enraptured the young ladies of 1840 was not the Johann of "Blue Danube" fame, but his father, who was the first waltz king of the Continent. From his native Vienna, where the older Strauss's waltzes were introduced, they spread rapidly to France, and then leaped over the English Channel, where the young ladies of London were ravished by the dulcet strains in 3/4 time. Several of Strauss's melodies were introduced by the adapter, Philip Klitz, who wrote the verses as well. They commence:

> John Strauss, John Strauss, the girls are all mad,
> Whirling, and twirling, tis really too bad,
> From night till morning, the great and the grand,
> Do nothing but Waltz to John Strauss' band.

A subject constantly before the American public from the 1830's on was temperance. In the early 1840's temperance societies sprang up along the eastern seaboard from New England to Maryland, and they gave much concern to those people who felt that the use of alcohol was an important right of citizens, not to be tampered with.

Many comic songs, ridiculing the efforts of the antialcohol groups, found favor with the public. For one, "The Tee-to-tal Society" (see page 314), published in 1840, Currier did a title page with four Cruikshankian illustrations, making us wonder whether they might have been originally inspired by that great English caricaturist. The song, introduced at the Park Theater in New York, has no kind word for anybody; but is full of sly wit and broad innuendo. For example:

> I'm come to exhort you so free,
> All you that so fond of the bottle, are,
> And when you my argument see,
> Ev'ry one will become a *Tee-To-Tal-Er*
> Of gin, brandy, rum, wine or beer
> To drink is a great impropriety,
> Of trash, I'd have you steer clear,
> And join the *Tee-to-tal Society*.

An old man that was troubled with corns,
That scarcely the stairs could he hobble up,
He used to drink beer out of horns,
And all sorts of liquors would gobble up.
His corns have all left one by one,
And now he's the pink of sobriety,
And pray how was all this done?
Why? He joined the *Teetotal Society*.

From the personal standpoint Nathaniel Currier was a gentlemanly and liberal man whose ideas were far ahead of his time. He had a remarkable awareness of public taste and good business sense. His attractive personality made him many friends. Among those who frequented his shop were Henry Ward Beecher, Horace Greeley, and P. T. Barnum. At his summer home in Amesbury, Massachusetts, he was visited often by John Greenleaf Whittier.

In 1852, Nathaniel and his brother Charles hired a twenty-eight-year-old bookkeeper named James Merritt Ives. He fitted so well into the expanding firm that five years later he was made a partner, and an all-American team had come into being. Alas, no sheet-music covers bear the imprint of Currier *and Ives*.

The neat letters "N. Currier's Lith., N.Y." appear on song covers with pictures of pretty girls, militia, royalty, maritime subjects, and ballerinas. But even more entertaining, and more popularly appealing, are the title pages of those comical topical songs in the era when America was young.

MY LONG TAIL BLUE,

NEW YORK.

Published by J. L. Hewitt & Co. 137, Broadway.

My Long Tail'd Blue

I've come to town to see you all, I ask you how d'ye do? I'll sing a song not ve-ry long, A-

bout my long tail blue. Oh! for the long tail blue. Oh! for the long tail blue. I'll sing a song

not ve-ry long a-bout my long tail blue.

2. Some Niggers they have but one coat,
But you see I've got two;
I wears a jacket all the week,
And Sunday my long tail blue.
O! for the long tail blue, &c.

3. Jim Crow is courting a white gall,
And yaller folks call her Sue;
I guess she back'd a nigger out,
And swung my long tail blue.
O! for the long tail blue, &c.

4. Jim Crow got mad and swore he'd fight,
With sword and pistol too;
But I guess I back'd the nigger out,
When he saw my long tail blue.
O! for the long tail blue, &c.

5. As I was a gwoin up Market Street,
I holler'd arter Sue,
The watchman came and took me up,

And spilte [split] my long tail blue.
O! for the long tail blue, &c.

6. I took it to a Tailor's shop,
To see what he could do;
He took a needle and some thread,
And mended my long tail blue.
O! for the long tail blue, &c.

7. If you want to win the Ladie's hearts,
I'll tell you what to do;
Go to a tip top Tailor's shop
And buy a long tail blue.
O! for the long tail blue, &c.

8. Now all you chaps that wantsa wife,
And don't know how to do;
Just look at me and I'll show you how,
For to swing your long tail blue.
O! for the long tail blue, &c.

THE "TABLE D'HOTE"

N. Currier's Lith.

A COMIC SONG

WRITTEN & SUNG BY Mr C. HILL

of the

Theatre Royal Covent Garden

The Music by

AUBER

Price 50 cts.

Pub. by James L. Hewitt & Co. No 239 Broadway. N.York.

The Table d' Hote

Hail to the hour when the cir-cling bowl, and the laugh and the fest-al chor-us, Fills with de-light each jo-vial soul, and drives dull care be-fore us When the friend-ly toast, and the ro-sy wine and the thril-ling song, and the strain di-vine, give zest to the hour when the cir-cling bowl, and the laugh and the fest-al chor-us, fills with de-light each jo-vial soul, and drives dull care be-fore us.

(*Spoken*)* "Major, shall I have the pleasure of taking a glass of wine with you?" SCOTCHMAN: "Maister Hodges, I'll trouble you for a few of them broths."—"Upon my life here's a mess."—"What's the matter Major?—What are you grumbling at?"—"Why, who ever heard of egg sauce with carp?"—"Oh, that's what you're carping at, eh?—Come, that's very well done of me." OLD GENT: "Well done, is it? I wish I could say as much of this pork." MAJOR: "By the bye, why ar'n't there no Eggs in St. Domingo?—Oh, 'cos they've thrown off the yoke, and don't allow us no whites." FOP: "I declare these chickens are not half roasted." MAJOR: "Why are they like innocent criminals? 'Cos they're hardly done by, and ought to be respitted." SNUFFLING GENT: "Waiter, hand my plate to the Chairman, and ask him for the Parson's nose, if you please." OLD GENT: "I wish, Mr. Snuffle, you'd blow your nose, it's very unpleasant." SNUFFLE: "Blow it yourself, Sir, it's quite as near to you as it is to me." (*Dog yelps.*) "Oh! Crimony! here's a lark!—I'm blow'd if the waiter hasn't fallen over Mounseer's poodle dog, and upset all the Egg sauce down Mr. Dennis McHogg's back."—MAJOR: "McHogg, did you say?—Then serve him up on a clean plate, for now we've made eggs and bacon of him."—So,

"Hail to the hour when circling bowl," &c. &c. &c.

* Not all speakers are identified.

2. Now merily ring the tables round,
   The Chairman calls to silence;
   In the mirthful hour that the wine has crown'd,
   We may hear their hurrahs aye a mile hence,
   Soon the morn will break, and the day star lamp
   Will light us home, and our revels damp,
   Then merily ring the tables round,
   The Chairman calls to silence;
   In the mirthful hour that the wine has crown'd,
   We may hear their hurrahs aye a mile hence.

(*Spoken*)* "Order, Chair, Chair, Order,—attention for Mr. Snuffle's song." (*Mr. Snuffle sings a verse of "Has she then failed in her truth."*)—"Bravo, bravo." IRISH GENT: "Faith it's Mr. Snuffle that can sing like a tay-kettle, and here's a toast I'll be giving him after it,—'May the man who draws his sword on his friend, find he's left it at home.' "—"Bravo, bravo,—Order, Gentlemen, order,—Sit down, Mr. Briggs, I'm happy to inform you, you've been drunk in your absence."—MAJOR: "Now, Briggs, my boy, get up and make a speech." BRIGGS (*very timid*): "I never made a speech in all my life." MAJOR: "Stand up, I'll prompt you,—Gentlemen unaccustomed as I am to—" BRIGGS: "Unaccustomed as I am to—" MAJOR: "Speak out—" BRIGGS: "Speak out—" MAJOR: "I feel—" BRIGGS: "I feel—" MAJOR: "Take your hands out of your pockets." BRIGGS: "Take your hands out of your pockets." MAJOR: "Pooh, sit down—ha, ha, ha,— "Bravo Briggs,"—"Order, attention, Gentlemen, and Mr. Markham will favor the company with a song." [MR. MARKHAM]: "Gentlemen, I'll attempt 'The pilgrim of love'—hem,—'Orynthia my beloved'—(*dog howls*) 'I call in vain'—(*dog*) 'Orynthia' —(*dog*) Turn the dog out—'Orynthia'—(*dog howls again*) 'Echo hears and calls again' —(*dog*) 'A mimic voice repeats the name around.' "—(*The dog howls is supposed to be kicked, yelps, &c.*)

"Now merrily rings the table round," &c. &c. &c.

All The World Is Scheming

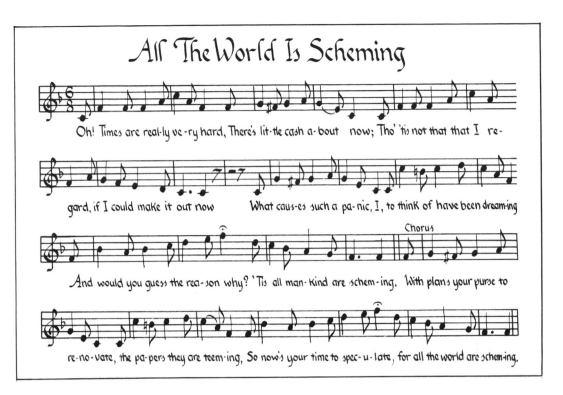

Oh! Times are real-ly ve-ry hard, There's lit-tle cash a-bout now; Tho' 'tis not that that I re-gard, if I could make it out now What caus-es such a pa-nic, I, to think of have been dream-ing And would you guess the rea-son why? 'Tis all man-kind are schem-ing. With plans your purse to

Chorus

re-no-vate, the pa-pers they are teem-ing, So now's your time to spec-u-late, for all the world are schem-ing.

2. They say, it's all because Reform
Has pass'd the House of Commons,
Where promises they ne'er perform,
They're such a set of rum 'uns;
They'd vote a Joint-Stock Property,
Those Radical debaters,
And organise a Company
For selling "Hot baked 'Taters."
With plans your purse to renovate,
The Papers they are teeming.
So now's your time to speculate;
For all the world are scheming.

3. There's Brown, who drives an Omnibus
From Greenwich up to London,
He's always making such a fuss
And says as how he's undone;
"Those Rail-way Companies," says he
"Sarves me in such a manner,
No *Tradesmen* ever rides with me

While they takes ev'ry *Tanner*.
With plans, &c.

4. There's even the poor Watermen,
They say it a disgrace is,
Those Steam-boat Companies should
plan
To ruin all their places;
There's such a lot of Steam about
To do what they require,
That the *River boils*, and soon no doubt
They'll "set the Thames a-fire."
With plans, &c.

5. Our Youths no more take rapid strides
In Boarding-school or College,
A Joint-stock Company provides
Them all with useful knowledge;
The Penny-Magazine in thrall
Their faculties has taken,

The Blacksmiths study *Locke*, and all
The Cheesemongers know *Bacon*.
With plans, &c.

6. A Company that all must praise
Supplies the Town with Water,
A Dairy-Company conveys
New Milk to ev'ry quarter;
And just because they thrive so well,
Hear what they mean to do now,
Get up a Company to sell
A *union of the two* now.
With plans, &c.

7. 'Tis not in life alone that we
These Companies need dread, Sir,
There's a Cemetery-company

Provides for us when dead, Sir,
You may be taken unawares
By Burying concoctors,
For I'm assured that all the Shares
Are *bought up by the Doctors*.
With plans, &c.

8. There's one thing tho' that puzzles me,
You'll own it is surprising,
A Joint-stock Banking-Company
We here and there see rising,
That folks have Money 'twould denote
Tho' I am more for thinking
What they call *Capital afloat*,
Is Capital *a sinking*.
With plans, &c.

THE HANDSOME MAN
Comic Song

"To shun these female plagues I'd be,
Deformed and rude as Pan.

"I wish they'd give me up, and say,
He's not a handsome Man."

Written by

JOHN FRANCES ESQ.

AUTHOR OF "THEY DONT PROPOSE"

Sung by Mr W. L. Hammond at the

New Strand Theatre in the Burletta.

THE MAN FOR THE LADIES

Composed by

J. BLEWITT

Pr. 50 Cts.

Published by James L. Hewitt & Co. 239 Broadway

NEW YORK.

The Handsome Man

My nose is very a-qui-line, My eyes are very grand, My teeth are ve-ry beau-ti-ful, and five feet eight I stand. My whis-kers black, mus-ta-chio's, too, My waist a child could span, My dark hair curls, my foot is small, I am a hand-some man, I am a ve-ry hand-some man, a ve-ry, ve-ry, ve-ry hand-some man, I am a ve-ry hand-some man, I am —— a hand-some man.

2. I wish my flirting nonsense were,
   Not told with such delight
   I wish my smiling gave no joy,
   My calling caus'd no fright,
   And would that I might be excus'd,
   From picking up each Fan,
   They're only dropt to be return'd,
   By such a handsome Man, &c.

3. I wish that I was very plain,
   I wish my eyes were green,
   I wish my hair was red and straight,
   My figure short and mean,

   To shun those female plagues I'd be
   Deformed, and rude as Pan;
   I wish they'd give me up and say
   He's not a Handsome Man, &c.

4. They take my Portrait on the sly,
   I don't know what to do;
   Letters in Scores come every day
   From lovers old and new:
   Each article of dress I wear,
   Most lovingly they scan;
   All clothes they look so well on me
   I'm such a handsome Man, &c.

OR

YANKEE WONDERS

Comic Song

sung by

Mr BUCKINGHAM

Written by

HENRY COLEMAN ESQ

(The American Boz)

The Music

Composed by

J. BLEWITT

A man sunk in absence of mind,
Took his boots off and laid them in bed sir
And not dreaming of aught of the kind
With the bootjack pull'd clean off his head sir

A man tied himself up for the clothes
And was sent to the washwomans daughter
And neer know it until his poor nose
Was fill'd full of soap-suds and water

A man there grew fifteen feet high
Tho' as thin and as pale as an adder
That when his collar but wanted a tie
He was forced to get up on a ladder

A waggoner dreaming of loads
With his harness himself put his dray in
And trotting along o'er the roads
Never stopp'd till he found himself neighing

NEW-YORK

HEWITT & JAQUES

N. Currier's Lith.

PUBLISHED BY

239 BROADWAY

Price 50 cts

Tarnation Strange

Yan-kee won-ders are now all the rage and I think with-out much con-tra-dic-tion I can prove in this e-ru-dite age that truth is much strang-er than fic-tion A man sunk in ab-sence of mind took his boots off and laid them in bed and not dream-ing of aught of the kind with the boot jack pull'd clean off his head (Oh yes) Is-n't it tar-na-tion strange (Oh yes) Is-n't it tar-na-tion strange?

2. There's a woman as large as a tree
   I can't say in what state they found her.
   But set off on a trot from her knee
   It will take you a week to get round her.
   There's a man cheats a cock of his crowing
   And he does it so shrill and so prime
   That the Sun was observ'd to be glowing
   Full two hours before its right time.
   Oh yes, &c.

3. Then a rifleman there's such a shot
   The birds when they see him a loading
   Come down and fall dead on the spot
   They can't bear the noise of exploding.
   A man there grew fifteen feet high
   Tho' as thin and as pale as an adder
   That when his collar but wanted a tie
   He was forc'd to get up on a ladder.
   Oh yes, &c.

4. Men take such a quantum of brandy,
   And inflame both their souls and their bodies,
   Buttons melt off their coats just like candy,
   With drinking so many hot toddies.
   A waggoner dreaming of loads,
   With his harness himself put his dray in,
   And trotting along o'er the roads,
   Never stopp'd till he found himself neighing.
   Oh yes, &c.

5. In the Post Office Box 'tother day,
   A Lady fast bound by Love's fetters,
   Threw herself without thinking they say,
   And got mixed up along with the letters;
   And off she'd been sent o'er the ocean
   With other dead letters to mingle,
   Had the Clerk not been seized with a notion
   To ask the fair dame was she single?
   Oh yes, &c.

6. A man tied himself up for the clothes,
   And was sent to the washwoman's daughter
   And ne'er knew it, until his poor nose
   Was fill'd full of soap-suds and water.
   Now I think I've described Yankee wonders,
   And my statement I never will change;
   You no doubt will think them all blunders,
   But you'll own they are "Tarnation Strange!"
   Oh yes, &c.

JOHN STRAUSS! JOHN STRAUSS!

"THE GIRLS ARE ALL MAD"

Comic Ballad,

Illustrative of the

BEAUTIES OF STRAUSS,

INTRODUCING   THE

GABRIELLE,

Hüldigung,

LA   ROSA   AND

PHILOMEL,

Ball Racketen,

ELIZABETHEN WALTZES.

WRITTEN & ADAPTED

BY

PHILIP KLITZ.

"Endearing Waltz to thy more melting tune,
Bow Irish Jig, and ancient Rigadoon;
Scotch Reels avaunt! and Country Dance, forego
Your future claims to each fantastic toe." *(Lord Byron)*

Pr. 75 cts.

NEW YORK

Published by HEWITT & JAQUES   239 Broadway.

N. Currier's Lith. N.Y.

John Strauss

John Strauss, John Strauss, the girls are all mad, Whirl-ing, and twirl-ing, 'tis real-ly too bad, From night till morn-ing, the great and the grand, do no-thing but waltz to John Strauss' band They say at Vi-en-na it's now such a rage, The King quits his throne, each stu-dent his page, Lack-a-dai-si-cal la-dies, who are not look-ing well, con-trive to keep twirl-ing to the Waltz "Phi-lo-mel."

2. Young Lady Maria who's just come from France,
   No wonder that she is so mad for the dance,
   A partner she has round her waist his arm's flung,
   And away they go twirling to the fam'd
   "Hül-Di-Gung."

3. And now as they thread, the gay mazy dance,
   Delighted they're swimming in pleasure's short trance,
   One lady has fainted, her beau's quite gallant,
   While the rest keep on twirling to
   "Les Fu-Sees Vo-lantes."

4. The Baronets wife has left her proud Lord,
   And prepares to commence, While the band strikes a chord,
   Delighted he smiles on his kind Cara Sposa,
   As she begins twirling to the Waltz call'd
   "La Rosa."

313

5. The man in moustachios seem'd ready to sink,
   Has refresh'd himself now, with a lemonade drink,
   One really would think they were tir'd to death,
   But still they keep twirling to th' Waltz
   "E-Li-Za-Beth."

6. The supper's now over, the lights are near out,
   We arrive at the end of this grand Waltzing rout,
   Musicians are tired and now may be seen,
   Nodding and fiddling,
   "God Save the Queen."

The Tee-to-tal Society

I'm come to ex-hort you so free, all you that so fond of the bot-tle are, and when you my ar-gu-ment see, ev'-ry one will be-come a Tee-to-tal-er Of gin, bran-dy, rum, wine, or beer to drink is a great im-pro-pri-e-ty, Of trash I'd have you steer clear, and join the Tee-to-tal So-ci-e-ty.

2. An old man that was troubled with corns, that scarcely the stairs could he hobble up,
   He used to drink beer out of horns, and all sorts of liquors would gobble up.
   His corns have all left one by one, and now he's the pink of sobriety.
   And pray how was all this done? *Why?* he joined the *Teetotal Society.*

3. Tother day my young pigs and old sow, I found to be far gone in liquor,
   In my family I this can't allow, to temperance being a sticker,
   They had with grain from the brewer been fed, but now they shall share in sobriety,
   Coffee grounds and tea leaves instead, and they shall join the *Teetotal Society.*

THE TEE-TOTAL SOCIETY,

His fireside in fact, was the picture of happiness

The sanctified Phiz of the Fellow persuaded him

AS SUNG

Mr CHAPMAN,

WITH THE

BY

AT THE

GREATEST APPLAUSE

PARK THEATRE.

The man that drinks water I'd have made a Pump of

When winter came on his great coat he grew thin in

His inside was stuffed full of Tea Leaves and Snow Water

Pr. 25 cts. Nt

New York ATWILL, *Publisher* 201 Broadway.

N Currier's Lith. N.Y.

4. A Teetotaler tother day died, the doctor his friend did entice out
Examined his stomach inside, and they say took a large lump of ice out.
This cant be true, for if ever we are ill, of Brandy we take a small moiety
And melt ice you know, *Brandy* it will, it has been tried by the *Teetotal Society*.

5. I wander about doing good, our society pays all my charges
Preaching two hours at least, to coal heavers working on barges.
But they said, "If you carried our coals, of beer you'll soon see the propriety."
But ah! they are sad wicked souls, they wont join the *Teetotal Society*.

6. Folks ask what makes my nose so red? I'll tell and end all this puzzling,
It 'ant drink what gets in my head, its blushing to see so much guzzling.
Drops of *Brandy* we take two or three, as medicine and no impropriety
And put some in our gruel and tea, its allowed by the *Teetotal Society*.

7. The people laugh at me oh! dear, and puts my mind in sad order works
And cries out whenever I appear, "How gets on the Temperance water works."
But I tells them I dont care dump, and preaches away on sobriety
And for example drinks out of the pump, since I joined the *Teetotal Society*.

8. In our progress there's nothing excells, in our efforts we never do slumber, sir,
We have dug six and fifty new wells! and erected of pumps a great number, sir,
I have here some Temperance tracts, of a most gratifying variety
That record some most wonderful facts, about the *Teetotal Society*.

9. A drunken beggar I very well know, quite lame and as thin as a rat he was
Led by a dog he would go, through the streets, for blind as a bat he was.
You'll scarcely believe what I say, he's now the pink of sobriety
He's got fat and can see as clear as day, since he joined the *Teetotal Society*.

10. One night in my house every week, I holds forth on the beauties of Temperance
Because when in public I speak, I'm subject to a good deal of imperance.
After a lecture on Coffee they sup, on Tea if they like for variety.
I charge a shilling a cup, since I joined the *Teetotal Society*.

Legacies from Grandma and Grandpa
10

IN THE DIM RECESSES of the minds of many of us there remain recollections of grandparents singing to us, when we were small, songs out of their own times or songs that they themselves heard as children from *their* grandparents.

Since up to a comparatively few years ago there were no computations of national ratings or figures on the number of records sold, I would venture that many of the songs sung to us by our grandparents were more popular with a greater proportion of the American people than are those whose records sales are highest today. Some of the best deserve inclusion in this chapter, and will bring back to mind melodies almost, but not quite, forgotten.

The oldest of these is "The Schoolmaster" (see page 327), which is scored as "a favorite glee for three voices." It was first published about 1834. The title page was designed by D. C. Johnston, the great American caricaturist of the period, who was known throughout New England and the East as the "American Cruikshank."

The melody is based on the second movement of Haydn's "Surprise" Symphony. Simple and catchy, it had been adapted many years before to the well-worn words of "Twinkle Twinkle Little Star."

Our glee starts:

> Come, come my children,
> I must see,
> How you can say your A B C.
> Go get your books
> And hither come to me
> And I will hear your E F G.

As the song continues, there is a trio to the same melody which just ticks off the letters of the alphabet. To help the rhyme scheme, it transposes the "W" and the "V," but apart from that, the author seems to know his letters without a slip.

The next well-known piece has been used for square dancing for many decades. The "Arkansas Traveller" (see page 330) was composed by Mose Case—whose name, incidentally, has never appeared elsewhere on a sheet of music and may therefore be pseudonymous. It combines a story, a dialogue, and a melody, nicely interwoven. The story, as printed on the first page of the sheet music, begins:

> This piece is intended to represent an Eastern man's experience among the inhabitants of Arkansas, showing their hospitality and the mode of obtaining it.
>
> Several years since he was travelling the State to Little Rock, the Capitol:— in those days Rail Roads had not been heard of and the Stage lines were very limited, so under the circumstances, he was obliged to travel the whole distance on foot. One evening about dusk he came across a small log house standing fifteen or twenty yards from the road and enclosed by a low rail fence, of the most primitive description. In the door sat a man playing a Violin; the tune was the "Arkansas Traveller," then, the most popular tune in that region. He kept repeating the first part of the tune over and over again, as he could not play the second part. At the time the traveller reached the house it was raining very hard, and he was anxious to obtain shelter from the storm;—the house looked anything but a shelter, as it was covered with clapboards and the rain was leaking into every part of it. The old man's daughter Sarah appeared to be getting supper, while a small boy was setting the table, and the old lady sat in the door near her husband, admiring the music.
>
> The Stranger on coming up, said:—"How do you do?"—the man merely glanced at him and continuing to play, said:—"I do as I please."

Then comes a bit of repartee between the stranger and the fiddler, in which the stranger can never impress on the old man his need for shelter. After evading every question asked the fiddler, to the Easterner's discomfort, the violinist starts again on his tune until the next question is raised. For example, when the stranger inquires:

> Give me some satisfaction if you please sir; where does this road go to?

The old man replies:

> Well it hain't moved a step since I've been here.

Then after another bit of fiddling, the stranger advances:

318

Why don't you cover your house? It leaks.

The old man replies:

Cause it's raining.

Stranger:

Then why don't you cover it when it's not raining?

Old man:

Cause it don't leak.

This was undoubtedly great repartee for stage performers one hundred years ago. After much such frustrating dialogue, interrupted by intermittent fiddling, the piece comes to an end with this final notation:

The stranger finding such poor accommodations, and thinking his condition could be bettered by leaving, soon left and finally succeeded in finding a Tavern with better fare. He has never had the courage to visit Arkansas since.

Another great song for our grandparents was "Billy Boy" (see page 332), published in 1847, arranged for the piano by Edward L. White, but with no clue to the author of the verses, the first of which goes as follows:

Oh where have you been Billy Boy, Billy Boy,
Oh, where have you been, charming Billy?
I have been to seek a wife,
She's the joy of my life,
She's a young thing and cannot leave her mother.

Each verse starts with a request for information about Billy's girl. Possibly the inquiry we remember best is:

Can she make a cherry pie, Billy Boy?

Another tremendously successful song of the 1840's, one which has been parodied through the years, was "Over There" (see page 334), not to be confused with the George M. Cohan masterpiece of World War I. As frequently happened, the song was either too well known or the author too modest for us to learn who wrote the words. Our piece was arranged by Charles Gossin, another unknown except for this most popular ditty, which ran through numerous editions and was distributed in thousands of copies.

319

One of the strange aspects of these verses is that apparently nobody is told where "Over There" *is*. They are only informed:

> Oh! Potatoes they grow small Over There!
> Oh! Potatoes they grow small Over There!
> Oh! Potatoes they grow small 'cause they plant 'em
>   in the fall,
> And then eats 'em tops and all over there!

With many of the reprints new verses were added, and these continued to accumulate well into the twentieth century, with some which might be classed as "curiosa," such as the one which starts: "The eagles they fly high, over there."

In the 1850's a very popular song was one "dedicated to all good children" and entitled "My Grandma's Advice." (See page 336.) It was a particular hit when delivered by a group of singers called the Tremaine Family. Its author remains unknown; the title page indicates only that the words and music are by "M." The melody is one of the catchiest of its day and the lyric is a real cutie. The first verse goes:

> My Grandma lives on yonder little green,
> Fine old lady as ever was seen;
> She often cautioned me with care,
> Of all false young men to beware.
> Tim–e–i tim–e um tum tim–e um pa ta
> Of all false young men to beware.

But after grandma has repeatedly discouraged her granddaughter from receiving the attentions of the young men, the girl finally thinks the thing through, and in the fifth verse comes up with a sage observation:

> Thinks I to myself there's some mistake,
> What a fuss these old folks make;
> If the boys and the girls had all been so fraid,
> *Then Grandma herself would have died an old maid.*

"Johnny Schmoker" (see page 338), which is still sung in small intimate groups and by college glee clubs, is the account of an old German musician making the sounds of a little German band. The song appeared in the 1860's and was advertised as having been "harmonized and arranged by B. F. Rix." Rix was certainly a pseudonym—many people believe for George F. Root, an important music publisher of Chicago. Root was one of the great Civil War song writers, producing some of the most stirring tunes of that time.

In addition to patriotic fervor, Root had a sense of humor. The fact that he himself wrote an introduction to "Johnny Schmoker," which was published by his firm, supports the conjecture that the song was Root's own.

The simple lyric was written in schoolboy German, and when it was sung nearly everyone knew what it meant. For example, the verse goes:

> Johnny Schmoker, Johnny Schmoker,
> Ich kann spielen, Ich kann spielen.

"Ich kann spielen" means "I can play," as a note at the bottom of the first page explains. That is all the singer needs to know. From then on the piece describes the sound of the drum, the fife, the triangle, the trombone, the cymbal, the violin and the toodle sach. The drum goes "rub a dub a dub," the trombone goes "bom, bom, bom," the triangle goes "knock, knock," the toodle sach goes "whack, whack, whack," and everybody has a wonderful time.

The English, who in the late eighteenth century introduced the first popular songs in this country, continued to entertain us with their own hit tunes.

"Vilikins and His Dinah" (see page 340) was a big music-hall hit in London, and when published in America in the middle 1850's was welcomed with enthusiasm. John Parry is named as the composer, as noted in chapter I. This pseudotragic ballad concerns a rich father who is anxious to marry off his daughter. The daughter is just as anxious to remain single, and solves her excruciating problem in the most drastic fashion. The touch of cockney in the verses and the overdramatic language give the song sly humor:

> As Dinah was a valiking the garden one day,
> Her papa he came to her, and thus did he say—
> "Go dress yourself, Dinah, in gorgeous array,
> And take yourself a husiband both galliant and gay."

These parental instructions are rejected dramatically, with ensuing disaster for all concerned.

Among the biggest English successes in the 1860's were "Captain Jinks of the Horse Marines" and "Up in a Balloon."

"Captain Jinks" (see page 343) was written by T. Maclagan and popularized in America by a great monologist and comic artist, William Horace Lingard. Lingard, an Englishman who came to the United States in the late 1860's, attained favor on the American stage at once. His repertoire included no character who was more appealing than Captain Jinks.

Captain Jinks was a smooth army man who lived handsomely off an income much too small and who in consequence was forever in debt. He tells his story in such a matter-of-fact fashion that he develops in his audience a grudging kind of sympathy on which Lingard slyly capitalized. Captain Jinks relates frankly, for example:

> I give my horse good corn and beans;
> Of course its quite beyond my means,
> Tho a Captain in the army.

And later:

> I join'd my corps when twenty-one,
> Of course I thought it capital fun;
> When the enemy came, then off I run,
> I wasn't cut out for the army.

A hundred years ago it was considered appropriate and amusing to burlesque a song which had proved a rousing hit. It should come as no surprise that "Captain Jinks" was so honored; and soon after the captain had been presented to his public, a female with the same name made her appearance. She was "Lady Jinks of the Foot Dragoons." (See page 345.) E. N. Slocum wrote the lyrics about the lady, setting them to the melody of "Captain Jinks." Lady Jinks has no secrets to hide from her musical patrons:

> I met the Captain on Parade,
> When first on him my eyes I laid;
> An exclamation then I made,
> He's the handsomest man in the Army.

"Up in a Balloon" (see page 348) was written by another great English composer named George Leybourne. Leybourne, in addition to being a song writer of talent, was a favorite actor in London and in the music halls of the provinces. As an interpreter of comic songs he was among the best in the business, portraying usually a "heavy swell" character, as the English put it. He liked to call himself the "Lion Comique." "Up in a Balloon" was probably the best known of his songs. It came to this country in 1868 and was widely distributed for a few years. Many minstrel troupes used it, for the simple melody was easy to remember.

Leybourne relates that one night he goes up in a balloon and, after climbing high over the housetops, finds himself surrounded by the planets and the constellations. Eventually the expected happens; he falls out of bed and realizes that his celestial voyage resulted from overindulgence at the table the evening before.

New verses were added to the original song, including a set for the ladies, one of whom complains that her Johnny went up in a balloon and never came back.

An English writer of the 1890's who gave us a winner which still evokes fond memories was Fred Gilbert, whose claim to fame is "The Man That Broke the Bank at Monte Carlo."

The song has an unusual background. Eighty years ago, the casino in Monte Carlo was anxious to promote its attractiveness to Londoners. Suddenly one day in 1891, a young man named Arthur De Coursey Brower began to appear ostentatiously all around town, scattering money as if it were scrap paper. Fashionably dressed and tossing his bills around with abandon, he started the rumor that he had broken the bank at Monte Carlo, which, of course, was the greatest publicity the bank could have.

While the excitement was at its peak, posters in the Strand were headlining "the man who broke the bank at Monte Carlo." The phrase caught the eye of Gilbert, and the following day he wrote the song, selecting as his title the words on the poster. (See page 351.) When he tried to find a performer, however, he was unsuccessful. He had hoped that the great English conductor Albert Chevalier would sponsor the song, but Chevalier turned him down, as did a number of music-hall performers. Discouraged, Gilbert finally called on a singing monologist named Charles Coburn. Coburn reacted as the others had, believing, he said afterward, that "it was too highbrow for the average music hall audience." But he thought it over later, regretted his action, went back to Gilbert, and bought the song from him for ten pounds.

Coburn put it into his act at the Tivoli Theater in London, where it received a lukewarm response. The first time he sang it, he tried too hard to win the audience. One music critic wrote that the act was so disgusting, it actually made him ill. Eventually the song was accepted as part of Coburn's regular routine, but he was unable to make it a solid hit. A short while later the great English comedienne Maggie Duggans appropriated the song and stampeded her audience with it.

About this time, two well-known American theatrical performers, Charles E. Evans and William Hoey, were in London. They heard Coburn's rendition of the song and decided that Hoey, a man with a great fund of humor, could put it across successfully in America. They brought it home with them and introduced it in a lively review at the Bijou Theater in New York in September, 1892.

In the second act Hoey walked on the stage dressed in a white box coat, plaid trousers, silk hat, diamond-buckled shoes, and diamond-studded tie—looking indeed like a man who might have "broken the bank." At the end of the performance, the audience rose cheering to its feet, and from that day on, "The Man That Broke the Bank at Monte Carlo" was Hoey's trademark. He was obliged to sing it whenever he appeared on a stage.

The swinging chorus in 6/8 time caught the whimsicality of the day. Even now the song is heard occasionally, and there are people who still remember the words:

> As I walk along the *Bois Boo-long*
> With an independent air
> You can hear the girls declare
> "He must be a millionaire."
> You can hear them sigh,
> And wish to die,
> You can see them wink the other eye
> At the man that broke the Bank at Monte Carlo.

In 1889 a run-of-the-mill vaudeville team by the name of Sheridan and Flynn was making the rounds of the country's stages. Very little is known about either of these men, but they did publish one song with the inscription "Sheridan and Flynn's greatest hit." Joe Flynn wrote the words and music. Apparently he never achieved another hit, but he certainly had a winner in "Down Went McGinty." (See page 352.)

"McGinty" was published and republished, as a song, as a schottische, and as a waltz. Poor McGinty was the original hard-luck man; his story is an excruciating series of disasters. At the outset, Dan McGinty meets a friend, Pat McGann, and offers to bet him that Pat cannot carry him on his back up a ladder to the top of a wall. McGinty's misfortunes commence when he falls off Pat's back, and from there he continues on a constant downgrade taking one fall after another.

After getting drunk, he falls into a coal hole; then when he tries to get out, the driver of the coal cart gives the load a start, and of course it descends on McGinty. Finally he is released, to return home and find that his wife and child have deserted him. This is the last straw, so he goes to the river bank, jumps in, and sinks to the bottom. One thing must be pointed out: McGinty is always well dressed. Each time McGinty "went down," his attire was the best he owned. Even when he finally jumps into the river, the chorus goes:

> Down went McGinty to the bottom of the say [sea],
> And he must be very wet
> For they haven't found him yet,
> But they say his ghost comes round the docks
> Before the break of day,
> Dress'd in his best suit of clothes.

For a long time after the song was written, superstitious longshoremen claimed that his ghost could be seen at the docks early each morning; but apparently this claim was never proved.

The variety stage of the nineties was the springboard from which a promising ballad leaped into popularity, riding on the performance of a glamorous figure. No singer of the day captivated an audience more completely than Maggie Cline, a gargantuan lady of Irish parentage. Maggie first attempted to go on the stage at fifteen. Three times she ran away from her home in Massachusetts; three times her father dragged her back. Eventually she broke into burlesque and created a sensation. No wonder: she tipped the scale at 230 pounds and had a voice to match her avoirdupois.

Tony Pastor, Broadway's greatest impresario of variety shows, took Maggie under his wing—not literally, of course; not even a giant condor could proffer a wing large enough to clutch so monumental a woman.

When she was in her early thirties and a headliner at Pastor's, she was approached one day by a leading song writer of the day, John W. Kelly, who offered her his latest, a number called "Throw Him Down McCloskey." (See page 355.) Maggie was not exactly free with her money; she tendered a two-dollar bill to Kelly, who, needing another drink badly, took the money. For the two dollars she got the story of a prizefight, and a chorus starting:

> "Throw him down, McCloskey," was to be the battle cry,
> "Throw him down, McCloskey," you can lick him if you try.

"McCloskey" became her greatest hit. When she took a deep breath and, swinging her powerful arms, bellowed, "Throw him down, McCloskey," every stagehand in the wings would hurl to the floor whatever prop he had in his hand. The crash would resound through the theater, and Maggie, completing the chorus, would swagger off the stage while the gallery-goers rose to their feet and whistled and yelled for more. At times when the tumultuous applause would not die down, Maggie would reappear, step to the front of the stage, and say modestly, "You will have to excuse me from repeating it. I am too refined for this business."

But "McCloskey" wasn't Maggie's only claim to fame. Another song that attained near-immortality because of her rendition of it, "Drill Ye Tarriers, Drill" (see page 357), was one of the merriest songs in her repertoire. Thomas Casey, who wrote it, started out himself as a tarrier (unskilled Irish laborer) in a blasting gang, and he was familiar with the steam drills which cut into and removed the rock. In the evenings he used to sing in amateur theatricals, and later he performed for political organizations and concert halls, which were the forerunners of nightclubs.

Apparently the first comedian to introduce "Tarriers" was Charles H. Hoyt, who in October, 1888, found a place for it in a play called *A Brass Monkey*, in which three actors dressed as rock drillers sang it to an appreciative audience. The audience was so enthusiastic about the song, in fact, that Hoyt retained it for four seasons. Subsequently, comedians in vaudeville and burlesque used it, the most famous being Maggie Cline. The melody is catchy and the words, too, appealed to the listener.

> Then drill, ye tarriers, drill,
> Drill, ye tarriers, drill.
> Oh it's work all day without sugar in your tay
> When ye work beyant on the railway,
> And drill, ye tarriers drill.

Joseph J. Sullivan was a blackface comedian, the son of a dairy farmer with a small place on Long Island, who used the barn for rehearsals for his shows. He was always looking for effective costumes for his performances. One day he tried on an old-fashioned high hat which was several sizes too small. As he walked down the street, some small boys saw him, jeered, threw rocks, and yelled, "Where did you get that hat?" This caused Sullivan to retreat to the barn. But the youngsters had given him an idea for the first song which had a hat for a "hero." (See page 358.)

The song relates the story of the death of the singer's grandfather, who has left all his money to his grandson provided he agrees always to wear the hat. Naturally he agrees, but everywhere he goes, the question is hurled at him, "Where did you get that hat?"

Sullivan introduced the song at Miner's Eighth Avenue Theater in New York in 1888, and it captivated his audience. For four years the ballad was demanded of Sullivan wherever he went, and the phrase, along with the

326

melody of the first bar of the song, became a trademark. Like so many others who had produced hits, Sullivan was a one-song man; but it kept him before the public for four decades.

When these old favorites are played today, many of us become nostalgic, thinking of our childhood days. Their melodies are catchy, easy to whistle, and easy to learn. They will very likely be around, singable and playable, for many years to come.

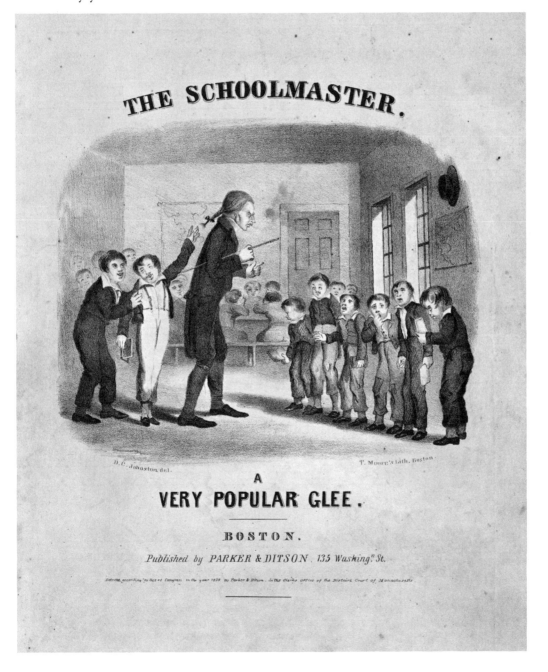

THE SCHOOLMASTER.

A
VERY POPULAR GLEE.

BOSTON.

Published by PARKER & DITSON, 135 Washingn. St.

The Schoolmaster

2. Don't you be so much alarm'd
   Dont you cry you shant be harm'd
   Dont you laugh you rogue at me,
   Mind I say your A B C
   Else I will whip you and send you out of school
   For you are a naughty boy and do not mind my rule.

3. Take good care, now, shut your books,
   On your master fix your looks,
   If you miss whate'er I tell you
   And dont say the words I spell you
   Then I shall whip you and beat you all around;
   Silence, softly, silence, let me not hear a sound.

4. Nothing else but letters telling
   Ruling books and hard words spelling;
   Pens a making, boys a shaking,
   Reading writing scolding fighting,
   Coaxing on the stubborn ones, and pushing on the lazy,
   Toils like these are hard enough to drive a poor man crazy.

THE

ARKANSAS TRAVELLER

BY

MOSE CASE.

3

BOSTON.

Published by *Oliver Ditson & Co.* 277 *Washington St.*

Cin.   N. York.   Boston.   Phil*
J. Church Jr.   W. A. Pond & Co.   J. C. Haynes & Co.   J. E. Gould.

The Arkansas Traveller

(*Spoken*)

STRANGER: How long have you been living here?

OLD MAN: D'ye see that mountain there? Well, that was there when I come here.

STRANGER: Can I stay here tonight?

OLD MAN: No! ye can't stay here.

STRANGER: How long will it take me to get to the next Tavern?

OLD MAN: Well, you'll not get thar at all if you stand thar foolin with me all night.

(*Plays.*)

STRANGER: Well, how far do you call it to the next Tavern?

OLD MAN: I reckon its upwards of some distance.

(*Plays.*)

STRANGER: I am very dry, do you keep any spirits in your house?

OLD MAN: Do you think my house is haunted? they say there's plenty down in the Grave-yard.

(*Plays.*)

STRANGER: How do they cross this river ahead?

OLD MAN: The ducks all swim across.

(*Plays.*)

STRANGER: How far is it to the forks of the road?

OLD MAN: I've been living here nigh on twenty years and no road aint forked yit.

(*Plays.*)

STRANGER: Give me some satisfaction if you please sir; where does this road go to?

OLD MAN: Well, it hain't moved a step since I've been here.

(*Plays.*)

STRANGER: Why don't you cover your house? it leaks;

OLD MAN: Cause its raining.

STRANGER: Then why don't you cover it when its not raining?

OLD MAN: Cause it don't leak.

331

(Plays.)

STRANGER: Why don't you play the second part of that tune?

OLD MAN: If you're a better player than I am you can play it yourself. I'll bring the Fiddle out to you, I don't want you in here.

(Stranger plays the second part of the tune.)

OLD MAN: Git over the fence and come in and sit down, I didn't know you could play. You can board here if you want to—kick that dog off that stool and set down and play it over, I want to hear it again.

(Stranger plays second part again.)

OLD MAN: Our supper is ready now, won't you have some with us?

STRANGER: If you please!

OLD MAN: What will you take, Tea or Coffee?

STRANGER: A cup of Tea if you please!

OLD MAN: Sall, git the grubbin hoe and go dig some sassafras, quick!

(Old Man plays the first part.)

STRANGER: *(To the little boy)*: Bub give me a knife and fork if you please.

BOY: We haint got no knives and forks sir.

STRANGER: Then give me a spoon.

BOY: We haint got no spoons neither.

STRANGER: Well then, how do you do?

BOY: Tolerable, thank you, how do you do sir?

Billy Boy

Oh where have you been Billy boy, Billy boy, Oh, where have you been, charming Billy?

I have been to seek a wife, She's the joy of my life, She's a young thing and cannot leave her

mother.

2. Did she bid you to come in, Billy boy, Billy boy,
   Did she bid you to come in, charming Billy?
   Yes, she bade me to come in,
   Theres a dimple in her chin,
   She's a young thing, &c.

3. Did she set for you a chair, Billy boy, Billy boy,
   Did she set for you a chair, charming Billy?
   Yes, she set for me a chair,
   She has ringlets in her hair,
   She's a young thing, &c.

4. Can she make a cherry pie, Billy boy, Billy boy,
   Can she make a cherry pie, charming Billy?
   She can make a cherry pie
   Quick as a cat can wink her eye;
   She's a young thing, &c.

5. Is she often seen at church, Billy boy, Billy boy,
   Is she often seen at church, charming Billy?
   Yes she's often seen at church
   With a bonnet white as birch;
   She's a young thing, &c.

6. How tall is she, Billy boy, Billy boy,
   How tall is she, charming Billy?
   She's as tall as any pine,
   And as straight as a pumpkin vine,
   She's a young thing, &c.

7. Are her eyes very bright, Billy boy, Billy boy
   Are her eyes very bright, charming Billy?
   Yes her eyes are very bright,
   But alas, they're minus sight,
   She's a young thing, &c.

8. How old is she, Billy boy, Billy boy,
   How old is she, charming Billy?
   She's three times six, four times seven,
   Twenty-eight and eleven,
   She's a young thing, &c.

OVER THERE!

"A DOLEFUL BALLAD,"
ONE OF THE "OLDEN TIME."

Arranged for the Piano Forte,

BY CHARLES GOSSIN.

New York:

PUBLISHED AT ATWILL'S MUSIC REPOSITORY.

Over There

Oh! Po-ta-toes they grow small Over there! Oh! Po-ta-toes they grow small Over there!

Oh! Po-ta-toes they grow small 'cause they plant 'em in the fall, and then eats 'em tops and all over

there!

2. Oh! the candles they are small
Over there!
Oh! the candles they are small
Over there!
Oh! the candles they are small,
For they dips 'em *lean* and *tall*—
And then burns 'em sticks and all
Over there!

3. Oh! I wish I was a geese,
All forlorn!
Oh! I wish I was a geese,
All forlorn!

Oh! I wish I was a geese,
'Cause they lives and dies in peace
And accumulates much grease
Eating corn!

4. Oh! they had a clam pie
Over there!
Oh! they had a clam pie
Over There!
Oh! they had a clam pie,
And the crust was made of *rye*—
You must eat it! or must *die,*
Over there!

335

To all good children

MY
Grandma's Advice.
SONG

Sung with great applause by the

Tremaine Family

Words & Music by

M

Arranged for the Piano by

EDWARD KANSKI

BOSTON
Published by OLIVER DITSON & Co 277 Washington St

C.C.CLAPP & Co.
Boston

BECK & LAWTON.
Philad'a

TRUAX & BALDWIN.
Cincinnati

S.T. GORDON.
N.York

H. WATERS. Agt. N.York.

My Grandma's Advice

My Grand-ma lives on yon-der lit-tle green Fine old la-dy as ev-er was seen; She of-ten

cau-tioned me with care Of all false young men to be-ware. Tim-e-i tim-e-um tum

tim-e um pa ta. Of all false young men to be-ware

2. These false young men they flatter and deceive,
   So my love you must not believe;
   They'll flatter, they'll coax, 'till you are in their snare,
   And away goes poor old grandma's care.
   Tim–e–i tim–e um tum tim–e um pa ta
   And a–way goes poor old grandma's care.

3. The first came a courting was little Johny Green,
   Fine young man as ever was seen;
   But the words of my Grandma run in my head,
   And I could not hear one word he said.
   Tim–e–i tim–e um tum tim–e um pa ta
   And I could not hear one word he said.

4. The next came a courting was young Ellis Grove,
   'Twas then we met with a joyous love;
   With a joyous love I couldn't be afraid,
   You'd better get married than die an old maid.
   Tim–e–i tim–e um tum tim–e um pa ta
   You'd better get married than die an old maid.

5. Think I to myself there's some mistake,
   What a fuss these old folks make;
   If the boys and the girls had all been so fraid,
   Then Grandma herself would have died an old maid.
   Timei time um tum time um pa ta
   Then Grandma herself would have died an old maid.

Johnny Schmoker

John-ny Schmo-ker, John-ny Schmo-ker Ich kann spiel-en Ich kann spiel-en Ich kann

spiel mein klein-e Drum-mel Rub a dub a dub, das ist mein Drum-mel.

2. Fifie.
   Pilly willy wink, das ist mein Fifie.
   Rub a dub a dub, das ist mein Drummel.
   Mein Rub a dub a dub,
   Mein Pilly willy wink, das ist mein Fifie.

3. Tic Knock Knock, das ist Triangle,
   Pilly willy wink, das ist mein Fifie.
   Rub a dub a dub, das ist mein Drummel.
   Mein rub a dub a dub,
   Mein Pilly Willy wink,
   Mein Tic, knock, knock, das ist Triangle.

4. Bom, bom, bom, das ist mein Trombone.
   Tic, knock, knock, das ist Triangle
   Pilly, willy, wink das ist mein Fifie.
   Rub, a dub, a dub, das ist mein Drummel.
   Mein Rub, a dub, a dub,
   Mein Pilly, Willy, wink
   Mein Tic, knock, knock,
   Mein Bom, bom, bom, das ist mein Trombone.

5. Zoom, zoom, zoom, das ist mein Cymbal.
   Bom bom bom, das ist mein Trombone.
   Tic knock knock, das ist Triangle
   Pilly willy wink, das ist mein Fifie,
   Rub a dub a dub, das ist mein Drummel.
   Mein Rub a dub a dub.
   Mein Pilly willy wink,
   Mein Tic knock knock,
   Mein Bom bom bom,
   Mein Zoom zoom zoom, das ist mein Cymbal.

338

6. Fal lal lal, das ist mein Viol.
   Zoom zoom zoom, das ist mein Cymbal.
   Bom, bom, bom das ist mein Trombone.
   Tic, knock, knock, das ist Triangle.
   Pilly, willy, wink, das ist mein Fifie.
   Rub, a dub, a dub, das ist mein Drummel.
   Mein rub, a dub, a dub,
   Mein Pilly, willy, wink,
   Mein Tic, knock, knock,
   Mein Bom, bom, bom,
   Mein Zoom, zoom, zoom,
   Mein fal, lal, lal, das ist mein Viol.

7. Toodle-Sach.
   Whack, whack, whack, das ist mein Toodle Sach.
   Fal, lal, lal, das ist mein Viol,
   Zoom, zoom, zoom, das ist mein Cymbal,
   Bom, bom, bom, das ist mein Trombone,
   Tic, knock, knock, das ist Triangle,
   Pilly, willy, wink, das ist mein Fifie.
   Rub a dub a dub, das ist mein Drummel.
   Mein Rub a dub a dub,
   Mein Pilly willy wink,
   Mein Tic knock knock
   Mein Bom, bom, bom,
   Mein Zoom, zoom, zoom,
   Mein Fal, lal, lal,
   Mein Whack, whack, whack,
   Das ist mein Toodle Sach.

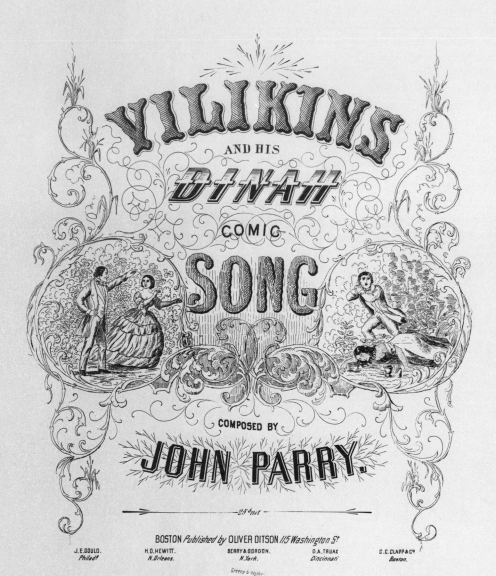

VILIKINS

AND HIS

DINAH

COMIC

SONG

COMPOSED BY

JOHN PARRY.

25¢ net

BOSTON *Published by* OLIVER DITSON *115 Washington St*

J.E.GOULD.
Philad?

H.O.HEWITT.
N.Orleans.

BERRY&GORDON.
N.York.

O.A.TRUAX
Cincinnati

C.C.CLAPP&C?
Boston.

Greene & Walker.

Vilikins & His Dinah

'Tis of a rich mer-chant who in Lon-don did dwell, He had but one daugh-ter an un-kim-mon nice young gall; Her name it was Din-ah, scarce six-teen years old; with a ve-ry large for-tune in silver and gold. Sing-ing to lal lol la rol lall to ral lal la. Sing-ing to la lol la rol lall to ral lol la.

2. As Dinah vas a valiking the garden one day,
   Her papa he came to her, and thus he did say—
   "Go dress yourself Dinah, in gorgeous array,
   And take yourself a husiband both galliant and gay!"
   Singing to la lol, &c.

3. "Oh papa, Oh papa, I've not made up my mind,
   And to marry just yet, why, I don't feel inclined;
   To you my large fortune I'll gladly give o'er,
   If you'll let me live single a year or two more.
   Singing to la lol, &c.

4. "Go, go, boldest daughter," the parient replied;
   "If you wont consent to be this here young man's bride
   I'll give your large fortune to the nearest of kin,
   And you shan't reap the benefit of one single pin."
   Singing to la lol, &c.

5. As Vilikins vas valiking the garden around,
   He spied his dear Dinah laying dead upon the ground,
   And the cup of cold pison it lay by her side,
   With a billet-dux a stating 'twas by pison she died.
   Singing to la lol, &c.

341

6. He kissed her cold corpus a thousand times o'er
   And called her his Dinah though she was no more,
   Then swallowed the pison like a lovyer so brave
   And Vilikins and his Dinah lie both in one grave.
   Singing to la lol, &c.

    MORAL: Now all you young maidens take warning by her,
                 Never not by no means disobey your govenor,
                 And all you young fellows mind who you claps eyes on,
                 Think of Vilikins and Dinah and the cup of cold pison.
                 Singing to la lol, &c.

CAPTAIN JINKS.
[OF THE HORSE MARINES.]

Piano
Guitar.

WRITTEN & SUNG BY
T. MACLAGAN.

Captain Jinks

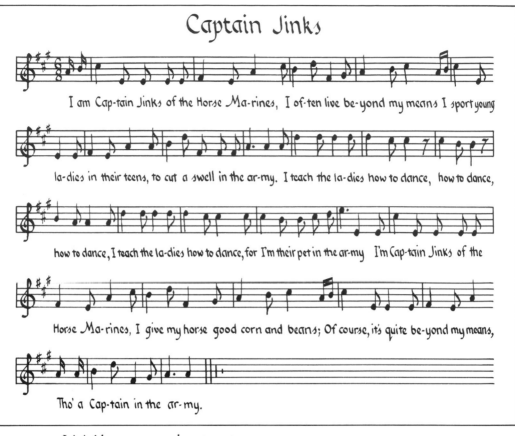

I am Cap-tain Jinks of the Horse Ma-rines, I of-ten live be-yond my means I sport young la-dies in their teens, to cut a swell in the ar-my. I teach the la-dies how to dance, how to dance, how to dance, I teach the la-dies how to dance, for I'm their pet in the ar-my I'm Cap-tain Jinks of the Horse Ma-rines, I give my horse good corn and beans; Of course, it's quite be-yond my means, Tho' a Cap-tain in the ar-my.

2. I join'd my corps when twenty-one,
   Of course I thought it capital fun;
   When the enemy came, then off I run,
   I wasn't cut out for the army.
   When I left home mama she cried, mama she cried, mama she cried,
   When I left home mama she cried, "He ain't cut out for the army."

   Chorus

3. The first day I went out to drill
   The bugle sound made me quite ill.
   At the Balance step my hat it fell,
   And that wouldn't do for the army.
   The officers they all did shout, they all cried out, they all did shout,
   The officers they all did shout, "Oh that's the Cure of the army!"

   Chorus

344

4. My Tailor's bills came in so fast
   Forc'd me one day to leave at last,
   And ladies too no more did cast
   Sheep's eyes at me in the army.
   My Creditors at me did shout, at me did shout, at me did shout,
   My Creditors at me did shout, "Why kick him out of the army."

CHORUS

(*Spoken*) Yes indeed! my dear Captain Jinks is the pet of the Army, and of the fair sex also. He says I must not be jealous of the attention paid him by the ladies. I tell him certainly not, for every one knows:

CHORUS

2. I met the Captain on Parade,
    When first on him my eyes I laid;
    An exclamation then I made,
    He's the handsomest man in the Army.
    He saw the conquest he had made, that he had made, that he had made,
    He heard the compliment I paid,
    To him the pride of the army.

(*Spoken*) I really did think he was the handsomest, I think so yet for the matter of that. Some people think I married him for the title of Lady. But not so; for it was love at first sight, if not how could I be:

CHORUS

3. Together we some times promenade,
    And hear remarks about us made
    And often we have heard it said
    They're the pride and boast of the Army.
    The officers they also shout, they also shout, they also shout,
    The officers they all cry out,
    Oh! they're the pride of the Army.

(*Spoken*) I am quite positive we are the pride of the Army. They all tell us so and why shouldn't we believe it. Who hasn't heard of Captain Jinks of the Horse Marines? And I hope in the future you will always warmly welcome, Yours most respectfully:

CHORUS

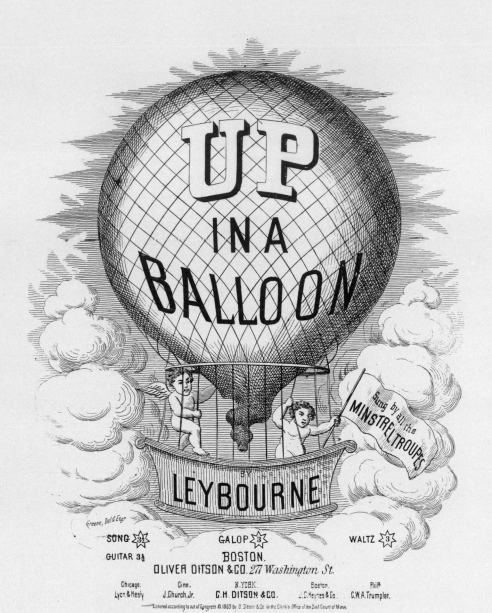

Up In A Balloon

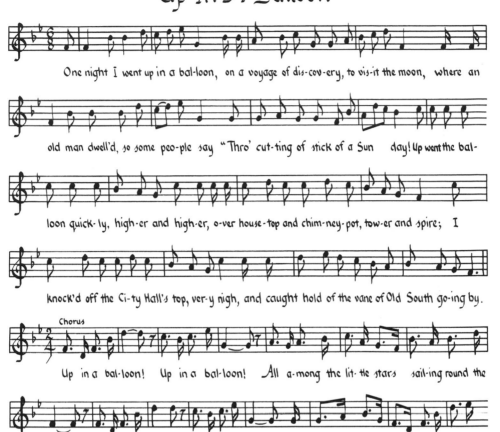

One night I went up in a bal-loon, on a voyage of dis-cov-ery, to vis-it the moon, where an old man dwell'd, so some peo-ple say "Thro' cut-ting of stick of a Sun day! Up went the bal-loon quick-ly, high-er and high-er, o-ver house-top and chim-ney-pot, tow-er and spire; I knock'd off the Ci-ty Hall's top, ver-y nigh, and caught hold of the vane of Old South go-ing by.

Chorus

Up in a bal-loon! Up in a bal-loon! All a-mong the lit-tle stars sail-ing round the moon. Up in a bal-loon! Up in a bal-loon! It's something awful jolly, to be up in a bal-loon.

2. Up, up, I was borne with terrible pow'r,
   At the rate of ten thousand five hundred an hour;
   The air was cold, the wind blew loud,
   I narrowly escaped being choked by a cloud;
   Still up I went 'till surrounded by stars,
   And such planets as Jupiter, Venus and Mars;
   The big and the little Bear loudly did growl,
   And the Dog-star, on seeing me, set up a howl.

CHORUS

349

3. I met shooting stars, who were bent upon sport,
   But who "shot" in a very strange manner, I thought;
   And one thing beat all by chalks, I must say,
   That was when I got into the "Milky Way";
   I counted the stars, 'till at last I thought
   I'd found out how much they were worth by the quart.
   An unpolite "Aerolite," who ran against my car,
   Wouldn't give me "e'er a light" to light my cigar.

CHORUS

4. Next a comet went by, 'midst fire, like hail;
   To give me a lift, I seized hold of his tail;
   To where he was going, I didn't enquire;
   We'd gone past the moon, 'till we couldn't get higher;
   Yes, we'd got to the furthermost!—don't think I joke,
   When somehow I felt a great shock! I awoke!
   When, instead of balloon, moon and planets, I saw,
   I'd tumbled from off my bed to the floor.

   And there was no balloon,—there was no balloon;
   There were not any planets, there wasn't any moon;
   So never sup too heavy, or by jingo very soon
   You're like to fancy you are going up in a balloon.

The Man That Broke The Bank At Monte Carlo

I've just got here through Pa-ris, from the sunny southern shore; I to Monte Carlo went, just to raise my winter's rent; Dame Fortune smiled up on me as she'd never done before, and I've now such lots of money, I'm a gent. — Yes, I've now such lots of money, I'm a gent. — As I walk a-long the Bois Boo-long with an in-de-pen-dent air You can hear the girls de-clare "He must be a mil-lion-aire" You can hear them sigh, and wish to die, You can see them wink the oth-er eye at the man that broke the Bank at Mon-te Car - lo —

2. I stay indoors till after lunch, and then my daily walk
   To the great Triumphal Arch is one grand triumphal march.
   Observ'd by each observer with the keenness of a hawk,
   I'm a mass of money, linen, silk and starch
   I'm a mass of money, linen, silk and starch.

   CHORUS

3. I patronized the tables at the Monte Carlo hell,
   Till they hadn't got a sou for a Christian or a Jew;
   So I quickly went to Paris for the charms of mad'moiselle,
   Who's the loadstone of my heart what can I do,
   When with twenty tongues she swears that she'll be true.

   CHORUS

Sheridan & Flynn's Greatest Hit!

DOWN WENT
McGINTY

Dressed in His Best Suit of Clothes

COMIC SONG.

—WORDS AND MUSIC—

—BY—

JOSEPH FLYNN.

SONG, 40.   SCHOTTISCHE, 40.   WALTZ, 40.

BROOKLYN, N. Y.:

PUBLISHED BY **SPAULDING & KORNDER,** 487 FULTON ST.

Down Went McGinty

Sun-day morn-ing just at nine, Dan Mc-Gin-ty dress'd so fine, stood look-ing up at a ver-y

high stone wall; When his friend young Pat Mc-Cann, says, I'll bet five dol-lars, Dan,

I could carry you to the top with-out a fall; So on his shoul-ders he took Dan, To climb the

lad-der he be-gan, and he soon com-menc'd to reach up near the top; When Mc-Gin-ty, cute old

rogue, to win the five he did let go, nev-er think-ing just how far he'd have to drop

Chorus

Down went Mc-Gin-ty to the bot-tom of the wall, and tho' he won the five, he was more dead than a-

live, Sure his ribs and nose and back were broke from get-ting such a fall, Dress'd in his best suit of clothes.

2. From the hospitle Mac went home,
   When they fix'd his broken bones,
   To find he was the father of a child;
   So to celebrate it right,
   His friends he went to invite,
   And he soon was drinking whisky fast and wild;
   Then he waddled down the street
   In his Sunday suit so neat,
   Holding up his head as proud as John the Great,
   But in the sidewalk was a hole,

To receive a ton of coal,
That McGinty never saw till just too late.

Down went McGinty to the bottom of the hole,
Then the driver of the cart
Give the load of coal a start,
And it took us half an hour to dig
McGinty from the coal,
Dress'd in his best suit of clothes.

3. Now McGinty raved and swore,
About his clothes he felt so sore,
And an oath he took he'd kill the man or die;
So he tightly grabb'd his stick
And hit the driver a lick,
Then he raised a little shanty on his eye;
But two policemen saw the muss
And they soon join'd in the fuss,
Then they ran McGinty in for being drunk;
And the Judge says with a smile,
We will keep you for a while
In a cell to sleep upon a prison bunk.

Down went McGinty to the bottom of the jail
Where his board would cost him nix,
And he stay'd exactly six,
They were big long months he stopp'd
For no one went his bail,
Dress'd in his best suit of clothes.

4. Now McGinty thin and pale
One fine day got out of jail,
And with joy to see his boy was nearly wild;
To his house he quickly ran
To meet his wife Bedaley Ann,
But she'd skipp'd away and took along the child;
Then he gave up in despair,
And he madly pull'd his hair,
As he stood one day upon the river shore,
Knowing well he couldn't swim,
He did foolishly jump in,
Although water he had never took before.

Down went McGinty to the bottom of the say,
And he must be very wet
For they haven't found him yet,
But they say his ghost comes round the docks
Before the break of day,
Dress'd in his best suit of clothes.

Throw Him Down M'Closkey

'Twas down at Dan Mc De-vitt's at the cor-ner of this street, There was to be a prize fight and both par-ties were to meet; To make all the ar-range-ments and see ev-ry-thing was right, Mc Clos-key and a na-gur were to have a fin-ish fight; The rules were Lon-don Prize Ring and Mc Clos-key said he'd try, To bate the na-gur wid one punch or in the ring he'd die; The odds were on Mc Clos-key tho' the bet-ting it was small, 'Twas on Mc Clos-key ten to one, On the na-gur, none at all. "Throw him down Mc Clos-key," was to be the bat-tle cry Throw him down Mc Clos-key, you can lick him if you try, And fu-ture gen-e-ra-tions, with won-der and de-light, will read on his-try's pa-ges of the great Mc Clos-key fight.

1. 'Twas down at Dan McDevitt's at the corner of this street,
   There was to be a prize fight and both parties were to meet;
   To make all the arrangements and see ev'rything was right,
   McCloskey and a nagur were to have a finish fight;

The rules were London Prize Ring and McCloskey said he'd try,
To bate the nagur wid one punch or in the ring he'd die;
The odds were on McCloskey tho the betting it was small,
'Twas on McCloskey ten to one, On the nagur, none at all.

CHORUS

"Throw him down McCloskey," was to be the battle cry,
Throw him down McCloskey, you can lick him if you try,
And future generations, with wonder and delight,
Will read on hist'ry's pages of the great McCloskey fight.

2. The fighters were to start in at a quarter after eight,
    But the nagur did not show up and the hour was getting late;
    He sent around a messenger who then went on to say,
    That the Irish crowd would jump him and he couldn't get fair play;
    Then up steps Pete McCracken, And said that he would fight.
    Stand up or rough and tumble if McCloskey didn't bite?
    McCloskey says I'll go you, then the seconds got in place,
    And the fighters started in to decorate each others face.

CHORUS

3. They fought like two hyenas 'till the forty seventh round,
    They scattered blood enough around by gosh, to paint the town,
    McCloskey got a mouthful of poor McCrackens jowl.
    McCracken hollered 'murther' and his seconds hollered 'foul'!
    The friends of both the fighters that instant did begin,
    To fight and ate each other the whole party started in,
    You couldn't tell the dif'rence in the fighters if you'd try,
    McCracken lost his upper lip, McCloskey lost an eye.

CHORUS

Drill, Ye Tarriers, Drill!

Oh! ev'ry morn at seven o-'clock there are twenty tarriers on the rock. The boss comes a-

long and says "be still and put all your power in the cast steel drill." Then drill, ye tarriers, drill,

Drill, ye tarriers, drill. Oh it's work all day with-out sug-ar in your tay when ye work be-yant on

the rail-way, and drill, ye tarriers, drill.

(*Spoken*) Stand out there with the flag, Sullivan. Stand back there! Blast! Fire! All over!

2. The boss was a fine man all around
   But he married a great, big, fat far down,
   She baked good bread and baked it well,
   And baked it hard as the hobs of H—l.

(*Spoken*) Stand out forninst the fence with the flag, McCarthy. Stand back, etc.
   Chorus

3. The new foreman is Dan McCann,
   I'll tell you sure he's a blame mean man,
   Last week a premature blast went off,
   And a mile in the air went big Jim Goff:

(*Spoken*) Where's the fuse, McGinty? What, he lit his pipe with it! Stop the belt car coming down. Stand back, etc.
   Chorus

4. When pay day next it came around,
   Poor Jim's pay a dollar short he found,
   "What for?" says he then came this reply,
   "You were docked for the time you were up in the sky."

(*Spoken*) More oatmeal in the bucket, McCue. What's that your reading, Duffy, the Staats Zeitung? Get out there with the flag, etc.
   Chorus

357

JOSEPH J. SULLIVAN'S
Celebrated
COMIC SONG

WHERE DID YOU GET THAT HAT?

NEW-YORK:
HARDING'S MUSIC OFFICE.

FOR SALE AT ALL MUSIC STORES.

Where Did You Get That Hat?

Now how I came to get this hat 'tis ve-ry strange and fun-ny: Grand-fa-ther died and left to me his prop-er-ty and mon-ey. And when the will it was read out, they told me straight and flat; If I would have his mon-ey, I must al-ways wear his hat! Where did you get that hat? Where did you get that tile? Is-nt it a nob-by one, and just the prop-er style? I should like to have one just the same as that! Wher-e'er I go they shout "Hel-lo!" Where did you get that hat?

2. If I go to the op'ra house, in the op'ra season,
   There's someone sure to shout at me, without the slightest reason.
   If I go to a "chowder club," to have a jolly spree;
   There's someone in the party, who is sure to shout at me:

   Chorus

3. At twenty one I thought I would to my sweetheart be married;
   The people in the neighborhood had said too long we'd tarried.
   So off to church we went right quick, determin'd to get wed;
   I had not long been in there, when the parson to me said:

   Chorus

Bibliography

Newspapers

Boston Herald. July 1, 1923.

Boston Transcript. June 29, 1895.

Christian Science Monitor. March 19, 1920.

Cleveland Plain Dealer. February 2, 1870.

Frank Leslie's Illustrated Newspaper. "Mr. and Mrs. Howard Paul," November 10, 1866, p. 124.

Newark Sunday Call. June 19, 1938.

New York Daily News. October 25, 1938.

New York Dramatic Mirror. November 20, 1897.

New York Evening Sun. December 14, 1889; December 28, 1889.

New York Herald Tribune. January 28, 1936; January 11, 1946; April 12, 1946.

New York Times. December 2, 1933; June 12, 1934; October 4, 1938; October 26, 1938; January 11, 1946; April 12, 1946.

Philadelphia Press. William Winter, "The Wallet of Time," November 20, 1891.

St. Louis Republic. March 12, 1899.

Times (London) *Literary Supplement.* "An English Singer in America" (review of Emilie Marguerite Cowell, *The Cowells in America, being the diary of Mrs. Sam Cowell during her husband's concert tour in the years 1860–1861,* ed. by M. Willson Disher [London, Oxford University Press, 1934]), December 6, 1934.

Magazines

Ford, James L. "The Father of Ragtime," *Bookman,* Vol. XLIII (August, 1916), 616–18.

Illustrated American, Vol. XIII, No. 174 (June 17, 1893).

Matlaw, Myron. "Pastor and His Flock," *Theatre Arts Magazine,* Vol. XLII, No. 8 (August, 1958).

"The Month," *Goodspeed's,* Vol. VII, No. 4 (January, 1936).

"A Southern Singer," *Musician,* Vol. XI, No. 10 (October, 1906), 491.

Vail, R. W. G. "Random Notes on the History of the Early American Circus," *American Antiquarian Society Proceedings,* new series, Vol. XLIII, No. 1 (1934), 116–85.

Adams, James Truslow. *Dictionary of American History*. Vols. II and V. New York, Chas. Scribner's Sons, 1940.

Beecher, Henry Ward. *An American Portrait*. Foreword by Sinclair Lewis. New York, The Press of the Readers Club, 1942.

Bellows, George K. *A Short History of Music in America*. New York, Thomas Y. Crowell & Co., 1957.

British Musical Biography. Birmingham, England, S. S. Stratton & Son, 1897.

Chindahl, George L. *A History of the Circus in America*. Caldwell, Idaho, The Caxton Printers Ltd., 1959.

Clapin, Sylvia. *A New Dictionary of Americanisms, Being a glossary of words supposed to be peculiar to the United States and the Dominion of Canada*. New York, Louis Weiss & Co., 1902.

Dichter, Harry, and Elliott Shapiro. *Early American Sheet Music: Its Lure and Its Lore*. New York, R. R. Bowker Co., 1941.

Dillon, William A. *Life Doubles in Brass*. Ithaca, New York, The House of Nollid, 1944.

Engel, Lehman. *The American Musical Theatre*. The C. B. S. Legacy Collection. New York, The Macmillan Co., 1967.

Ewen, David. *Panorama of American Popular Music*. Englewood Cliffs, New Jersey, Prentice-Hall, 1957.

———. *Popular American Composers from Revolutionary Times to the Present*. New York, H. W. Wilson Co., 1962.

Geller, James J. *Famous Songs and Their Stories*. New York, The Macauley Co., 1931.

Gilbert, Douglas. *American Vaudeville, Its Life and Times*. New York, McGraw-Hill Cook Co., Inc., 1940.

———. *Lost Chords*. Garden City, N.Y., Doubleday, Doran & Co., 1942.

Goldberg, Isaac. *Tin Pan Alley, A Chronicle of the American Popular Music Racket*. New York, The John Day Company, 1930.

Harris, Charles K. *After the Ball: 40 Years of Melody*. New York, Frank-Maurice, Inc., 1926.

Howard, John Tasker. *Our American Music. A Comprehensive History from 1620 to the Present*. New York, Thomas Y. Crowell Co., 1965.

Johnson, Allen, and Dumas Malone, eds. *Dictionary of American Biography*. New York, Charles Scribner's Sons, 1929.

Kahn, E. J., Jr. *The Merry Partners. The Age and Stage of Harrigan and Hart*. New York, Random House, 1955.

Klement, Frank L. *The Copperheads in the Middle West*. Chicago, University of Chicago Press, 1960.

Loesser, Arthur. *Humor in American Song*. New York, Howell, 1942.

Marks, Edward Bennett. *They All Sang: From Tony Pastor to Rudy Vallee*. New York, Viking Press, 1934.

Mathews, Mitford M., ed. *Dictionary of Americanisms on Historical Principles.* Vols. I and II. Chicago, University of Chicago Press, 1951.

Memoir of Madame Vestris. London, G. Virtue, 1826.

Paskman, Dailey, and Sigmund G. Spaeth. *Gentlemen Be Seated.* Garden City, New York, Doubleday Doran & Co., 1928.

Rice, Edw. LeRoy. *Monarchs of Minstrelsy, From "Daddy" Rice to Date.* New York, Kenny Publishing Co., 1911.

Scroggs, William O. *Filibusters and Financiers. The Story of William Walker and His Associates.* New York, The Macmillan Co., 1916.

Smith, Cecil. *Musical Comedy in America.* New York, Theatre Arts Books: Robert M. MacGregor, 1950.

The Songs in Howard Paul's Musical, Comical, and Fanciful Entertainment. 30th ed. New York, Proprietor at Irving Hall, c. 1894.

Songs of the Florences; comprising the original melodies of those distinguished delineators of the Irish boy and Yankee girl. New York, Dick and Fitzgerald, 1860.

Spaeth, Sigmund. *History of Popular Music in America.* New York, Random House, 1948.

Stowe, Lyman Beecher. *Saints, Sinners and Beechers.* New York, Blue Ribbon Books, Inc., 1934.

Thompson, David and Kathleen. *Songs that Mother Used to Sing.* Chicago, A. C. McClurg & Co., 1931.

Vallandigham, James L. *A Life of Clement L. Vallandigham.* Baltimore, Turnbull Brothers, 1872.

Wilson, James Grant, ed. *Appletons' Cyclopedia of American Biography.* New York, D. Appleton & Co., 1901.

Ziff, Stanley Green. *The World of Musical Comedy.* New York, Davis Publishing Co., 1960.

Index